Tried-and-True Recipes
Party Planning Fun and Easy

YOU'VE likely heard the saying "Third time's the charm". That statement couldn't be more true for this third edition of *Taste of Home's Holiday & Celebrations Cookbook*!

Like the previous two editions, this recipe-packed, photo-filled treasury will make your Christmas, Thanksgiving, Easter and other special occasions throughout the year even more memorable.

That's because inside *Taste of Home's Holiday & Celebrations Cookbook 2003* you'll find 270 wonderful recipes from cooks across the country and from our own home economists, all of whom prepare satisfying dishes for their families at home…just like you do. To minimize last-minute fuss, we also offer menu options and party-planning pointers.

'Tis the Season. Whether you're hosting a holiday brunch, ornament exchange, tree trimming get-together or Christmas Day dinner, you'll stir up magical memories with some of this chapter's 130 festive foods. From appetizers and breads to entrees and desserts, you'll find a merry array of dishes, including Chicken Cordon Bleu Crepes…Pesto Cream Cheese Spread…Cinnamon Swirl Loaves…Special Seafood Linguine…Peppermint Biscotti and Gift-Wrapped Chocolate Cake.

Giving Thanks. It's easy to prepare a Thanksgiving meal as good as Grandma's when you start with Herb-Glazed Turkey. Round out the meal with a seasonal selection of sides, such as Cranberry Spinach Salad, Buttermilk Corn Bread, Pineapple Sweet Potato Bake and Cheesy Zucchini Casserole. Palate-pleasing pies like Cherry Meringue Pie, Rustic Pear Tart and Caramel Chocolate Mousse Pie are hard to resist.

Easter Gatherings. For your Easter egg hunt or dinner, choose from an array of irresistible recipes, including Bacon 'n' Egg Bundles…Rabbit Rolls…Orange Barbecued Ham…and Lemon Ricotta Cheesecake. There are even ideas for using leftover hard-cooked eggs!

Special Celebrations. We also offer 79 family-favorite recipes for a host of other gatherings throughout the year. Warm up with a fun-filled fondue party, bring a bit of Irish luck to your table on St. Patrick's Day or fire up the grill for a July Fourth burger bar. For some awesome ethnic recipes, celebrate Mexico's Cinco de Mayo or the 2004 Summer Olympic Games in Greece. You'll also find delightful dishes for a 25th wedding anniversary gala and a haunting Halloween party.

Can-Do Decorating Ideas. There are dozens of ideas for simple centerpieces (turn to page 153 for a fast-to-fix Daffodil Topiary), great-looking garnishes (adorn cakes with the beautiful Chocolate Bow on page 72) and easy, impressive napkin folds (see page 17 for the Christmas Tree Napkin Fold).

With unforgettable fare, easy decorating ideas and perfect party menus, *Taste of Home's Holiday & Celebrations Cookbook 2003* will make entertaining fun for you…and unforgettable for your family!

WOULD YOU like to see one of your family-favorite recipes featured in a future edition of this timeless treasury? See page 256 for details!

HOLIDAY & *Celebrations* COOKBOOK 2003

Editor: Julie Schnittka
Art Director: Linda Dzik
Food Editor: Janaan Cunningham
Craft Editor: Jane Craig
Associate Editors: Kristine Krueger, Heidi Reuter Lloyd
Associate Food Editor: Coleen Martin
Senior Recipe Editor: Sue A. Jurack
Recipe Editor: Janet Briggs
Test Kitchen Director: Karen Johnson
Senior Home Economist: Karen Wright
Test Kitchen Home Economists: Sue Draheim,
Tamra Duncan, Peggy Fleming, Wendy Stenman
Test Kitchen Assistants: Rita Krajcir, Megan Taylor
Food Stylists: Julie Herzfeldt, Joylyn Jans, Kristin Koepnick
Food Photography: Rob Hagen, Dan Roberts
Senior Food Photography Artist: Stephanie Marchese
Food Photography Artist: Julie Ferron
Photo Studio Manager: Anne Schimmel
Graphic Art Associates: Ellen Lloyd, Catherine Fletcher
Chairman and Founder: Roy Reiman
President: Russell Denson

Taste of Home Books
©2003 Reiman Media Group, Inc.
5400 S. 60th St., Greendale WI 53129
International Standard Book Number: 0-89821-383-5
International Standard Serial Number: 1535-2781
All rights reserved.
Printed in U.S.A.

For additional copies of this book, write *Taste of Home* Books, P.O.
Box 908, Greendale WI 53129. Or to order by credit card, call
toll-free 1-800/344-2560 or visit our Web site at
www.reimanpub.com.

PICTURED ON THE COVER: Glazed Cornish Hens (p. 20), Apricot
Rice Stuffing (p. 22), Sparkling White Grape Juice (p. 24), Orange-
Caramel Ice Cream Sauce (p. 21) and Chocolate Dessert Cups (p. 20).

'Tis the Season

With all the hustle and bustle of Christmas,
the last thing you need to worry about is what to make
for your holiday happenings. Whether you're hosting a
Christmas Day brunch, a dinner later that day,
a casual tree trimming get-together or a festive
ornament exchange, this chapter has you covered.
You'll also find an assortment of appealing appetizers,
oven-fresh breads, hearty main courses and
sweet treats to round out every merry menu.

Bright-Eyed Christmas Brunch

AFTER the little ones have huddled around the evergreen and opened Santa's gifts on Christmas morning, continue the merry mood by gathering around the table for a mouth-watering brunch.

To tantalize tired taste buds, present your famished family with such delightful dishes as Red Pepper Cornmeal Souffle, Canadian Bacon with Apples and Chilled Christmas Punch. (All recipes shown at right.)

With the festive yet fuss-free foods featured here, early-in-the-day entertaining is a snap!

MERRY MID-MORNING
MEAL
(Top to bottom)

Red Pepper Cornmeal Souffle (p. 9)

Chilled Christmas Punch (p. 8)

Canadian Bacon with Apples (p. 8)

Chilled Christmas Punch

(Pictured on page 6)

A blend of juices gives this punch a little pizzazz. For a more tart flavor,
substitute cranberry juice for the cran-apple juice.
—Edna Hoffman, Hebron, Indiana

  2 cups water
3/4 cup sugar
1/2 teaspoon ground cinnamon
  1 can (46 ounces) pineapple
    juice, chilled
  4 cups cran-apple juice, chilled
  1 liter ginger ale, chilled

In a saucepan, bring the water, sugar and cinnamon to a boil; stir until sugar is dissolved. Chill. Just before serving, combine the syrup mixture, juices and ginger ale in a punch bowl or large pitcher. Serve over ice. **Yield:** 3-3/4 quarts (15-20 servings).

Canadian Bacon with Apples

(Pictured on page 6)

When the holidays roll around, I'd rather spend time with family and friends
than be stuck in the kitchen. So I've come to rely on easy-to-fix recipes like this.
No one can resist Canadian bacon and apples coated with a brown sugar glaze.
—Paula Marchesi, Lenhartsville, Pennsylvania

1/2 cup packed brown sugar
  1 tablespoon lemon juice
1/8 teaspoon pepper
  1 large unpeeled red apple
  1 large unpeeled green apple
  1 pound sliced Canadian bacon

In a large skillet, combine the brown sugar, lemon juice and pepper; mix well. Cook and stir over medium heat until sugar is dissolved. Cut each apple into 16 wedges; add to brown sugar mixture. Cook over medium heat for 5-7 minutes until tender, stirring occasionally. Remove apples to a serving platter with a slotted spoon; keep warm.

Add Canadian bacon to the skillet; cook over medium heat for 3 minutes or until heated through, turning once. Transfer to platter. Pour remaining brown sugar mixture over apples and bacon. Serve immediately. **Yield:** 6 servings.

Red Pepper Cornmeal Souffle

(Pictured at right and on page 6)

I use the vegetables from our garden in all my cooking. Dotted with parsley and red pepper, this souffle is a favorite.
—*Janet Eckhoff, Woodland, California*

1 large onion, chopped
1 cup chopped sweet red pepper
1/4 cup butter *or* margarine
3 cups milk
2/3 cup cornmeal
1 cup (4 ounces) shredded
    sharp cheddar cheese
2 tablespoons minced fresh
    parsley
1 teaspoon salt, *divided*
1/2 teaspoon white pepper
2 egg yolks, beaten
7 egg whites
1/2 teaspoon cream of tartar

In a large saucepan, saute the onion and red pepper in butter until tender. Add the milk. Bring to a boil. Gradually whisk in cornmeal; whisk constantly until thickened, about 5 minutes. Add the cheese, parsley, 1/2 teaspoon salt and pepper. Add 1 cup of the cornmeal mixture to the egg yolks; mix well. Return all to the saucepan.

In a large mixing bowl, beat egg whites, cream of tartar and remaining salt until stiff peaks form. Fold into the cornmeal mixture. Transfer to a greased 2-qt. souffle dish. Bake at 375° for 35-40 minutes or until golden brown. **Yield:** 8-10 servings.

STIRRING UP SUCCESSFUL SOUFFLE BATTERS

PROPERLY preparing the batter is one of the keys to creating a standout souffle. Follow these tips for a distinctive dish guests are sure to fall for!

- When separating eggs, make sure no yolks get into the egg whites, or they won't beat properly.
- Let egg whites stand at room temperature for 30 minutes before beating. They will expand more than cold egg whites and will give you better volume.
- Be sure that the beaters and bowl are clean and dry before they touch the whites.
- When beaten, the whites should be just firm enough to form and hold a stiff peak when the beaters are lifted.
- When adding the egg whites to the yolk base, first fold in a third of the egg whites until blended. Then fold in the remaining whites just until combined.

Coffee Cream Cheese Spread

(Pictured on opposite page)

Even folks who don't care for coffee can't resist this mild-flavored spread.
It's a fun way to dress up homemade breads.
—Ruth Hastings, Louisville, Illinois

2 packages (3 ounces *each*)
  cream cheese, softened
1/4 cup confectioners' sugar
1/2 teaspoon instant coffee
  granules

In a small mixing bowl, beat cream cheese, confectioners' sugar and coffee granules until light and fluffy. Serve with bread, bagels or toast. Store in the refrigerator. **Yield:** 1 cup.

Cherry Cream Cheese Spread

Dotted with pretty maraschino cherries, this spread is
an attractive complement to your holiday table.
—Ruth Hastings

1 package (3 ounces) cream
  cheese, softened
1 teaspoon milk
1/8 teaspoon almond extract
1 tablespoon chopped
  maraschino cherries

In a small mixing bowl, beat the cream cheese, milk and extract until fluffy. Fold in cherries. Serve with bread, bagels or toast. Store in the refrigerator. **Yield:** 1/3 cup.

Honey Butter Spread

Honey lovers will gobble up this spread in a snap! In addition to bread and bagels,
try serving it alongside warm biscuits or pancakes.
—Ruth Hastings

1/2 cup butter (no substitutes),
  softened
1/2 cup honey

In a small mixing bowl, beat the butter until light and fluffy. Add the honey; beat just until blended. Serve with bread, bagels or toast. Store in the refrigerator. **Yield:** 1-1/4 cups.

Cinnamon Swirl Loaves

(Pictured at right)

When I was growing up, my mom made this bread quite often. The irresistible aroma of cinnamon will call your clan to the kitchen.
—Lynn Callahan
Rosemount, Minnesota

1/3 cup shortening
1-1/2 cups plus 2 tablespoons sugar, *divided*
3 eggs
1-1/2 teaspoons vanilla extract
3 cups all-purpose flour
1-1/2 teaspoons baking powder
3/4 teaspoon baking soda
3/4 teaspoon salt
1-1/2 cups buttermilk
1 tablespoon ground cinnamon

In a large mixing bowl, cream shortening and 1-1/2 cups sugar. Add eggs, one at a time, beating well after each addition. Beat in vanilla. Combine the flour, baking powder, baking soda and salt; add to creamed mixture alternately with buttermilk.

Spread half of the batter in two greased and floured 8-in. x 4-in. x 2-in. loaf pans. Combine cinnamon and remaining sugar; sprinkle half over batter. Spread with the remaining batter; sprinkle with remaining cinnamon-sugar. Bake at 350° for 50-55 minutes or until a toothpick inserted near the center comes out clean. Cool for 10 minutes before removing from pans to wire racks. **Yield:** 2 loaves.

Fluffy Orange Spread

(Pictured above)

With its pleasant orange flavor, this simple spread perfectly tops a variety of breads. Each bite has just the right amount of sweetness.
—Ruth Hastings

2 packages (3 ounces *each*) cream cheese, softened
1/4 cup orange juice
1 tablespoon sugar
1 tablespoon grated orange peel

In a small mixing bowl, beat cream cheese and orange juice until smooth and creamy. Add sugar and orange peel; mix well. Serve with bread, bagels or toast. Store in the refrigerator. **Yield:** 1 cup.

Frosted Round Johns

These delightful doughnuts are less greasy than some store-bought varieties, plus they're easy to prepare. My mother and I make the brown sugar frosting in a cast-iron skillet.
—Darlene Brenden, Salem, Oregon

1 package (1/4 ounce) active
  dry yeast
1 cup warm water (110° to
  115°)
3 tablespoons sugar
3 tablespoons shortening
1 egg
1/2 teaspoon salt
3 to 3-1/2 cups all-purpose flour
BROWN SUGAR FROSTING:
3/4 cup packed brown sugar
1/4 cup butter (no substitutes)
3 tablespoons milk
1 teaspoon vanilla extract
2 to 2-1/2 cups confectioners'
  sugar
Oil for deep-fat frying

In a large mixing bowl, dissolve yeast in warm water. Add the sugar, shortening, egg, salt and 1 cup flour; beat until blended. Stir in enough of the remaining flour to form a soft dough. Turn onto a floured surface; knead until smooth and elastic, about 6-8 minutes. Place in a greased bowl, turning once to grease top. Cover and let rise in a warm place until doubled, about 1 hour.

For frosting, combine the brown sugar and butter in a saucepan. Bring to a boil; cook and stir for 2 minutes or until sugar is dissolved. Remove from the heat; stir in the milk and vanilla. Add the confectioners' sugar; beat with a portable mixer for 1 minute or until smooth. Set aside.

Punch dough down. Turn onto a lightly floured surface; divide into 20 pieces. Shape each piece into a ball; pat each ball into a 3-in. circle about 1/4 in. thick. In an electric skillet or deep-fat fryer, heat oil to 375°. Drop dough circles, four to five at a time, into oil. Fry for 1-2 minutes or until browned, turning once. Drain on paper towels. Frost while warm. **Yield:** about 1-1/2 dozen.

Eggnog Pancakes

During the holidays, my family is delighted when they awake to a platter piled high with these featherlight flapjacks. Pancakes made from a mix just can't compare to these homemade delights.
—Marilyn Mueller, Fayetteville, Arkansas

2 cups all-purpose flour
4 teaspoons baking powder
1/2 teaspoon salt
1/4 teaspoon ground nutmeg,
  optional
2 eggs
1-1/2 cups eggnog*
2 tablespoons butter *or*
  margarine, melted

In a bowl, combine flour, baking powder, salt and nutmeg if desired. In another bowl, beat eggs, eggnog and butter; stir into dry ingredients just until moistened. Pour batter by 1/4 cupfuls onto a lightly greased hot griddle. Turn when bubbles form on top; cook until the second side is golden brown. **Yield:** 1 dozen.

*Editor's Note: This recipe was tested with commercially prepared eggnog.

Chicken Cordon Bleu Crepes

(Pictured at right)

I came up with these crepes one day as a way to use up leftover chicken and ham. It's an elegant dish that only looks like you fussed.
—Susan Kemmerer, Telford, Pennsylvania

1 cup all-purpose flour
2 eggs
1-1/4 cups milk
FILLING:
    2 cups coarsely chopped cooked chicken
    2/3 cup chopped fully cooked ham
    1 cup (4 ounces) shredded Swiss cheese
SAUCE:
    2 tablespoons butter *or* margarine
    2 tablespoons all-purpose flour
    1 teaspoon chicken bouillon granules
1-1/2 cups milk
    1/4 cup shredded Swiss cheese
    2 tablespoons chopped fully cooked ham
Minced fresh parsley

In a bowl, whisk the flour, eggs and milk until smooth. Cover and refrigerate for 1 hour.

Heat a lightly greased 7-in. skillet. Pour about 2 tablespoons batter into the center of skillet; lift and tilt pan to evenly coat bottom. Cook until top appears dry; turn and cook 15-20 seconds longer. Remove to a plate. Repeat with remaining batter, adding oil to the skillet as needed. Place waxed paper between crepes. Sprinkle chicken, ham and Swiss cheese over crepes. Roll up tightly. Place seam side down in a greased 13-in. x 9-in. x 2-in. baking dish.

For sauce, in a small saucepan, melt butter. Stir in the flour and bouillon until blended. Gradually whisk in milk. Bring to a boil; cook and stir for 1-2 minutes or until thickened and bubbly. Remove from the heat. Stir in Swiss cheese and ham until cheese is melted. Pour 2/3 cup sauce over crepes. Bake, uncovered, at 350° for 15-20 minutes or until bubbly and heated through. Sprinkle with parsley. Serve with remaining sauce. **Yield:** *7 servings.*

FREEZING CREPES

CHICKEN Cordon Bleu Crepes are a wonderful way to dress up a special-occasion brunch. But you can avoid some of the last-minute preparation with a little planning.

Stack unfilled crepes between layers of waxed paper or white paper towel. Cool; place in an airtight container. Refrigerate for 2 to 3 days or freeze for 4 months. (Thaw frozen crepes overnight in the refrigerator when ready to use.)

In addition, you can make the cheese sauce the day before; cover and refrigerate. The next morning, fill the crepes as directed; cover with plastic wrap and chill. Just before baking, top crepes with the sauce.

Spiced Fruit Compote

My sister shared this recipe with me years ago. It's a must for my family at Christmas.
—*Elaine Nichols, Mesa, Arizona*

1 can (29 ounces) sliced peaches
1 can (15 ounces) apricot halves
1 tablespoon whole allspice
1 to 1-1/2 teaspoons whole cloves
3/4 cup packed brown sugar
1/3 cup white vinegar
5 cinnamon sticks (3 inches)
1 can (20 ounces) pineapple chunks, drained

Drain peaches and apricots, reserving juice. Set fruit aside. Place allspice and cloves on a double thickness of cheesecloth; bring up corners of cloth and tie with kitchen string to form a bag. In a large saucepan, combine the brown sugar, vinegar, and reserved juice. Add spice bag and cinnamon sticks. Bring to a boil; boil for 5 minutes. Discard spice bag and cinnamon. Add the pineapple, peaches and apricots. Bring to a boil. Reduce heat; simmer, uncovered, for 5 minutes or until heated through. Serve warm or at room temperature. **Yield:** 8-10 servings.

MAKING A SPICE BAG

TO KEEP spices together so they can be removed from a saucepan or kettle, place them on several thicknesses of cotton cheesecloth that has been cut into 3-inch squares. Tie with kitchen string to form a bag.

Ham and Cheese Frittata

This frittata is a nice change of pace from traditional scrambled eggs.
Plus, it looks so pretty on a buffet table.
—*Ivy Abbadessa, Loxahatchee, Florida*

1 cup diced fully cooked ham
1/2 cup diced sweet red *or* green pepper
1/2 cup chopped onion
6 eggs, lightly beaten
3/4 cup cottage cheese
1/4 teaspoon pepper
2 plum tomatoes, sliced
1/4 cup shredded cheddar cheese

In a large ovenproof skillet coated with nonstick cooking spray, saute the ham, red pepper and onion until ham is lightly browned and vegetables are tender.

In a bowl, combine the eggs, cottage cheese and pepper; pour over ham mixture. As eggs set, lift edges, letting uncooked portion flow underneath. When the eggs are almost set, broil 4-6 in. from the heat for 1 minute or until top is set. Top with tomatoes and cheddar cheese. Broil 1 minute longer or until cheese is melted. **Yield:** 6 servings.

Veggie Sausage Strata

(Pictured at right)

As a retired home economics teacher, I've made quite a few recipes through the years. This hearty casserole is a favorite of my family.
—*Dorothy Erickson, Blue Eye, Missouri*

   2 pounds bulk Italian sausage
   2 medium green peppers,
     coarsely chopped
   1 medium onion, chopped
   8 eggs
   2 cups milk
   2 teaspoons salt
   2 teaspoons white pepper
   2 teaspoons ground mustard
  12 slices bread, cut into 1/2-inch
     pieces
   1 package (10 ounces) frozen
     chopped spinach, thawed and
     squeezed dry
   2 cups (8 ounces) shredded
     Swiss cheese
   2 cups (8 ounces) shredded
     cheddar cheese
   1 medium zucchini, cut into
     1/4-inch slices

In a large skillet, cook the sausage, green peppers and onion over medium heat until meat is no longer pink; drain. In a large bowl, whisk the eggs, milk, salt, pepper and mustard. Stir in the sausage mixture, bread, spinach, cheeses and zucchini. Transfer to a greased 13-in. x 9-in. x 2-in. baking dish. Cover and refrigerate overnight.

   Remove from the refrigerator 30 minutes before baking. Cover and bake at 350° for 40 minutes. Uncover; bake 40-45 minutes longer or until a knife inserted near the center comes out clean. **Yield:** 10-12 servings.

All Hearts Come Home for Christmas

CHRISTMAS TREE NAPKIN FOLD

SPRUCE UP the place settings on your Christmas brunch table with napkins folded to resemble evergreen trees. This fold works best with a stiff square cloth napkin that holds a crease. Spray starch or sizing can be used to stabilize lightweight or soft fabrics. Start by placing the napkin with the seam side up on a flat surface.

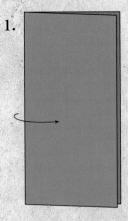

1. Fold napkin in half from left to right to make a rectangle with the fold on the left.

2. Fold the top corners to meet at the center. Repeat with the bottom corners.

3. Fold the top point down and the bottom point up to make a square.

4. Fold the square in half from top to bottom to make a rectangle.

5. Take the top layer of the lower right corner and bring it to the lower left corner, forming a large triangle. Crease the napkin.

6. Fold the left point of the triangle back to the right and align points.

7. Take the top layer of the lower left corner and bring it to the lower right corner, forming a large triangle. Crease the napkin.

8. Take the top layer of the lower right corner and bring it to the lower left corner and align points.

9. Stand the napkin up, evenly spreading the four folds to resemble pine boughs. Tie gold metallic cording into a double bow. Place bow on top of tree napkin.

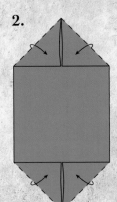

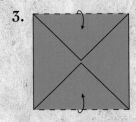

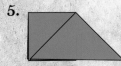

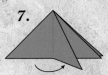

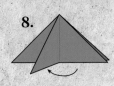

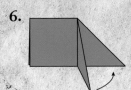

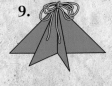

Teapot Poinsettia

(Pictured at right and on page 7)

When hosting a brunch during the holidays, don't just set a potted poinsettia on your table for a centerpiece. Instead play upon the breakfast theme by using a teapot or coffeepot as a vase for cut poinsettias.

Poinsettia plant
Melted candle wax*
Floral foam
Teapot
Fresh ivy and ferns *or* **other greens**

Cut poinsettia bracts with stems from plant (we used only one). Immediately dip the end of each stem into melted candle wax to seal and then place stems in cool water. Cut the foam to fit inside teapot. Soak foam following manufacturer's instructions; place inside teapot. Add cut poinsettia bracts. Fill in the arrangement with ivy and ferns.

***Editor's Note:** The stems of cut poinsettias secrete sap, which can prevent them (and other flowers or greens in the arrangement) from absorbing water. So after cutting poinsettia bracts from the plant, the stems must be sealed. We sealed ours with melted candle wax, but they can also be sealed by singeing them with an open flame or by placing them in rubbing alcohol for 10 minutes. Place stems in cool water immediately after sealing.

'TIS THE *Season*

Dazzling Christmas Day Dinner

NO ONE in your family will have a blue Christmas when you set a stunning table and serve an unforgettable meal.

Your favorite goblets will shine even brighter when filled with a refreshing beverage like Sparkling White Grape Juice.

For the mouth-watering main course, place golden Glazed Cornish Hens on top of a bed of flavorful Apricot Rice Stuffing.

Chocolate Dessert Cups filled with ice cream and topped with Orange-Caramel Ice Cream Sauce are an elegant treat everyone will rave about for Christmases to come. (All of the recipes are shown at right.)

TRUE-BLUE MENU

(Clockwise from top right)

Sparkling White Grape Juice (p. 24)

Glazed Cornish Hens (p. 20)

Apricot Rice Stuffing (p. 22)

Orange-Caramel Ice Cream Sauce (p. 21)

Chocolate Dessert Cups (p. 20)

Glazed Cornish Hens

(Pictured on page 18)

If you're looking to add a touch of elegance to your Christmas dinner table, our Test Kitchen home economists suggest these Cornish game hens topped with a sweet apricot glaze.

2 Cornish game hens (20 ounces *each*), split lengthwise
1/4 teaspoon salt
1/8 teaspoon white pepper
1/3 cup 100% apricot spreadable fruit, warmed
1 tablespoon orange juice

Place hens, breast side up, on a rack in a shallow roasting pan. Sprinkle with salt and pepper. Bake, uncovered, at 350° for 30 minutes. In a small bowl, combine spreadable fruit and orange juice. Spoon some of the apricot mixture over the hens. Bake 30-35 minutes longer or until golden brown and juices run clear, basting several times with remaining apricot mixture. Let stand for 5 minutes before serving. **Yield:** 4 servings.

Chocolate Dessert Cups

(Pictured on opposite page and page 18)

Our home economists assure that your guests will be delighted with these edible dessert cups, which can be used to serve ice cream, pudding, fresh fruit and more. You can make them a week in advance, then refrigerate in an airtight container.

6 squares (1 ounce *each*) semisweet chocolate
1 teaspoon shortening

Cut out four 6-in. circles from waxed paper; place on a baking sheet. In a microwave, melt chocolate and shortening; stir until smooth. Pour 2 tablespoons melted chocolate into the center of each circle; spread chocolate to within 1 in. of edge. Refrigerate for 3-4 minutes or until chocolate does not spread when handled.

Drape circles, waxed paper side down, over inverted 6-oz. custard cups or small bowls. Shape edges if desired. Chill for 10 minutes. Carefully peel waxed paper from chocolate cups. **Yield:** 4 servings.

MAKING CHOCOLATE DESSERT CUPS

POUR melted chocolate onto a circle of waxed paper. Chill 3-4 minutes. With waxed paper side down, drape circle over inverted custard cup. Chill for 10 minutes before removing paper.

Orange-Caramel Ice Cream Sauce

(Pictured at right and on page 18)

Instead of topping ice cream with a store-bought sauce, our Test Kitchen presents this simple homemade version. The subtle orange flavor pairs well with any type of ice cream.

1 cup packed brown sugar
1 cup heavy whipping cream
1/2 cup sweetened condensed milk
1/2 teaspoon orange extract
Butter pecan ice cream
Orange spirals, optional

In a saucepan, cook and stir brown sugar and cream over medium heat until sugar is dissolved. Bring to a boil; cook for 5 minutes or until mixture is reduced by half. Remove from the heat. Stir in milk and orange extract. Cover and refrigerate. Just before serving, warm over low heat. Serve over ice cream. Garnish with orange spirals if desired. **Yield:** 1-1/3 cups.

GARNISHING WITH ORANGE SPIRALS

ORANGE SPIRALS (pictured above) make an attractive and fragrant garnish for any type of dessert.

To make orange spirals, use a citrus stripper to remove the peel of an orange in one continuous motion, working from end to end. Tightly wind strip around a straw; trim and secure ends with waterproof tape. Use the remaining orange peel strip to wrap more straws. Let wrapped straws stand for at least 20 minutes. (The longer the strips are wrapped around the straw, the longer they'll hold their shape after the straw is removed.)

To make the spirals a day in advance, place the wrapped straws in a large resealable plastic bag and add a dampened white paper towel. Seal the bag and refrigerate.

Before using as a garnish, remove the tape and unwind the spirals from the straws. You can cut the spirals to any desired length.

Apricot Rice Stuffing

(Pictured on page 18)

This fruity rice stuffing accompanies roast duck as part of our traditional New Year's Day dinner.
It's also an attractive side dish to serve alongside Cornish game hens and chicken.
—Katrina Forar, Lakewood, Colorado

1/2 cup finely chopped onion
1/2 cup finely chopped celery
1/4 cup butter *or* margarine
 3 cups cooked rice
3/4 cup chopped dried apricots
1/4 cup minced fresh parsley
1/2 teaspoon salt
1/4 teaspoon pepper
1/4 teaspoon dried thyme
1/4 teaspoon ground nutmeg
1/8 teaspoon ground cloves

In a large skillet, saute onion and celery in butter until tender. Stir in the rice, apricots, parsley and seasonings. Transfer to a greased 1-qt. baking dish. Cover and bake at 350° for 30 minutes. Uncover; bake 5-10 minutes longer or until heated through. **Yield:** 4 servings.

Basil Beans

Since I grow lots of green beans and basil in my garden, this is a popular
side dish in my home. These flavored beans round out a variety of meals.
—Sue Gronholz, Columbus, Wisconsin

1 pound fresh green beans,
 trimmed
1 tablespoon minced fresh basil
 or 1 teaspoon dried basil
1 tablespoon butter *or*
 margarine
1/2 teaspoon salt
1/8 teaspoon pepper

Place beans in a saucepan and cover with water; bring to a boil. Cook, uncovered, for 8-10 minutes or until crisp-tender; drain. Place beans in a serving dish. Add the basil, butter, salt and pepper. Toss until butter is melted and beans are evenly coated. Serve immediately. **Yield:** 4 servings.

Crunchy Breadsticks

(Pictured at right)

These thin, crisp breadsticks created in our Test Kitchen add a bit of elegance to a holiday dinner. Each bite is perfectly seasoned with thyme and coarse salt.

2 cups all-purpose flour
1-1/2 teaspoons baking powder
1/2 teaspoon salt
3 tablespoons shortening
1/2 to 3/4 cup ice water
1 tablespoon olive *or* vegetable oil
1/4 teaspoon coarse salt
1/4 teaspoon dried thyme

In a food processor, combine the flour, baking powder, salt and shortening; cover and process until mixture resembles coarse crumbs. While processing, gradually add water until dough forms a ball.

Transfer to a floured surface. Roll dough into a 10-in. x 8-in. rectangle. Cut into 10-in. x 1/2-in. strips. Twist each strip four times and place on baking sheets. Brush with oil. Combine coarse salt and thyme; sprinkle over breadsticks. Bake at 350° for 18-20 minutes or until golden brown. Cool on a wire rack. **Yield:** 16 breadsticks.

Sesame Ginger Vinaigrette

(Pictured above)

Our home economists enliven an ordinary green salad with a vinaigrette featuring orange juice, ginger and balsamic vinegar.

1/3 cup orange juice
3 tablespoons olive *or* vegetable oil
1 tablespoon sugar
1 tablespoon balsamic vinegar *or* red wine vinegar
2 teaspoons sesame seeds, toasted
1/2 teaspoon sesame oil

1/4 teaspoon ground ginger *or* 1-1/2 teaspoons grated fresh gingerroot
1/4 teaspoon salt
Torn salad greens, halved cherry tomatoes and sliced cucumbers

In a jar with a tight-fitting lid, combine the first eight ingredients; shake well. Serve over salad. **Yield:** 1/2 cup.

Sparkling White Grape Juice

(Pictured on page 19)

*The bubbles from the lemon-lime soda cling to the grape "ice cubes", giving this
refreshing beverage from our Test Kitchen lots of sparkle.*

2-1/3 cups chilled white grape juice
4-2/3 cups chilled lemon-lime soda
Green grapes

In a pitcher, combine grape juice and soda. Pour into glasses. Thread grapes on skewers; add to each glass. **Yield:** 7 servings.

COUNTDOWN TO CHRISTMAS DINNER

A Few Weeks Before:
- Prepare two grocery lists—one for non-perishable items to purchase now and one for perishable items to purchase a few days before Christmas Day.
- Make the Fire-and-Ice Centerpiece (see page 25).

One Week Before:
- Make the Chocolate Dessert Cups. Remove waxed paper and place cups in an airtight container; chill.

Two to Three Days Before:
- Buy remaining grocery items.
- Cook the rice for Apricot Rice Stuffing; refrigerate in a covered container.

Christmas Eve:
- Set the table.
- Prepare the Sesame Ginger Vinaigrette; chill.
- Make the orange spirals; place in a resealable plastic bag along with a dampened paper towel and refrigerate.
- Prepare the Orange-Caramel Ice Cream Sauce; cover and chill.
- Wash and trim the fresh green beans for Basil Beans. Refrigerate in a resealable plastic bag.
- Prepare and combine the stuffing ingredients; cover and chill.
- Bake the Crunchy Breadsticks; cool and store in an airtight container at room temperature.

Christmas Day:
- In the morning, combine the salad ingredients in a bowl; cover with plastic wrap and refrigerate.
- Shortly before guests arrive, remove the Fire-and-Ice Centerpiece from the freezer and arrange on a tray with fresh greens. Light the candles just before sitting down to dinner.
- Prepare and serve Sparkling White Grape Juice.
- Bake Glazed Cornish Hens. After 30 minutes, put the stuffing in the oven.
- Remove the salad dressing from the refrigerator 30 minutes before serving. Shake well and serve over salad.
- Set out the breadsticks.
- A few minutes before the Cornish hens are done baking, cook the Basil Beans.
- For dessert, scoop butter pecan ice cream into Chocolate Dessert Cups. Top with warmed Orange-Caramel Ice Cream Sauce; garnish with orange spirals.

Fire-and-Ice Centerpiece

(Pictured at right and on page 18)

Guests will be in awe when they catch sight of this unique holiday centerpiece. Hostesses will appreciate that there's no pressure to have it looking perfect because the items will shift any which way as the water freezes. But the end result will definitely be stunning!

Artificial *or* natural pine greens and pinecones
Small gold plastic balls
Gold string beads
Freezer-safe container with smooth straight sides
Distilled water
Tea light candles in clear containers
Edged tray to hold centerpiece
Fresh greens

Place greens, pinecones, gold balls and beads in a freezer-safe container, using enough so they stay in place when water is added and arranging them so they touch the sides of the container. Carefully add distilled water to within 1 in. of the top of the container. Float tea lights on top of the water. Place on a flat surface in the freezer; freeze for several days or until solid.

About 15 minutes before unmolding, remove container from the freezer. Let stand at room temperature until ice releases from the sides of container.

Trim or fold paper towel so it is a bit smaller than the centerpiece and place on tray. Place the centerpiece on top of paper towel to keep it from sliding. Add fresh greens around the base of the centerpiece. Remove water from the tray as needed.

MAKING THE FIRE-AND-ICE CENTERPIECE

1. Place greens, pinecones, balls and beads in the freezer-safe container.

2. Carefully add distilled water to within 1 inch of the top of the container. Freeze until solid.

Hearty Holiday Appetizers

CHRISTMAS is a terrific time of year to toast the people who are nearest and dearest to you.

So gather your closest friends and present them with an intimate evening of good conversation and appealing appetizers.

On the following pages, you'll uncover an elegant assortment of tray toppers, such as Crab Corn Pudding, Coconut Shrimp and Pesto Cream Cheese Spread. (All recipes shown at right.)

Not only are the Yuletide yummies in this chapter guaranteed to be good, many can be made ahead and either frozen or refrigerated. So seasonal snacking couldn't be easier!

FINGER FOOD
WITH FLAIR
(Clockwise from bottom)

Crab Corn Pudding (p. 28)

Coconut Shrimp (p. 29)

Pesto Cream Cheese Spread (p. 31)

Crab Corn Pudding

(Pictured on page 26)

This special dish is a wonderful first course for a small gathering of friends around the holidays.
—Shawn Solley, Lawton, Oklahoma

1/2 cup finely chopped green onions
2 tablespoons butter *or* margarine
2-1/2 cups frozen corn, thawed and patted dry
1-3/4 cups half-and-half cream
6 eggs, lightly beaten
2 cans (6 ounces *each*) crabmeat, drained, flaked and cartilage removed
1/4 cup grated Parmesan cheese
3 tablespoons all-purpose flour
1-1/2 teaspoons salt
1 teaspoon sugar
1/4 teaspoon white pepper
1/4 teaspoon ground nutmeg

Lightly grease eight 8-oz. custard cups; set aside. In a skillet, saute green onions in butter until tender; set aside.

Spread corn on an ungreased baking sheet. Bake, uncovered, at 350° for 20 minutes. In a blender or food processor, combine corn and cream; cover and process for 1-2 seconds. Add the eggs, crab, Parmesan cheese, flour, salt, sugar, pepper, nutmeg and reserved onions. Cover and process 10-20 seconds longer. Pour into prepared custard cups.

Place cups in a large baking pan. Add 1 in. of boiling water to pan. Bake, uncovered, at 350° for 45-50 minutes or until a knife inserted near the center comes out clean. **Yield:** 8 servings.

Chicken Bacon Bites

Ginger and orange marmalade give these rumaki-style snacks wonderful flavor.
I marinate the wrapped chicken earlier in the day and broil them when guests arrive.
—Betty Pierson, Wellington, Florida

12 bacon strips, halved
10 ounces boneless skinless chicken breasts, cut into 24 cubes
1 can (8 ounces) sliced water chestnuts, drained
1/2 cup orange marmalade
1/4 cup soy sauce
2 garlic cloves, minced
1/4 teaspoon ground ginger *or* 1 teaspoon grated fresh gingerroot

Place bacon on a broiler rack. Broil 4 in. from the heat for 1-2 minutes on each side or until partially cooked; cool. Wrap a piece of bacon around a chicken cube and water chestnut slice; secure with a toothpick. In a large resealable plastic bag, combine the marmalade, soy sauce, garlic and ginger. Add wrapped chicken; carefully turn to coat. Seal and refrigerate for 2 hours.

Drain and discard marinade. Broil chicken for 3-4 minutes on each side or until juices run clear and bacon is crisp. Serve warm. **Yield:** 2 dozen.

Coconut Shrimp

(Pictured at right and on page 26)

Guests are always impressed when I serve these restaurant-quality shrimp. A selection of sauces served alongside adds the perfect touch.
— Tacy Holliday
Germantown, Maryland

1-1/4 cups all-purpose flour
  1/4 teaspoon seafood seasoning
    1 egg, beaten
  3/4 cup pineapple juice
    1 package (14 ounces) flaked
      coconut
    1 pound large shrimp, peeled
      and deveined
Oil for deep-fat frying
Sweet-and-sour sauce, plum sauce
  or Dijon mustard, optional

In a bowl, combine the flour, seafood seasoning, egg and pineapple juice until smooth. Place coconut in a shallow bowl. Dip shrimp into batter, then coat with coconut.

    In an electric skillet or deep-fat fryer, heat oil to 375°. Fry shrimp, a few at a time, for 1-1/2 minutes or until golden brown, turning occasionally. Drain on paper towels. Serve with dippng sauce or mustard if desired. **Yield:** about 1-1/2 dozen.

Cucumber Ham Roll-Ups

I came across this recipe when looking for a new dish to take to a card party. Everyone loves these refreshing roll-ups...even the kids!
— Debbie Smith, Urbana, Ohio

1 medium cucumber
1 package (8 ounces) cream
  cheese, softened
2 tablespoons prepared mustard
1 teaspoon dill weed
8 thin rectangular slices
  deli ham

Peel cucumber; cut in half lengthwise. Scoop out seeds with a spoon. Cut each half lengthwise into four strips; set aside. In a small mixing bowl, combine the cream cheese, mustard and dill. Spread about 2 tablespoons over each ham slice. Place a cucumber strip on the wide end; roll up tightly jelly-roll style. Cut off any cucumber that extends beyond ham slice. Wrap tightly in plastic wrap and refrigerate for at least 2 hours. Cut into 3/4-in. slices. **Yield:** about 4 dozen.

Savory Christmas Cutouts

This recipe is always a success because the dough is easy to work with and cuts well.
The appetizers can be made year-round using cookie cutter shapes to suit the season.
—*J.R. Smosna, Warren, Pennsylvania*

2 cups all-purpose flour
1 cup (4 ounces) shredded
  Swiss cheese
1 teaspoon sugar
1 teaspoon salt
1/2 teaspoon ground mustard
1/8 to 1/4 teaspoon cayenne
  pepper
1/2 cup plus 2 teaspoons cold
  butter (no substitutes)
9 tablespoons dry white wine *or*
  chicken broth
1 egg, lightly beaten
Sesame seeds *and/or* poppy seeds

In a bowl, combine the first six ingredients; cut in butter until the mixture resembles coarse crumbs. Gradually add wine or broth, tossing with a fork until dough forms a ball.

On a lightly floured surface, roll out dough to 1/8-in. thickness. Cut with 2-in. cookie cutters dipped in flour. Place 1 in. apart on ungreased baking sheets. Brush tops with egg; sprinkle with sesame and/or poppy seeds. Bake at 400° for 10-12 minutes or until lightly browned. Remove to wire racks to cool. **Yield:** 6 dozen.

Artichoke Wonton Cups

I came up with this recipe by combining several artichoke dip recipes.
Wonton cups add a fancy look that's perfect for special occasions.
If you're serving a large crowd, you may want to double the recipe.
—*Paige Scott, Murfreesboro, Tennessee*

1 cup grated Parmesan cheese
1 cup mayonnaise
1/2 teaspoon onion powder
1/2 teaspoon garlic powder
2 cups (8 ounces) shredded
  mozzarella cheese
1 can (14 ounces) water-packed
  artichoke hearts, drained and
  chopped
1 package (12 ounces) wonton
  wrappers

In a small mixing bowl, combine the Parmesan cheese, mayonnaise, onion powder and garlic powder; mix well. Stir in the mozzarella cheese and artichokes; set aside.

Coat one side of each wonton wrapper with nonstick cooking spray; press greased side down into miniature muffin cups. Bake at 350° for 5 minutes or until edges are lightly browned. Fill each cup with 1 tablespoon artichoke mixture. Bake 5-6 minutes longer or until golden brown. Serve warm. **Yield:** about 4 dozen.

Pesto Cream Cheese Spread

(Pictured at right and on page 27)

This is a terrific appetizer to serve when hosting an Italian-theme meal. People may be a little hesitant to try it, but once they dip in, they won't be able to stop!
—Cynthia Emshoff, Sarasota, Florida

- 1 package (8 ounces) cream cheese, softened
- 1/8 teaspoon garlic powder
- 1/3 cup grated Parmesan cheese
- 3 tablespoons butter *or* margarine, softened
- 1/2 cup minced fresh parsley
- 1 garlic clove, minced
- 1 teaspoon dried basil
- 1/2 teaspoon dried marjoram
- 1/4 cup finely chopped walnuts
- 3 tablespoons olive *or* vegetable oil

Assorted crackers

Line a 5-3/4-in. x 3-in. x 2-in. loaf pan with plastic wrap. In a small mixing bowl, combine cream cheese and garlic powder until blended; set aside. In a bowl, combine Parmesan cheese, butter, parsley, garlic, basil and marjoram until blended. Stir in walnuts. Gradually stir in oil.

Spread about 1/4 cup cream cheese mixture in prepared pan. Carefully spread with a third of the Parmesan mixture. Repeat layers twice. Top with remaining cream cheese mixture. Cover and refrigerate for at least 5 hours. Unmold; serve with crackers. **Yield:** about 1-1/2 cups.

A SPREAD WITH LOVELY LAYERS

THE LAYERS in your Pesto Cream Cheese Spread can look as lovely as the photo above if you have a little extra time.

Here's the trick: After evenly spreading 1/4 cup cream cheese mixture in the prepared pan, cover and refrigerate until firm. Evenly spread a third of the Parmesan cheese mixture on top; cover and refrigerate until firm. Repeat layers as the recipe directs, making sure each layer is flat and even, and refrigerating after adding each layer.

Marvelous Stuffed Mushrooms

My mother-in-law would make these savory stuffed mushrooms every Christmas.
Pouring whipping cream over them before baking makes each morsel extra moist and rich.
—Gail Anderson, Cantonment, Florida

1 **pound large fresh mushrooms**
1/3 **cup butter *or* margarine, softened**
4-1/2 **teaspoons all-purpose flour**
1 **tablespoon finely chopped onion**
1 **tablespoon minced fresh parsley**
1 **tablespoon Dijon mustard**
1/2 **teaspoon salt**
Dash to 1/8 teaspoon cayenne pepper
Dash ground nutmeg
1 **cup heavy whipping cream**

Remove stems from mushrooms; set caps aside. Finely chop stems. In a small mixing bowl, combine the butter, flour, onion, parsley, mustard, salt, cayenne, nutmeg and chopped stems. Fill mushroom caps. Place in a greased shallow 2-qt. baking dish. Pour cream over mushrooms. Bake, uncovered, at 375° for 30-35 minutes or until mushrooms are tender, basting twice. **Yield:** about 2 dozen.

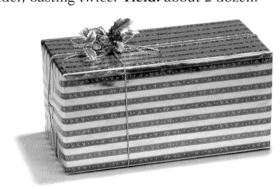

Southwest Corn Spread

My Aunt Christine shared this recipe with me at a family reunion a few years ago.
The thick spread's Southwestern flavor has mass appeal.
—Rebecca Sue Dickinson, Iredell, Texas

2 **packages (8 ounces *each*) cream cheese, softened**
1/4 **cup lime juice**
1 **can (4 ounces) chopped green chilies**
3 **green onions, thinly sliced**
1 **tablespoon ground cumin**
1 **teaspoon cayenne pepper**
1 **teaspoon pepper**
1/2 **to 1 teaspoon salt**

1 **can (8-3/4 ounces) whole kernel corn, drained**
1 **cup chopped walnuts, optional**
Crackers *or* tortilla chips

In a mixing bowl, combine cream cheese and lime juice until smooth. Beat in the chilies, onions, cumin, cayenne, pepper and salt. Stir in corn and walnuts if desired. Cover and refrigerate for at least 4 hours. Serve with crackers or chips. **Yield:** about 3 cups.

Spicy Chili Dip

(Pictured at right)

With chili powder, red pepper flakes and picante sauce, this dip has plenty of kick! I like to take it to parties and never have to worry about bringing home leftovers.
—Joan Kittler, Western Springs, Illinois

  1 package (8 ounces) cream
     cheese, softened
  2 cups (16 ounces) sour cream
1/2 cup finely chopped onion
  2 garlic cloves, minced
  1 tablespoon chili powder
1/2 teaspoon crushed red pepper
     flakes
1-1/2 cups picante sauce
  1 cup (4 ounces) shredded
     mozzarella cheese
Fresh vegetables and corn *or*
   tortilla chips

In a small mixing bowl, beat cream cheese and sour cream until smooth. Beat in the onion, garlic, chili powder and pepper flakes. Stir in picante sauce and mozzarella cheese. Cover and refrigerate for at least 4 hours. Serve with vegetables and chips. **Yield:** about 5 cups.

Sherry Fruit Dip

A fruit appetizer is a nice change of pace from the rich, savory snacks so prevalent around the holidays. It's a no-fuss favorite I take to many get-togethers.
—Sandy Oldendick, Cincinnati, Ohio

  1 package (8 ounces) cream
     cheese, softened
1/3 cup heavy whipping cream
1/4 cup sherry *or* apple juice
1/4 teaspoon vanilla extract
1-1/3 cups confectioners' sugar
Fresh fruit

In a small mixing bowl, combine the cream cheese, cream, sherry or apple juice and vanilla. Gradually beat in confectioners' sugar. Cover and refrigerate for 8 hours or overnight. Serve with fruit. **Yield:** about 1-1/2 cups.

Swiss Cheese Canape Cups

Guests will think you spent hours making these impressive-looking canapes.
You don't have to tell them they're actually easy to prepare!
Horseradish and mustard give these bite-size snacks a little zip.
— Carol Harkins, Casper, Wyoming

8 slices sandwich bread, crusts removed
1/4 cup butter *or* margarine, softened
1 tablespoon minced fresh parsley
1 teaspoon prepared horseradish
1 teaspoon Dijon mustard
1 cup (4 ounces) shredded Swiss cheese
1 egg white, lightly beaten

Cut each slice of bread into four squares. Press squares into greased miniature muffin cups. In a bowl, combine the butter, parsley, horseradish and mustard. Stir in cheese. Add egg white; mix well. Place about 3/4 teaspoonful in each bread cup. Bake at 400° for 6-8 minutes or until filling is set and edges of bread are golden brown. Serve warm. **Yield:** 32 appetizers.

   Editor's Note: Baked cheese cups may be frozen for up to 4 months. Thaw in the refrigerator. Place on ungreased baking sheets and bake at 350° for 4-6 minutes or until heated through.

Marinated Olives

Our son often made these olives for holiday get-togethers.
They're simple to make and add a little zest to the buffet table offerings.
— Marguerite Shaeffer, Sewell, New Jersey

2 cups large stuffed olives, drained
1 cup pitted kalamata olives, drained
1 cup pitted medium ripe olives, drained
1/4 cup olive *or* vegetable oil
2 tablespoons lemon juice
1 tablespoon minced fresh thyme *or* 1 teaspoon dried thyme
2 teaspoons grated lemon peel
2 teaspoons minced fresh rosemary *or* 1/2 teaspoon dried rosemary, crushed
4 garlic cloves, slivered
Pepper to taste

Place olives in a bowl. Combine the remaining ingredients; pour over olives and stir. Cover and refrigerate for 1-2 days before serving, stirring several times each day. Olives may be refrigerated for 2 weeks. Serve with a slotted spoon. **Yield:** 4 cups.

WHAT ARE KALAMATA OLIVES?

KALAMATA OLIVES are purple-black, almond-shaped olives native to Greece. They're usually packed in either olive oil or vinegar, giving them a stronger flavor than most other olives. Kalamata olives can be found in larger supermarkets as well as smaller ethnic grocery stores.

Spinach Dip With Cajun Pita Chips

(Pictured at right)

I learned to make Cajun Pita Chips while working for a caterer. They're deliciously different dippers for my rich and creamy spinach dip.
—Julia Morgan, Flatwoods, Kentucky

> 2 cups (16 ounces) sour cream
> 1 package (10 ounces) frozen chopped spinach, thawed and squeezed dry
> 1/4 cup finely chopped sweet red pepper
> 1/4 cup chopped green onions
> 1 garlic clove, minced
> 1/4 teaspoon salt
> 1/4 teaspoon hot pepper sauce

CHIPS:
> 5 pita breads (6 inches), halved and split
> 1/2 cup butter *or* margarine, melted
> 1/2 teaspoon Cajun seasoning
> 1/4 teaspoon ground cumin

In a bowl, combine the sour cream, spinach, red pepper, onions, garlic, salt and hot pepper sauce. Cover and refrigerate for at least 1 hour.

Meanwhile, for chips, cut each pita half into four wedges. Combine the butter, Cajun seasoning and cumin; brush over rough side of pita wedges. Place on ungreased baking sheets. Bake at 400° for 8-10 minutes or until chips are golden brown and crisp. Serve with dip. **Yield:** about 2-1/3 cups dip (6-1/2 dozen pita chips).

Swiss Cherry Bruschetta

This recipe is a spin-off of a cherry chicken main dish my husband adores.
The combination of sweet, tart and salty flavors provides a contrast that's hard to resist.
—*Shelly Platten, Amherst, Wisconsin*

2 large onions, chopped
1 garlic clove, minced
4 teaspoons olive *or*
    vegetable oil
1 tablespoon balsamic vinegar
    or red wine vinegar
1 teaspoon brown sugar
1/2 teaspoon garlic salt
2-1/2 cups pitted dark sweet
    cherries, coarsely chopped
16 slices French bread (1/2 inch
    thick), lightly toasted

1-1/2 cups (6 ounces) shredded Swiss cheese
2 tablespoons minced fresh parsley

In a large skillet, saute onions and garlic in oil until tender, about 6 minutes. Add the vinegar, brown sugar and garlic salt; reduce heat. Cook for 3-4 minutes or until onions are caramelized. Stir in the cherries; cook 5 minutes longer or until sauce is syrupy.

Place toasted bread on a baking sheet; spoon cherry mixture evenly over toast. Sprinkle with cheese and parsley. Broil 3-4 in. from the heat for 1-2 minutes or until cheese is melted. **Yield:** 16 servings.

Hot Cauliflower Crab Spread

Many of our favorite recipes feature vegetables, especially cauliflower and broccoli.
This spread from my sister-in-law is a great special-occasion meal starter.
—*Ruth Bartman, Nordman, Idaho*

1 package (16 ounces) frozen
    cauliflowerets, thawed
1 can (6 ounces) crabmeat,
    drained, flaked and cartilage
    removed *or* 1 cup chopped
    imitation crabmeat
1 cup mayonnaise*
1 cup grated Parmesan cheese
1/2 teaspoon garlic salt
1/2 teaspoon lemon-pepper
    seasoning

1 to 2 tablespoons chopped pimientos
Assorted crackers

In a bowl, combine the cauliflower, crab, mayonnaise, Parmesan cheese, garlic salt and lemon-pepper. Transfer to an ungreased 9-in. pie plate. Sprinkle with pimientos. Bake, uncovered, at 350° for 25-30 minutes or until bubbly and edges are golden brown. Serve with crackers. **Yield:** 4 cups.

*Editor's Note: Reduced-fat or fat-free mayonnaise may not be substituted for regular mayonnaise in this recipe.

Honey-Garlic Glazed Meatballs

(Pictured at right)

My husband and I raise cattle on our farm here in southwestern Ontario, so it's no surprise that we're fond of these saucy meatballs. I know your family will like them, too.
—*Marion Foster, Kirkton, Ontario*

  2 eggs
3/4 cup milk
  1 cup dry bread crumbs
1/2 cup finely chopped onion
  2 teaspoons salt
  2 pounds ground beef
  4 garlic cloves, minced
  1 tablespoon butter *or* margarine
3/4 cup ketchup
1/2 cup honey
  3 tablespoons soy sauce

In a large bowl, combine eggs and milk. Add the bread crumbs, onion and salt. Crumble beef over mixture and mix well. Shape into 1-in. balls. Place in two greased 15-in. x 10-in. x 1-in. baking pans. Bake, uncovered, at 400° for 12-15 minutes or until meat is no longer pink.

Meanwhile, in a large saucepan, saute garlic in butter until tender. Stir in the ketchup, honey and soy sauce. Bring to a boil. Reduce heat; cover and simmer for 5 minutes. Drain meatballs; add to sauce. Carefully stir to evenly coat. Cook for 5-10 minutes. **Yield:** about 5-1/2 dozen.

Water Chestnut Cheese Bites

Water chestnuts and olives make these baked cheese snacks deliciously different.
They're best served fresh from the oven.
—Rebecca Banks, White, Georgia

1 cup (4 ounces) shredded
 cheddar cheese
2 tablespoons butter *or*
 margarine, softened
1/2 cup all-purpose flour
1/4 cup chopped stuffed olives
Dash cayenne pepper
1 egg

1 can (8 ounces) water chestnuts, drained and
 finely chopped

In a small mixing bowl, beat cheese and butter on low speed until blended. Add the flour, olives and cayenne; mix well. Beat in the egg and water chestnuts until combined. Drop by teaspoonfuls onto greased baking sheets. Bake at 400° for 10-12 minutes or until light golden brown. Serve warm. **Yield:** 2-1/2 dozen.

Rhubarb Chutney Appetizer

My husband is a true-blue rhubarb lover, so I'm sure to make this spread often each spring.
With frozen rhubarb, it's a terrific take-along appetizer for holiday gatherings.
—Joyce Pappenfus, St. Cloud, Minnesota

1 cup packed brown sugar
1/2 cup finely chopped fresh *or*
 frozen rhubarb, thawed and
 drained
1/2 cup raisins
1/2 cup diced peeled apples
1/2 cup cider vinegar
1 teaspoon ground allspice
1/2 teaspoon ground cinnamon
1/8 teaspoon ground cloves
1 package (8 ounces) cream
 cheese, softened
1 tablespoon milk

4 green onions, thinly sliced
1/2 cup dry roasted peanuts, chopped
Assorted crackers

For chutney, combine the first eight ingredients in a saucepan. Bring to a boil over medium heat, stirring occasionally. Reduce heat; simmer, uncovered, for 35 minutes or until thickened. Cool. Cover and refrigerate until chilled.

In a small mixing bowl, beat cream cheese and milk until smooth. Spread over a serving platter. Spread chutney over cream cheese. Top with onions and peanuts. Serve with crackers. **Yield:** about 3 cups.

Mozzarella Marinara

(Pictured at right)

My husband and I enjoy mozzarella marinara at our state fair and thought we'd try to make our own version at home. Our recipe calls for convenient egg roll wrappers instead of a messy batter. The homemade marinara sauce is fast and flavorful.
—Ellen Borst, Genoa City, Wisconsin

1 small onion, chopped
1 garlic clove, minced
3 tablespoons olive *or* vegetable oil
1 can (14-1/2 ounces) diced tomatoes, undrained
1 can (6 ounces) tomato paste
1 cup water
2 teaspoons sugar
1/2 teaspoon salt
1 bay leaf
24 egg roll wrappers
24 pieces string cheese
Oil for deep-fat frying

In a large saucepan, saute onion and garlic in oil. Add the tomatoes, tomato paste, water, sugar, salt and bay leaf. Bring to a boil. Reduce heat; simmer, uncovered, for 20-30 minutes or until thickened.

Meanwhile, place an egg roll wrapper on a work surface with a point facing you. Place a piece of cheese near the bottom corner. Fold bottom corner of wrapper over cheese; roll up just until cheese is enclosed. Fold sides of wrapper over top. Using a pastry brush, wet the top corner with water. Roll up tightly to seal, forming a tube. Repeat.

In an electric skillet or deep-fat fryer, heat oil to 375°. Fry mozzarella sticks, a few at a time, for 1 minute or until golden brown, turning occasionally. Discard bay leaf from marinara sauce. Serve with the mozzarella sticks. **Yield:** 2 dozen (3 cups sauce).

Speedy Salsa

*With a small list of ingredients, this salsa is a snap to prepare on a moment's notice
I've also served it over baked potatoes for a light lunch.*
—*Carolyn Hayes, Johnston City, Illinois*

2 cans (10 ounces *each*) diced
tomatoes and green chilies,
undrained
1 can (15 ounces) black beans,
rinsed and drained
1 can (11 ounces) Mexicorn,
drained

Sour cream and sliced green onions
Tortilla *or* corn chips

In a serving bowl, combine the tomatoes, beans and corn. Garnish with sour cream and green onions. Serve with chips. **Yield:** 3 cups.

MAKE-AHEAD APPETIZER IDEAS

HOSTING an appetizer buffet involves serving several foods at the same time. In addition to offering appetizers that need to be assembled just as guests arrive, look for recipes that can be frozen weeks in advance or prepared the day before.

Here are some suggestions for do-ahead appetizers found in this chapter:

Freezer Favorites. The following appetizers can be fully or partially prepared and frozen.
- Mozzarella Marinara (page 39). After deep-frying the mozzarella sticks, place in a single layer in a baking pan; cool, then freeze. Transfer to a resealable plastic bag; freeze. The day before the party, make the marinara sauce; refrigerate. Bake frozen mozzarella sticks at 400° for 10-15 minutes or until golden and hot. Reheat the sauce; serve with mozzarella sticks.
- Honey-Garlic Glazed Meatballs (page 37). Bake the meatballs as directed; cool. Freeze in a single layer in a baking pan. Transfer to a resealable plastic bag and freeze. The day before the party, thaw the meatballs in the refrigerator and make the honey-garlic

sauce. In the morning, reheat the meatballs and sauce in a slow cooker on low.
- Swiss Cheese Canape Cups can be made ahead and frozen. See the recipe on page 34 for instructions.

Do-Ahead Delights. These snacks are convenient because they can be prepared a day— or more!—in advance.
- Marinated Olives (page 34) can be made and stored in the refrigerator for 2 weeks.
- Spinach Dip with Cajun Pita Chips (page 35). Prepare the dip; cover and refrigerate overnight. Bake the chips as directed; cool and store in an airtight container at room temperature.
- Pesto Cream Cheese Spread (page 31), Spicy Chili Dip (page 33), Cucumber Ham Roll-Ups (page 29) and Southwest Corn Spread (page 32) can be prepared, covered and refrigerated overnight.
- Artichoke Wonton Cups (page 30). Prepare the artichoke mixture; cover and refrigerate overnight. Bake the wonton cups; cool and store in an airtight container at room temperature. Fill cups with the artichoke mixture just before baking.

Christmas Candle Cheese Spread

(Pictured at right)

My sister shared this recipe with me when I was in school and still learning to cook. It's an excellent appetizer that's remained a favorite through the years.
— Patty Glasgow, Dresden, Ontario

1 package (8 ounces) cream cheese, softened
3 cups (12 ounces) shredded cheddar cheese
1/4 cup sour cream
1/4 cup finely chopped green onions
1/8 teaspoon Worcestershire sauce
1/8 teaspoon hot pepper sauce
2 tablespoons minced fresh parsley
1/3 cup sesame seeds, toasted
1 *each* medium green and sweet red pepper
Assorted crackers

In a mixing bowl, combine the cream cheese, cheddar cheese, sour cream, onions, Worcestershire and hot pepper sauce until blended. Using 1/2 cup cheese mixture, form a 4-in. circle. Coat with parsley.

Form the remaining cheese mixture into a cylinder; roll in sesame seeds. Place on top of circle. Cut a piece of red pepper to resemble a flame; insert into the top of the candle. Cut one ring from the green pepper; cut in half. Position one half on the side for handle. (Save remaining peppers for another use.) Refrigerate until serving. Serve with crackers.
Yield: 4-1/2 cups.

'TIS THE *Season*

A Bounty of Yuletide Breads

NOTHING can bring back happy memories of Christmases past quite like the aroma of breads, rolls and muffins baking in the oven.

So when your clan is home for the holidays, don an apron, reach for the flour and take them back in time with this classic collection of home-baked goodies.

Christmas Cranberry Rolls, Walnut-Filled Stollen and Cranberry Pumpkin Muffins (shown at right) are just three of this chapter's sweet breads that will awaken tired taste buds on Christmas morning.

Or to round out lunch and dinner, you'll find a savory selection laden with herbs, seasonings, cheeses and more.

SEASONAL SWEET BREADS
(Clockwise from top)

Christmas Cranberry Rolls (p. 46)

Walnut-Filled Stollen (p. 44)

Cranberry Pumpkin Muffins (p. 48)

Walnut-Filled Stollen

(Pictured on opposite page and page 43)

*Mary Falk's grandmother made date stollen every Christmas. Over the years,
the Cambridge, Wisconsin cook replaced her grandmother's date filling with nuts.
On the next page, our home economists show how you can top off this sweet yeast bread with
either a vanilla glaze, drizzle or frosting to suit your family's tastes.*

1 **package (1/4 ounce) active
dry yeast**
1 **cup warm milk (110° to 115°)**
1/2 **cup butter *or* margarine,
softened**
1/2 **cup sugar**
2 **eggs**
1 **teaspoon salt**
4 **to 4-1/2 cups all-purpose flour**
FILLING:
3 **cups chopped walnuts**
1 **cup packed brown sugar**
2 **tablespoons half-and-half
cream**
1 **tablespoon vanilla extract**
2 **teaspoons ground cinnamon**
**Vanilla Glaze, Vanilla Drizzle *or*
Vanilla Frosting (recipes on
opposite page)**

In a large mixing bowl, dissolve yeast in warm milk. Add the butter, sugar, eggs, salt and 2 cups flour; beat until smooth. Stir in enough remaining flour to form a soft dough. Turn onto a floured surface; knead until smooth and elastic, about 6-8 minutes. Place in a greased bowl, turning once to grease top. Cover and let rise in a warm place until doubled, about 1-1/4 hours.

Punch dough down; divide into thirds. Shape each portion into a 12-in. x 7-in. oval. In a bowl, combine the walnuts, brown sugar, cream, vanilla and cinnamon. Spread down the middle third of each stollen. Fold a long side over to within 1 in. of opposite side; press edge lightly to seal. Place on greased baking sheets; curve ends slightly. Cover and let rise until nearly doubled, about 45 minutes.

Bake at 350° for 15-20 minutes or until golden brown. Remove to wire racks to cool. Top with vanilla glaze, drizzle or frosting. **Yield:** 3 loaves.

Vanilla Glaze

(Pictured at right, top)

1 cup confectioners' sugar
2 tablespoons milk
1/4 teaspoon vanilla extract

In a small bowl, combine the sugar, milk and vanilla. Stir until smooth. Let stand 5 minutes to thicken if desired. Spoon over bread. **Yield:** 1/2 cup.

Vanilla Drizzle

(Pictured at right, middle)

1-1/2 cups confectioners' sugar
1/4 teaspoon vanilla extract
5 to 5-1/2 teaspoons milk

In a small bowl, combine the sugar, vanilla and enough milk to achieve desired consistency. Stir until smooth. Drizzle over bread. **Yield:** 1/2 cup.

Vanilla Frosting

(Pictured at right, bottom)

2 cups confectioners' sugar
2 tablespoons butter *or* margarine, softened
2 tablespoons milk
1/2 teaspoon vanilla extract

In a mixing bowl, combine the sugar, butter, milk and vanilla. Beat on medium speed until smooth and fluffy. Spread over bread. **Yield:** 1 cup.

Christmas Cranberry Rolls

(Pictured on page 43)

Cranberries are one of my family's favorite foods, and this is a much-requested recipe.
I've been making these pretty sweet rolls for almost 3 years.
—Margery Rice, Bedford, New Hampshire

3-3/4 cups all-purpose flour
1/4 cup sugar
1 package (1/4 ounce) active
   dry yeast
1 teaspoon salt
1-1/4 cups milk
1/4 cup vegetable oil
1 egg
3 tablespoons butter *or*
   margarine
3/4 cup packed brown sugar
3 tablespoons corn syrup
1 cup fresh cranberries, halved
1/2 cup chopped citron *or* mixed
   candied fruit
1/2 cup chopped pecans
2 teaspoons grated lemon peel
TOPPING:
2/3 cup sugar
1 teaspoon ground cinnamon
6 tablespoons butter *or*
   margarine, melted

In a large mixing bowl, combine 1-3/4 cups flour, sugar, yeast and salt. In a saucepan, heat milk and oil to 120°-130°. Add to the dry ingredients; mix well. Add egg; beat well. Add enough remaining flour to form a soft dough. Turn onto a floured surface; knead until smooth and elastic, about 6-8 minutes. Place in a greased bowl, turning once to grease top. Cover and let rise until doubled, about 1 hour.

Meanwhile, melt butter in a small saucepan; stir in brown sugar and corn syrup. Spread into two greased 9-in. round baking pans; set aside. Combine cranberries, citron, pecans and lemon peel; sprinkle over brown sugar mixture.

Punch dough down; turn onto a lightly floured surface. Divide into 30 pieces; roll each piece into a 1-1/2-in. ball. In a small bowl, combine sugar and cinnamon. Place melted butter in another bowl. Roll each ball in butter, then in cinnamon-sugar. Place 15 balls in each pan. Cover and let rise until doubled, about 1 hour. Bake at 375° for 22-27 minutes or until golden brown. Cool for 5 minutes before inverting onto serving plates. **Yield:** 2-1/2 dozen.

CANDIED FRUIT FACTS

WHETHER used to adorn fruitcake, breads, desserts or cookies, candied fruits are the hallmark of the holiday season. To keep candied fruit fresh, freeze in an airtight container for up to 6 months.

Basil Cheddar Scones

(Pictured at right)

Our Test Kitchen home economists suggest you tuck these oven-fresh savory scones into a napkin-lined gift basket, along with a package of pasta and jar of spaghetti sauce.

2-1/4 cups all-purpose flour
   2 teaspoons baking powder
1/2 cup cold butter *or* margarine,
   cubed
   1 egg
   1 cup milk
   1 cup (4 ounces) shredded
   cheddar cheese
1/4 cup prepared pesto sauce

In a bowl, combine the flour and baking powder. Cut in butter until mixture resembles coarse crumbs. In another bowl, combine the egg, milk, cheese and pesto. Stir into flour mixture just until moistened.

Turn onto a lightly floured surface; knead 8-10 times. Transfer to a greased baking sheet. Pat into a 10-in. circle; cut into eight wedges but do not separate. Bake at 400° for 20-25 minutes or until golden brown. Serve warm. **Yield:** 8 scones.

Maraschino Mini Muffins

These cherry-studded mini muffins never last long around our house.
—Stephanie Moon, Nampa, Idaho

1/3 cup butter *or* margarine,
   softened
2/3 cup sugar
   1 egg
   1 cup milk
   1 tablespoon maraschino cherry
   juice
   1 teaspoon vanilla extract
1/4 teaspoon almond extract
2-1/2 cups all-purpose flour
   4 teaspoons baking powder
3/4 teaspoon salt

1/2 cup vanilla *or* white chips
1/3 cup finely chopped maraschino cherries

In a mixing bowl, cream butter and sugar. Add egg and mix well. Combine the milk, cherry juice and extracts. Combine the flour, baking powder and salt; add to creamed mixture alternately with milk mixture. Fold in the chips and cherries.

Fill greased or paper-lined miniature muffin cups two-thirds full. Bake at 375° for 12-15 minutes or until a toothpick comes out clean. Cool for 5 minutes before removing from pans to wire racks. **Yield:** 4 dozen.

Cranberry Pumpkin Muffins

(Pictured on page 42)

The delicate pumpkin flavor of these muffins is enhanced with tart, juicy cranberries.
I sometimes dust the tops with powdered sugar for added sweetness.
—Sue Ross, Casa Grande, Arizona

2-1/4 cups all-purpose flour
1 teaspoon baking soda
1 teaspoon pumpkin pie spice
1/2 teaspoon salt
2 eggs
2 cups sugar
1 cup canned pumpkin
1/2 cup vegetable oil
1 cup fresh *or* frozen
  cranberries, chopped

In a large bowl, combine the first four ingredients. In a mixing bowl, beat the eggs and sugar; add the pumpkin and oil and mix well. Stir into the dry ingredients just until moistened. Fold in the cranberries. Fill foil- or paper-lined muffin cups three-fourths full. Bake at 400° for 18-22 minutes or until a toothpick comes out clean. Cool for 5 minutes before removing from pans to wire racks. **Yield:** 2 dozen.

Orange Mocha Muffins

I've developed many mouth-watering muffin recipes through the years, but this one remains
a favorite. With their rich chocolate taste, these muffins also make a terrific dessert.
—Sandy Szwarc, Albuquerque, New Mexico

1-2/3 cups whole wheat flour
1/2 cup baking cocoa
1/4 cup oat bran
1/4 cup sugar
1/4 cup packed brown sugar
2 tablespoons nonfat dry milk
  powder
1 tablespoon instant coffee
  granules
1 teaspoon baking powder
1 teaspoon baking soda
1/4 teaspoon salt
2 eggs

2 cups (16 ounces) plain yogurt
6 tablespoons butter *or* margarine, softened
1 tablespoon finely grated orange peel
3/4 cup semisweet chocolate chips

In a large bowl, combine the first 10 ingredients. In another bowl, beat the eggs, yogurt, butter and orange peel. Stir into dry ingredients just until moistened. Fold in chocolate chips. Fill greased or paper-lined muffin cups two-thirds full. Bake at 375° for 15-20 minutes or until a toothpick comes out clean. Cool for 5 minutes before removing from pans to wire racks. Serve warm. **Yield:** 1-1/2 dozen.

Honey Rolls

(Pictured at right)

*With just the right touch of honey,
these golden rolls appear on many
of my holiday tables.*
*—Kathleen Taugher
Franklin, Wisconsin*

> 3 packages (1/4 ounce *each*)
>   active dry yeast
> 2 cups warm water (110° to
>   115°)
> 1/4 cup honey
> 2 tablespoons vegetable oil
> 1 tablespoon salt
> 2 eggs
> 1 egg, *separated*
> 7-3/4 to 8-1/2 cups bread flour
> 1/2 teaspoon cold water

In a large mixing bowl, dissolve yeast
in warm water; let stand for 5 min-
utes. Add the honey, oil, salt, eggs, egg yolk and 5 cups flour;
beat until smooth. Stir in enough remaining flour to form a
stiff dough. Turn onto a lightly floured surface; knead until
smooth and elastic, about 6-8 minutes. Place in a greased
bowl, turning once to grease top. Cover and let rise in a
warm place until doubled, about 1 hour.

Punch dough down; turn out onto a lightly floured surface. Divide and form the dough into desired shapes (see below). Cover and let rise until doubled, about 40 minutes.

Beat egg white and cold water; brush over the dough.
Bake at 350° for 20-25 minutes or until golden brown. Remove from pans to wire racks. **Yield:** 3 dozen.

SHAPING YEAST ROLLS

WHEN making most yeast rolls, you can shape the dough into any form you prefer, such as
knots, cloverleafs and crescents. Here's how to create those three classic shapes:

For knots: Divide dough in
half; divide each portion into
12 pieces. Roll each piece into a 10-inch rope; tie into a
knot. Tuck ends under. Place
knots 3 inches apart on a
greased baking sheet.

For cloverleafs: Divide the
dough in half; divide each portion into 36 pieces. Roll into
balls and make smooth by
pulling the edges under. Place
three balls, smooth side up, in
each greased muffin cup.

For crescents: Divide dough
into thirds; roll each portion
into a 12-inch circle. Cut into 12 wedges. Roll up wedges
from the wide end; place
pointed side down 2 inches
apart on a greased baking
sheet. Curve ends down to
form crescent shape.

Almond Cherry Ring

I first made this coffee cake for Christmas brunch a few years ago and it was a hit.
Each bite is bursting with the classic pairing of cherry and almond flavors.
—Michelle Delgado, Newnan, Georgia

1 cup dried cherries *or*
    cranberries
1 cup cold water
1/2 cup sugar, *divided*
1 package (1/4 ounce) active
    dry yeast
1/4 cup warm water (110° to
    115°)
1/2 cup milk
3 tablespoons butter *or*
    margarine
1 tablespoon grated lemon peel
1/2 teaspoon salt
2-1/2 to 2-3/4 cups all-purpose flour
1 egg
FILLING/GLAZE:
1/2 cup almond filling
1 egg
2 tablespoons milk, *divided*
1/2 cup confectioners' sugar
1/4 teaspoon vanilla extract

In a saucepan, combine the cherries, cold water and 1/4 cup sugar. Cook and stir until mixture comes to a boil. Remove from the heat; cover and let stand for 10 minutes. Drain and set aside.

In a large mixing bowl, dissolve yeast in warm water. In a saucepan, heat milk and butter to 110°-115°. Add the milk mixture, lemon peel, salt, remaining sugar and 1-1/2 cups flour to yeast mixture; beat until smooth. Add egg; beat on medium speed for 1 minute. Add enough remaining flour to form a firm dough. Turn onto a lightly floured surface; knead until smooth and elastic, about 6-8 minutes. Place in a greased bowl, turning once to grease top. Cover and let rise in a warm place until doubled, about 1 hour.

Punch dough down. Roll into an 18-in. x 8-in. rectangle. Spread almond filling to within 1/2 in. of edges. Sprinkle with reserved cherries. Roll up jelly-roll style, starting with a long side; pinch seam to seal. Place seam side down on a lightly greased baking sheet. Pinch ends together to form a ring.

With scissors, cut from outside edge to two-thirds of the way toward the center of the ring at 1-1/2-in. intervals. Separate strips slightly; twist so filling shows. Cover and let rise in a warm place until doubled, about 45 minutes.

In a bowl, combine egg and 1 tablespoon milk. Brush over dough. Bake at 350° for 25-30 minutes or until golden brown. Cool for 5 minutes before removing from pan to a wire rack to cool completely. For glaze, in a mixing bowl, beat confectioners' sugar, vanilla and remaining milk until smooth; drizzle over the ring. **Yield:** 10-12 servings.

FINDING ALMOND FILLING

ALMOND FILLING is typically used in pastries and specialty breads, like Almond Cherry Ring (above). Look for it near the canned pie fillings in most grocery stores.

Poppy Seed Sweet Rolls

(Pictured at right)

When I don't plan on serving these sweet rolls the same day I prepare them, I tuck them into the freezer. Then I can surprise my family with a batch when they least expect it!
—Ruth Stahl, Shepherd, Montana

2 tablespoons active dry yeast
1/4 cup warm water (110° to 115°)
3 tablespoons sugar, *divided*
1-1/2 cups warm buttermilk* (110° to 115°)
1/2 cup vegetable oil
1 teaspoon salt
1/2 teaspoon baking soda
4 to 4-1/2 cups all-purpose flour

FILLING:
1 package (8 ounces) cream cheese, softened
1/4 cup butter *or* margarine, softened
1 cup packed brown sugar
2 tablespoons all-purpose flour
1 teaspoon vanilla extract
1 cup chopped pecans
2 tablespoons poppy seeds

ICING:
2 cups confectioners' sugar
4 teaspoons milk
1 teaspoon vanilla extract

In a large mixing bowl, dissolve yeast in warm water. Add 1 tablespoon sugar; let stand for 5 minutes. Add buttermilk, oil, salt, baking soda, 3 cups flour and remaining sugar; beat until smooth. Stir in enough remaining flour to form a soft dough. Turn onto a lightly floured surface; knead until smooth and elastic, about 6-8 minutes. Place in a greased bowl, turning once to grease top. Cover and let rise in a warm place for 30 minutes.

Punch dough down. Turn onto a floured surface; divide in half. Roll each portion into a 15-in. x 9-in. rectangle. For filling, in a small mixing bowl, beat cream cheese and butter. Add the brown sugar, flour and vanilla; beat well. Stir in nuts and poppy seeds. Spread over rectangles. Roll up jelly-roll style, starting with a long side; pinch seams to seal.

Cut into 1-in. pieces. Place 2 in. apart on greased baking sheets. Cover and let rise for 30 minutes. Bake at 375° for 12-15 minutes. Remove from pans to wire racks to cool. Combine icing ingredients; drizzle over rolls. **Yield:** about 2-1/2 dozen.

*Editor's Note: Warmed buttermilk will appear curdled.

Apple Streusel Muffins

One day when I didn't have apples for my favorite dessert recipe, I used applesauce instead. I also put the batter in muffin cups so the men working cattle at our place could easily eat these treats in the field.
—*Beverly Medalen, Willow City, North Dakota*

1 package (18-1/4 ounces)
  yellow cake mix
3/4 cup all-purpose flour
3 eggs
3/4 cup water
1/3 cup vegetable oil
FILLING:
3/4 cup applesauce
1/4 cup sugar
1 teaspoon ground cinnamon
STREUSEL TOPPING:
1/4 cup sugar
1 teaspoon all-purpose flour

1 teaspoon ground cinnamon
1 teaspoon butter *or* margarine, softened

In a mixing bowl, combine cake mix, flour, eggs, water and oil. Beat on low speed for 30 seconds. Beat on medium for 2 minutes. Fill paper-lined muffin cups one-third full. Combine the filling ingredients; place 2 teaspoonfuls in the center of each muffin cup. Top with remaining batter. Combine the topping ingredients until crumbly; sprinkle over batter.

Bake at 350° for 18-22 minutes or until a toothpick comes out clean. Cool for 10 minutes before removing from pans to wire racks to cool completely. **Yield:** 2 dozen.

Golden Cornmeal Yeast Buns

This recipe is a great help to me when I don't have purchased buns on hand. We enjoy them with hamburgers at home and with luncheon meat when we're on the go.
—*Kathy Scott, Hemingford, Nebraska*

2 cups milk
1/2 cup butter *or* margarine,
  cubed
1/2 cup yellow cornmeal
1/2 cup sugar
1 teaspoon salt
2 packages (1/4 ounce *each*)
  active dry yeast
1/2 cup warm water (110° to
  115°)
4-3/4 to 5-1/2 cups all-purpose flour
3 eggs

In a saucepan, combine the milk, butter, cornmeal, sugar and salt. Cook and stir until butter is melted. Cool to 110°-115°. In a mixing bowl, dissolve yeast in warm water. Add 3 cups flour and milk mixture; beat until blended. Add eggs; beat until smooth. Stir in enough remaining flour to form a soft dough (dough will be slightly sticky). Turn onto a heavily floured surface; knead until smooth and elastic, about 6-8 minutes. Cover and let rise in a warm place until doubled, about 1 hour.

Punch dough down; turn onto a lightly floured surface. Divide into four portions; divide each portion into six pieces. With lightly floured hands, shape into buns. Place on greased baking sheets. Cover and let rise until doubled, about 40 minutes. Bake at 350° for 18-22 minutes or until golden brown. Remove from pans to wire racks to cool. **Yield:** 2 dozen.

Herb Swirl Bread

(Pictured at right)

This pretty and palate-pleasing bread is a nice alternative to garlic bread. I make it whenever we have lasagna or spaghetti, which is quite often!
—Laura Dix, Sylacauga, Alabama

2-3/4 to 3-1/4 cups all-purpose flour
   1 **tablespoon sugar**
   1 **package (1/4 ounce) active
      dry yeast**
   1 **teaspoon salt**
   1 **cup water**
   2 **tablespoons vegetable oil**
HERB FILLING:
 1/4 **cup butter (no substitutes),
      softened**
 1/3 **cup minced fresh parsley**
   1 **tablespoon minced chives**
   1 **teaspoon garlic powder**
   1 **teaspoon seasoned salt**
Cornmeal

In a large mixing bowl, combine 1-1/2 cups flour, sugar, yeast and salt. In a saucepan, heat the water and oil to 120°-130°. Add to dry ingredients; beat until well blended. Stir in enough remaining flour to form a soft dough. Turn onto a floured surface; knead until smooth and elastic, about 6-8 minutes. Place in a greased bowl, turning once to grease top. Cover and let rise in a warm place until doubled, about 1 hour.

In a small bowl, combine the butter, parsley, chives, garlic powder and seasoned salt. Punch dough down; turn onto a lightly floured surface. Roll into a 15-in. x 12-in. rectangle. Spread filling to within 1 in. of edges. Roll up jelly-roll style, starting with a short side; pinch seam to seal. Grease a baking sheet and sprinkle with cornmeal. Place loaf seam side down on prepared pan.

With a sharp knife, make several shallow diagonal slashes across top of loaf. Cover and let rise in a warm place until doubled, about 1 hour. Bake at 375° for 30-35 minutes or until golden brown. Remove from pan to a wire rack. **Yield:** 1 loaf.

Jumbo Cream Rolls

I always marveled at the sweet rolls served in coffee shops. When I came across this recipe, I couldn't wait to try it. They'll be a hit with anyone who has a weakness for sweet rolls!
—Marla Fogderud, Fargo, North Dakota

2 packages (1/4 ounce *each*) active dry yeast
1 cup warm water (110° to 115°)
1 cup warm milk (110° to 115°)
1/2 cup shortening
1 cup sugar
1 egg
2 teaspoons salt
6-1/2 to 6-3/4 cups all-purpose flour
FILLING:
1/2 cup packed brown sugar
1 to 2 tablespoons ground cinnamon
TOPPING:
1-1/2 cups packed brown sugar
3/4 cup heavy whipping cream

In a large mixing bowl, dissolve yeast in warm water. Add the milk, shortening, sugar, egg, salt and 3 cups flour; beat until smooth. Stir in enough remaining flour to form a soft dough. Turn onto a floured surface; knead until smooth and elastic, about 6-8 minutes. Place in a greased bowl, turning once to grease top. Cover and let rise in a warm place until doubled, about 1 hour.

Punch dough down; turn onto a lightly floured surface. Roll into an 18-in. x 12-in. rectangle. Combine filling ingredients; sprinkle over dough to within 1/2 in. of edges. Roll up jelly-roll style, starting with a long side. Cut into 12 slices. Combine the topping ingredients; pour into two greased 8-in. square baking dishes. Place rolls over topping. Cover and let rise for 45 minutes or until nearly doubled.

Bake at 350° for 35-40 minutes or until golden brown. Cool for 5 minutes before inverting onto serving platters. **Yield:** 1 dozen.

Italian Sweet Bread

The women in our family feel so blessed that my mom taught us how to make this Pane Dolce before she passed away. We do our best to carry on her loving tradition.
—Kathleen Schweihs, Lockport, Illinois

1 cup milk
1 cup sugar
1 cup butter *or* margarine, cubed
1 cup raisins
2 packages (1/4 ounce *each*) active dry yeast
1/2 cup warm water (110° to 115°)
4 eggs
6 teaspoons anise extract
2 teaspoons vanilla extract
1 cup chopped walnuts
1/2 cup chopped red and green candied cherries
8 cups all-purpose flour
ICING:
1 cup confectioners' sugar
4 teaspoons milk

In a saucepan, combine the first four ingredients. Cook and stir over medium heat until butter is melted. Remove from the heat; cool to 110°-115°.

In a mixing bowl, dissolve yeast in warm water. Add the cooled butter mixture, eggs, extracts, nuts and cherries; mix well. Add enough flour to form a soft dough. Turn onto a floured surface; knead until smooth and elastic, about 6-8 minutes. Place in a greased bowl, turning once to grease top. Cover and let rise in a warm place until doubled, about 1 hour.

Punch dough down; divide into thirds. Shape each portion into an oval loaf; place in three greased and floured 8-in. x 4-in. x 2-in. baking pans. Cover and let rise until doubled, about 45 minutes. Bake at 350° for 60-65 minutes or until golden brown. Cover loosely with foil if top browns too quickly. Remove from pans to wire racks to cool. Combine icing ingredients; drizzle over cooled loaves. **Yield:** 3 loaves.

Cherry Banana Mini Loaves

(Pictured at right)

This recipe has been passed down from my mom's mother. The addition of chocolate chips and dried cherries makes it stand out from ordinary banana bread. These are terrific gifts from the kitchen.
— *Diane Doll, West Bend, Wisconsin*

1/2 **cup butter *or* margarine, softened**
1 **cup sugar**
2 **eggs**
1 **cup mashed bananas (about 2 medium)**
2 **cups all-purpose flour**
1 **teaspoon baking soda**
1/4 **cup chopped walnuts**
1/4 **cup miniature semisweet chocolate chips**
1/4 **cup dried cherries *or* cranberries**

In a mixing bowl, cream butter and sugar. Add eggs and banana; mix well. Combine flour and baking soda; gradually add to the creamed mixture. Fold in the nuts, chips and cherries. Transfer to four greased 5-3/4-in. x 3-in. x 2-in. loaf pans. Bake at 350° for 32-37 minutes or until a toothpick inserted near the center comes out clean. Cool for 10 minutes before removing from pans to wire racks. **Yield:** 4 loaves.

Pumpkin Chip Loaf

This is a family favorite Mom made during the holidays. Once we smelled the wonderful aroma of this spiced pumpkin bread baking, we could hardly wait for her to slice it!
—Michele McFie, Salem, Oregon

1/2 cup butter *or* margarine, softened
1 cup sugar
2 eggs
1 cup canned pumpkin
1-3/4 cups all-purpose flour
1 teaspoon baking soda
1 teaspoon ground cinnamon
1/2 teaspoon salt
1/2 teaspoon ground nutmeg
1/4 teaspoon ground ginger
1/4 teaspoon ground cloves

1 cup miniature semisweet chocolate chips
1/2 cup chopped walnuts

In a mixing bowl, cream butter and sugar. Add eggs and pumpkin; mix well. Combine the flour, baking soda, cinnamon, salt, nutmeg, ginger and cloves; gradually add to creamed mixture. Stir in chips and walnuts; mix well.

Pour into a greased 9-in. x 5-in. x 3-in. loaf pan. Bake at 350° for 65-70 minutes or until a toothpick inserted near the center comes out clean. Cool for 10 minutes before removing from pan to a wire rack to cool completely. **Yield:** 1 loaf.

Herb Casserole Bread

I'm a fairly experienced baker and have tried many recipes through the years. My family and I put this tried-and-true casserole bread at the top of our list.
—Kelly Kirby, Westville, Nova Scotia

4-1/2 to 5 cups all-purpose flour
1/4 cup plus 1 teaspoon sugar
1 package (1/4 ounce) active dry yeast
1-1/2 teaspoons salt
1 teaspoon dried oregano
1/2 teaspoon dried basil
1/2 teaspoon dried thyme
1/4 teaspoon garlic powder
1 cup milk
1/2 cup water
1/4 cup plus 2 teaspoons butter *or* margarine, *divided*
1 tablespoon grated Parmesan cheese, optional

In a large mixing bowl, combine 3 cups flour, sugar, yeast, salt, oregano, basil, thyme and garlic powder. In a saucepan, heat the milk, water and 1/4 cup butter to 120°-130°. Add to the dry ingredients; beat until smooth. Stir in enough remaining flour to form a stiff dough. Turn onto a floured surface; knead until smooth and elastic, about 6-8 minutes. Place in a greased bowl, turning once to grease top. Cover and let rise in a warm place until doubled, about 1 hour.

Punch dough down; turn onto a lightly floured surface. Shape into a round loaf. Place in a greased 2-qt. round baking dish. Cover and let rise until doubled, about 40 minutes. Melt remaining butter; brush over dough. Sprinkle with Parmesan cheese if desired. Bake at 350° for 35-40 minutes or until golden brown. Remove to a wire rack to cool. **Yield:** 1 loaf.

Braided Onion Loaf

(Pictured at right)

This recipe won the blue ribbon for "Best Loaf of Bread" at our county fair a few years ago. One bite and you'll see why the tender savory slices appealed to the judges.
—Linda Knoll, Jackson, Michigan

  1 **package (1/4 ounce) active dry yeast**
3/4 **cup warm water (110° to 115°)**
1/2 **cup warm milk (110° to 115°)**
1/4 **cup butter *or* margarine, softened**
  1 **egg**
1/4 **cup sugar**
1-1/2 **teaspoons salt**
  4 **to 4-1/4 cups all-purpose flour**
FILLING:
1/4 **cup butter *or* margarine, softened**
3/4 **cup dried minced onion**
  1 **tablespoon grated Parmesan cheese**
  1 **teaspoon paprika**
  1 **teaspoon garlic salt, optional**
Melted butter

In a large mixing bowl, dissolve yeast in warm water. Add the milk, butter, egg, sugar, salt and 2 cups flour; beat until smooth. Add enough of the remaining flour to form a soft dough. Turn onto a floured surface; knead until smooth and elastic, about 6-8 minutes. Place in a greased bowl, turning once to grease top. Cover and let rise in a warm place until doubled, about 1 hour.

For filling, in a bowl, combine the butter, onion, Parmesan cheese, paprika and garlic salt if desired; set aside. Punch dough down; turn onto a lightly floured surface. Divide into thirds. Roll each portion into a 20-in. x 4-in. rectangle. Spread filling over rectangles. Roll up jelly-roll style, starting from a long side.

Place ropes on an ungreased baking sheet; braid. Pinch ends to seal and tuck under. Cover and let rise until doubled, about 45 minutes. Bake at 350° for 30-35 minutes or until golden brown. Brush with melted butter. Remove from pan to a wire rack. **Yield:** 1 loaf.

Main Courses for Christmas

MOST FOLKS would agree that the main attraction on a holiday dinner table is the entree.

From beef, chicken and game to turkey, seafood and pork, the possibilities for exciting eating are almost endless.

Looking for some special-occasion fare? Reach for Cranberry-Orange Roast Ducklings and Garlic Crab-Stuffed Chicken.

Or add some class (and a little kick!) to a casual get-together with Spicy Filet Mignon.

The hardest task you'll have this holiday season will be deciding just which of this chapter's merry main courses to make first!

MEATY MEDLEY
(Clockwise from top)

Cranberry-Orange Roast Ducklings (p. 61)

Spicy Filet Mignon (p. 60)

Garlic Crab-Stuffed Chicken (p. 63)

Spicy Filet Mignon

(Pictured on page 59)

I adapted this recipe from a seasoning I saw for blackened catfish. Because these steaks have a lot of kick, I make a more mellow side dish, like buttered potatoes or grilled fresh vegetables.
—*Vera Kobiako, Jupiter, Florida*

2 tablespoons paprika
2 teaspoons onion salt
1-1/2 teaspoons garlic powder
1-1/2 teaspoons dried basil
1 to 1-1/2 teaspoons cayenne
   pepper
1 teaspoon dried thyme
6 beef tenderloin steaks (about
   1-1/2 inches thick)

Combine the seasonings; rub over steaks. Grill, covered, over indirect medium heat for 9-11 minutes on each side or until meat reaches desired doneness (for rare, a meat thermometer should read 140°; medium, 160°; well-done, 170°). **Yield:** 6 servings.

Scandinavian Meatballs With Dill Sauce

This recipe is handwritten in a cookbook that's used so often, I have to hold it together with rubber bands! The meatballs have appealing old-world flavor.
—*Linda Swanson, Riverside, Washington*

2 eggs
1 cup heavy whipping cream
1/2 cup grated peeled apple
1/2 cup chopped raisins
1/2 cup cubed rye bread (1/4-inch
   cubes)
1/4 cup thinly sliced green onions
1/4 cup chopped almonds,
   optional
1 teaspoon salt
1 teaspoon pepper
2 pounds ground beef
SAUCE:
1/4 cup butter *or* margarine
1/4 cup all-purpose flour
2 cups beef broth

2 teaspoons snipped fresh dill *or* 1/2 to 1 teaspoon
   dill weed
1 cup (8 ounces) plain yogurt
1 can (8 ounces) sliced water chestnuts, drained

In a bowl, combine the eggs, cream, apple, raisins, bread, onions, almonds if desired, salt and pepper. Crumble meat over mixture and mix well. Shape into 2-in. balls. Place on a greased wire rack in a baking pan. Bake, uncovered, at 400° for 25-30 minutes or until meat is no longer pink.
   Meanwhile, in a saucepan, melt the butter. Stir in flour until smooth; gradually add the broth and dill. Bring to a boil over medium heat; cook and stir for 2 minutes or until thickened. Remove from the heat; stir in yogurt and water chestnuts. Serve over meatballs. **Yield:** 8-10 servings.

Cranberry- Orange Roast Ducklings

(Pictured at right and on page 59)

I came up with this recipe a few years ago. The first time I served it, there wasn't a speck of food left on the platter and I knew I had a winning recipe.
—Gloria Warczak, Cedarburg, Wisconsin

2 domestic ducklings (4 to 5 pounds *each*)
2 medium navel oranges, quartered
2 sprigs fresh rosemary
1-1/2 cups fresh *or* frozen cranberries, *divided*
4 cups orange juice
1 cup chicken broth
1/4 cup soy sauce
2 teaspoons sugar
1/4 teaspoon ground ginger *or* 1 teaspoon grated fresh gingerroot
2 garlic cloves, minced
2/3 cup orange marmalade

Prick skin of ducklings well. Place four orange quarters, one sprig of rosemary and 1/4 cup of cranberries in each cavity; tie drumsticks together. Place breast side up on a rack in a roasting pan.

In a large bowl, combine the orange juice, broth, soy sauce, sugar, ginger and garlic; mix well. Refrigerate 1/2 cup for the glaze. Pour 1 cup over the ducklings; sprinkle with the remaining cranberries. Cover and bake at 350° for 1 hour. Uncover; bake 1-1/2 hours longer, basting frequently with the remaining orange juice mixture. (Drain fat from pan as it accumulates.)

Combine the marmalade and reserved orange juice mixture; spread over ducklings. Bake, uncovered, 30-40 minutes longer or until a meat thermometer reads 180°. Discard the oranges, rosemary and cranberries from cavities. Let ducklings stand for 10 minutes before carving. **Yield:** 8-10 servings.

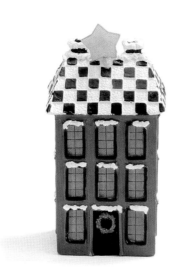

Italian-Style Round Steak

My family loves this Swiss steak with an Italian touch.
It's true comfort food that will appeal to your family as well.
—*Sharon Farnsworth, Longmont, Colorado*

1/4 cup all-purpose flour
1-1/2 teaspoons salt
1/4 teaspoon pepper
2 pounds boneless beef round steak, cut into serving-size pieces
2 to 3 tablespoons vegetable oil
1 cup water
1 garlic clove, minced
1 can (15 ounces) tomato sauce
1/2 pound fresh mushrooms, sliced
1 medium onion, sliced
1 small green pepper, julienned
2 teaspoons sugar

1/2 teaspoon dried oregano
1/8 teaspoon dried basil
1 package (7 ounces) spaghetti, cooked and drained
1/4 cup grated Parmesan cheese

In a large resealable plastic bag, combine the flour, salt and pepper. Add beef, a few pieces at a time, and shake to coat. In a Dutch oven, brown beef in batches in oil; drain. Add water and garlic. Bring to a boil. Reduce heat; cover and simmer for 1-1/2 hours.

Stir in the tomato sauce, mushrooms, onion, green pepper, sugar, oregano and basil. Cover and simmer 30-45 minutes longer or until the meat and vegetables are tender. Serve over spaghetti. Sprinkle with Parmesan cheese. **Yield:** 6-8 servings.

EASY GARNISHES FOR ENTREES

YOU don't need to take a class, buy special tools or even spend a lot of time to garnish entrees like an expert. Keep in mind that often the simplest garnishes are the most elegant.

- One of the easiest ways to garnish is by repeating ingredients used in the recipe. For example, fresh rosemary flavors the Cranberry-Orange Roast Ducklings (page 61), then sprigs of fresh rosemary are used as skewers for kumquats and cranberries. Escarole and star fruit slices are tucked in for added interest.
- Use garnishes to add splashes of color. For instance, Italian parsley, halved spiced apple rings and orange wedges contrast nicely with the brown colors of wild rice and Garlic Crab-Stuffed Chicken (page 63).

- Play upon the theme of the food. In the photo of Spicy Filet Mignon (page 59), fresh basil ties into the dried basil used in the recipe, while assorted hot peppers not only add color but hint at the steak's spiciness.
- Greens are always reliable garnishes. It's best to use sturdy greens that stand up to hot foods, like curly endive (see Honey-Mustard Pork Roast on page 69), kale, escarole, spinach and leaf lettuce.
- Don't feel you need to garnish every entree. The golden crust of Apple Turkey Potpie (page 65) is scrumptious enough.

If you'll be filling guests' plates with the entree and a side dish or salad, the blend of colors makes garnishing unnecessary (like Sausage-Topped Polenta on page 67).

Garlic Crab-Stuffed Chicken

(Pictured at right and on page 58)

I created this recipe as a way to make ordinary chicken extra special. To save time, you can roll up the chicken early in the day, refrigerate it, then dip in the egg, brown and bake later on.
—Dorothy Glaeser, Naples, Florida

6 large boneless skinless
  chicken breast halves
  (8 ounces *each*)
2 tablespoons minced garlic
2 cans (6 ounces *each*)
  crabmeat, drained, flaked and
  cartilage removed
8 ounces Jarlsberg *or* Gouda
  cheese, shredded
3 tablespoons minced fresh
  parsley
1 egg
1 tablespoon cold water
1-1/4 cups dry bread crumbs
2 tablespoons vegetable oil
1 cup apple juice
1 cup white wine *or* chicken
  broth
Wild rice, optional

Flatten chicken to 1/4-in. thickness. Spread 1 teaspoon garlic on one side of each chicken breast half. Place crab, cheese and parsley down the center of each. Roll up and tuck in ends; secure with toothpicks. In a bowl, beat egg and water. Place bread crumbs in another bowl. Dip chicken in egg mixture, then roll in crumbs.

In a large skillet, brown chicken in oil on both sides. Transfer to a greased 13-in. x 9-in. x 2-in. baking dish. Add apple juice and wine or broth. Bake, uncovered, at 350° for 35-40 minutes or until chicken juices run clear. Serve with wild rice if desired. **Yield:** 6 servings.

POUNDING CHICKEN BREASTS

PLACE a boneless chicken breast between two pieces of waxed paper. Starting in the center and working out to the edges, pound lightly with the flat side of a meat mallet until the chicken is even in thickness.

Peachy Orange Sauce for Ham

My mother and father made enough of this sauce to serve 250 people at my wedding!
Shortly after, my dad gave me my own copy of the recipe.
Holiday ham just isn't the same without this fruity sauce.
—Vivian Nelson, Lloydminster, Saskatchewan

1 can (28 ounces) sliced peaches
1 cup sugar
1/4 cup cornstarch
2 teaspoons ground mustard
1 teaspoon seasoned salt
1/2 teaspoon paprika
1 cup water
1/3 cup orange juice
1/4 cup cider vinegar

Drain peaches, reserving 1-1/2 cups syrup; set syrup and peaches aside. In a large saucepan, combine the sugar, cornstarch, mustard, seasoned salt and paprika. Stir in the water, orange juice, vinegar and reserved syrup until smooth. Bring to a boil; cook and stir for 2 minutes or until thickened. Add peaches. Reduce heat; simmer, uncovered, for 2-3 minutes or until heated through. Serve with ham. **Yield:** 5 cups.

Smoky Beef Brisket

A friend and I first ate this brisket at a restaurant, then came home and duplicated
it with great success. Leftovers make terrific sandwiches.
—Sue McQueen, Cameron, Missouri

2 to 4 tablespoons liquid smoke
1 teaspoon pepper
1/2 teaspoon salt
1 fresh beef brisket* (about 3 pounds)
1/4 cup packed brown sugar
1 teaspoon *each* celery salt, garlic salt and onion salt
1 teaspoon ground nutmeg
1 teaspoon paprika
1/2 cup barbecue sauce

In a large resealable plastic bag, combine the liquid smoke, pepper and salt; add the brisket. Seal bag and turn to coat; refrigerate for at least 4 hours or overnight.

Drain and discard marinade. Combine the brown sugar, celery salt, garlic salt, onion salt, nutmeg and paprika; rub over meat. Wrap in a large sheet of heavy-duty foil; seal tightly. Place in an ungreased 15-in. x 10-in. x 1-in. baking pan. Bake at 325° for 4 hours or until meat is tender.

Remove brisket to a warm serving platter; skim fat from pan juices. In a saucepan over medium heat, combine 1 cup pan juices with barbecue sauce; cook and stir until thickened. Thinly slice meat across the grain; serve with sauce. **Yield:** 6-8 servings.

*Editor's Note: This is a fresh beef brisket, not corned beef.

Apple Turkey Potpie

(Pictured at right)

I like to take leftover holiday turkey and turn it into this delicious potpie. Apples and raisins add sweetness.

—Georgia MacDonald
Dover, New Hampshire

1/4 cup chopped onion
1 tablespoon butter *or* margarine
2 cans (10-3/4 ounces *each*) condensed cream of chicken soup, undiluted
3 cups cubed cooked turkey
1 large unpeeled tart apple, cubed
1/3 cup golden raisins
1 teaspoon lemon juice
1/4 teaspoon ground nutmeg
Pastry for single-crust pie (9 inches)

In a large saucepan, saute onion in butter until tender. Add the soup, turkey, apple, raisins, lemon juice and nutmeg; mix well. Spoon into an ungreased 11-in. x 7-in. x 2-in. baking dish. On a lightly floured surface, roll out pastry to fit top of dish. Place over filling; flute edges and cut slits in top. Bake at 425° for 25-30 minutes or until crust is golden brown and filling is bubbly. **Yield:** 6 servings.

Cinnamon Pork Tenderloin

The marinade for this grilled pork tenderloin is laden with lots of wonderful flavors, like cinnamon, honey and garlic. It turns out perfectly every time and always impresses.
—Cathleen Bushman, Geneva, Illinois

3 tablespoons soy sauce
3 tablespoons sherry *or* chicken broth
1 tablespoon brown sugar
1-1/2 teaspoons honey
1 teaspoon ground cinnamon
1 garlic clove, minced
2 pork tenderloins (3/4 pound *each*)

In a large resealable plastic bag, combine the first six ingredients. Add the pork; seal bag and turn to coat. Refrigerate for 4-6 hours. Drain and discard marinade. Grill pork, uncovered, over medium heat for 15-20 minutes or until a meat thermometer reads 160°, turning occasionally. Let stand for 5 minutes before slicing. **Yield:** 4-6 servings.

Special Seafood Linguine

*When entertaining, I often rely on this hearty pasta dish. To avoid some last-minute fuss,
chop the onion and green pepper, and peel and devein the shrimp earlier in the day.*
—*Valerie Putsey, Winamac, Indiana*

1 large red onion, chopped
1/2 cup chopped green pepper
3 garlic cloves, minced
1/3 cup minced fresh parsley
1/4 cup olive *or* vegetable oil
1 can (28 ounces) diced
   tomatoes, undrained
1 can (10-3/4 ounces)
   condensed cream of shrimp
   soup, undiluted
1 tablespoon lemon juice
1 teaspoon dried basil
1 teaspoon dried oregano
1/4 teaspoon salt
1/4 teaspoon pepper

1 pound uncooked medium shrimp, peeled and
   deveined
2 cans (6 ounces *each*) crabmeat, drained, flaked
   and cartilage removed
1 package (16 ounces) linguine
1/4 cup shredded Parmesan cheese

In a large skillet, saute the onion, green pepper, garlic and parsley in oil until tender. Add the tomatoes, soup, lemon juice and seasonings. Bring to a boil. Reduce heat; simmer, uncovered, for 20 minutes.

Stir in the shrimp and crab; simmer for 10 minutes or until shrimp turn pink. Meanwhile, cook the linguine according to package directions; drain. Serve seafood mixture over linguine; sprinkle with Parmesan cheese. **Yield:** 6-8 servings.

Chicken with Tomato-Cream Sauce

*A creamy tomato sauce makes plain chicken an extraordinary dish for guests.
It's easy to double the recipe when cooking for a crowd.*
—*Agnes Cooper, Newark, Delaware*

8 boneless skinless chicken
   breast halves
1/4 cup butter *or* margarine
1 small onion, thinly sliced
2 garlic cloves, minced
2 tablespoons all-purpose flour
1 teaspoon salt
1 can (14-1/2 ounces) diced
   tomatoes, undrained
1 cup (8 ounces) sour cream
2/3 cup grated Parmesan cheese
Hot cooked noodles

In a large skillet, brown chicken in butter on both sides. Remove and set aside. Add onion and garlic; saute until tender. Stir in flour and salt until blended. Gradually add tomatoes, stirring until blended. Bring to a boil. Reduce heat; return chicken to pan. Cover and simmer for 30 minutes or until chicken juices run clear.

Remove chicken and keep warm. Reduce heat to low; stir in sour cream and Parmesan cheese. Heat through (do not boil). Serve chicken and sauce over noodles. **Yield:** 8 servings.

Sausage-Topped Polenta

(Pictured at right)

My Italian grandmother and mother have relied on this recipe for years. Many sauces can be served with polenta, but this tomato and sausage topping is our favorite.
—Joyce Riskedal, Earlville, Illinois

  1 **pound bulk pork sausage**
  1 **can (6 ounces) tomato paste**
1-1/2 **cups water**
  1 **tablespoon minced fresh parsley**
  1 **teaspoon sugar**
1/2 **teaspoon dried basil**
POLENTA:
  2 **cups water**
  1 **teaspoon salt**
  1 **cup cornmeal**
  1 **cup cold water**
  1 **cup (4 ounces) shredded brick *or* mozzarella cheese**

In a large skillet, cook sausage over medium heat until no longer pink; drain. Stir in the tomato paste, water, parsley, sugar and basil. Cover and simmer for 30 minutes, stirring occasionally.

Meanwhile, in a saucepan, bring water and salt to a boil. Combine cornmeal and cold water; stir into boiling water. Return to a boil, stirring constantly. Reduce heat; cover and simmer for 15 minutes, stirring occasionally. Spoon into a greased 9-in. round baking pan. Cool for 15-20 minutes or until set. Cut into wedges. Sprinkle with cheese and top with sausage mixture. **Yield:** 6 servings.

Poached Teriyaki Salmon

This easy, elegant entree comes from my mother-in-law, who's an excellent and innovative cook. The salmon doesn't take a lot of time to prepare, which I appreciate as a busy mom.
—Michelle Krzmarzick, Redondo Beach, California

  2 **cups orange juice**
1/3 **cup teriyaki sauce**
  6 **salmon fillets (6 ounces *each*), skin removed**
  6 **thin orange slices**
  2 **teaspoons cornstarch**
  4 **teaspoons cold water**

In a large nonstick skillet or electric skillet, bring orange juice and teriyaki sauce to a boil. Place salmon fillets in skillet; top each with an orange slice. Return to a boil. Reduce heat; cover and simmer for 15-20 minutes or until fish flakes easily with a fork. Remove fillets and keep warm.

Strain cooking liquid; return 3/4 cup to the skillet. Combine cornstarch and water until smooth; add to cooking liquid. Bring to a boil; cook and stir for 1-2 minutes or until thickened. Serve over salmon. **Yield:** 6 servings.

Broccoli Chicken Lasagna

When hosting a holiday buffet, consider serving this special lasagna. You can make it the night before and chill. Remove it from the refrigerator 30 minutes before baking.
—Carol Gaus, Itasca, Illinois

6 tablespoons butter *or*
    margarine, *divided*
1/4 cup all-purpose flour
2 cups milk
1 cup chicken broth
3 eggs, beaten
3/4 cup grated Parmesan cheese,
    divided
1 teaspoon salt, *divided*
Pinch *each* ground nutmeg and
    cayenne pepper
1 cup chopped onion
2 garlic cloves, minced
1-1/4 pounds boneless skinless
    chicken breasts, cut into thin
    strips
1 package (16 ounces) frozen
    broccoli cuts
1/2 cup shredded carrot
1/4 cup minced fresh parsley
1/4 teaspoon white pepper
9 lasagna noodles, cooked and
    drained
1 pound thinly sliced
    mozzarella cheese

In a large saucepan, melt 4 tablespoons butter; stir in flour until smooth. Gradually add milk and broth. Bring to a boil; cook and stir for 2 minutes or until thickened. Remove from the heat. Stir a small amount of sauce into the eggs; return all to pan, stirring constantly. Cook and stir over low heat until mixture reaches 160°, about 1 minute. Remove from the heat; stir in 1/2 cup Parmesan cheese, 1/2 teaspoon salt, nutmeg and cayenne. Set aside.

In a large skillet, saute onion and garlic in remaining butter until tender. Add chicken; cook and stir until juices run clear. Stir in the broccoli, carrot and remaining salt. Cover and cook over medium heat for 5 minutes or until vegetables are tender. Add parsley and pepper.

In a greased 13-in. x 9-in. x 2-in. baking dish, layer 1/2 cup of the sauce, three noodles, half of the chicken mixture, 1/2 cup sauce and a third of the mozzarella cheese. Sprinkle with 1 tablespoon Parmesan cheese. Top with three noodles, the remaining chicken mixture, half of the remaining mozzarella, 1 tablespoon Parmesan and 1/2 cup sauce. Top with the remaining noodles. Place the remaining mozzarella slices over noodles. Top with remaining sauce; gently lift noodles away from sides of the dish, letting sauce flow underneath. Sprinkle with remaining Parmesan.

Bake, uncovered, at 350° for 45-50 minutes or until bubbly and golden brown. Let stand for 15 minutes before cutting. **Yield:** 12 servings.

DRAINING LASAGNA NOODLES

TO KEEP lasagna from becoming watery when baking, it's important to drain the noodles well. Here's a good way to do that:

    Drain and rinse the cooked noodles in a colander. Take each noodle, shake off excess water and lay flat on pieces of waxed paper or paper towel until most of the water has evaporated.

Honey-Mustard Pork Roast

(Pictured at right)

Family and friends are surprised when I tell them this impressive-looking roast is easy to prepare. I simply marinate the roast a few hours, then pop it in the oven. While it bakes, I whip up the sauce to serve alongside.
—*Grace Brennfleck*
Clairton, Pennsylvania

3/4 cup beer *or* ginger ale
1/2 cup Dijon mustard
1/3 cup honey
1/4 cup olive *or* vegetable oil
 8 garlic cloves, minced
 2 tablespoons minced fresh rosemary *or* 2 teaspoons dried rosemary, crushed
 1 boneless pork loin roast (2 to 2-1/2 pounds)
1/2 cup heavy whipping cream

In a bowl, combine the beer, mustard, honey, oil, garlic and rosemary. Place the roast in a large resealable plastic bag; add marinade. Seal bag and turn to coat. Refrigerate for at least 2 hours.

Drain and reserve marinade; refrigerate for sauce. Place roast on a rack in a roasting pan. Bake, uncovered, at 350° for 1-1/2 to 1-3/4 hours or until a meat thermometer reads 160°. Let stand for 10 minutes before carving.

Strain reserved marinade into a saucepan. Add cream and pan drippings if desired. Bring to a rolling boil. Reduce heat; simmer, uncovered, for 15 minutes or until reduced to about 1-1/2 cups. Serve with sliced pork. **Yield:** 6-8 servings.

'TIS THE Season

Host an Ornament Exchange!

LIKE most people, you and your friends probably add a new ornament or two to your collection every Christmas.

Add a twist to that tradition this year by throwing an ornament exchange party!

As guests unwrap their pretty packages and "ooh" and "aah" over their new treasures, they can nibble on some delectable desserts.

For a sweet spread, set out Layered Coffee Ice Cream Dessert, Gift-Wrapped Chocolate Cake and Cream Puffs with Raspberry Sauce. (All recipes shown at right.) Guests are sure to be impressed!

Best of all, each of these recipes has time-saving tricks that won't keep you in the kitchen for hours.

DELIGHTFUL DESSERTS
(Clockwise from top)

Gift-Wrapped Chocolate Cake (p. 73)

Layered Coffee Ice Cream Dessert (p. 76)

Cream Puffs with Raspberry Sauce (p. 74)

Chocolate Bow

(Pictured on opposite page and page 71)

What a beautiful sight this is on top of your favorite cake! It takes some time to prepare but can be made a month in advance, then stored in an airtight container.
— *Debbie Gauthier, Timmins, Ontario*

1 cup plus 2 tablespoons vanilla
or* white chips, *divided
4 teaspoons shortening
1/2 large marshmallow

Cut three 6-in. squares from freezer paper. Cut each square into six 1-in. strips. Set aside four strips. Place remaining strips shiny side up on a waxed paper-lined work surface.

In a microwave, melt 1 cup vanilla chips and shortening; stir until smooth. Working quickly with a few strips at a time, spread chocolate beyond three sides of the strips onto the waxed paper, leaving 1/2 in. at one short end.

Immediately peel each strip from work surface; place on clean waxed paper. Let strips dry just until barely set but still pliable, about 1 minute. (If chocolate strips become too stiff, warm in the microwave for a few seconds.)

With paper side out, press ends of chocolate strips together. Stand strips on edges on a waxed paper-lined baking sheet. Chill until set, about 10 minutes. Carefully remove freezer paper.

For ribbons, coat four reserved strips with chocolate; peel strips from work surface. On an inverted 9-in. x 1-1/2-in. round baking pan, place strips, chocolate side down, at 90-degree angles to each other and drape 1-1/4 in. over side of pan. (If necessary, use a drop of chocolate under the bottom edge to hold in place. With a toothpick, press the strip onto the dab of chocolate.) Chill until set; remove freezer paper.

Melt remaining chips in the microwave. Fill a plastic bag with melted chocolate; cut a small hole in the corner. Place marshmallow half, cut side down, in the center of a piece of waxed paper. Secure six chocolate loops around edge of marshmallow with melted chocolate; press ends down. Layer five more loops on top with ends touching. Secure with chocolate. Coat top of marshmallow with remaining chocolate; place remaining loops in center, pressing down. Let dry for 1 hour or overnight. Carefully peel waxed paper from bow. Place ribbons and bow on top of cake. **Yield:** 1 chocolate bow for a 9-in. round or springform cake.

CREATING A CHOCOLATE BOW

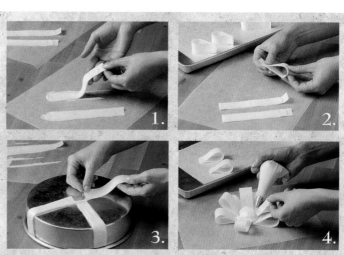

1. Spread chocolate onto strips of freezer paper. Immediately peel strips from work surface; place on clean waxed paper.

2. Press ends of strips together, paper side out. Stand on edges on a waxed paper-lined baking sheet.

3. Coat four reserved strips of freezer paper with chocolate. Peel from work surface. Place chocolate side down on an inverted 9-inch round baking pan.

4. Using additional melted chocolate, secure loops around the marshmallow.

Gift-Wrapped Chocolate Cake

(Pictured at right and on page 71)

Family and friends will be impressed when you present this rich, glazed cake from our Test Kitchen.

2 teaspoons plus 3/4 cup butter (no substitutes), softened, *divided*
1-1/2 cups sugar
3 eggs, *separated*
3 tablespoons water
3 tablespoons vegetable oil
1-1/2 teaspoons vanilla extract
1/2 cup all-purpose flour
1/2 cup plus 1 tablespoon baking cocoa
3/4 cup chopped pecans
1/8 teaspoon cream of tartar
1/8 teaspoon salt
GLAZE:
8 squares (1 ounce *each*) semisweet chocolate, chopped
1/2 cup heavy whipping cream
Chocolate Bow (recipe on opposite page)

Line the bottom of a 9-in. springform pan with foil; grease foil and sides of pan with 2 teaspoons butter; set aside. Melt remaining butter. In a mixing bowl, beat butter and sugar. Add egg yolks, one at a time, beating well after each. Beat in the water, oil and vanilla; mix well. Combine flour and cocoa; gradually add to egg mixture. Stir in pecans.

In another mixing bowl, beat egg whites on medium speed until foamy. Add cream of tartar and salt; beat on high until stiff peaks form. Fold into chocolate mixture. Pour into prepared pan. Bake at 350° for 45-50 minutes or until top begins to crack slightly and a toothpick comes out with moist crumbs. Cool on a wire rack for 10 minutes. Carefully run a knife around edge of pan to loosen; cool 1 hour longer. Refrigerate overnight.

To assemble, invert cake onto a waxed paper-lined baking sheet. Remove foil; set aside. In a heavy saucepan, heat chocolate and cream over very low heat until chocolate is melted (do not boil); stir until smooth. Remove from the heat. Cool if necessary until mixture reaches spreading consistency.

Slowly pour glaze over cake, smoothing sides with a metal spatula to evenly coat. Chill until set. Carefully transfer cake to a flat serving plate. Top with Chocolate Bow. Refrigerate leftovers. **Yield:** 10-12 servings.

Cream Puffs with Raspberry Sauce

(Pictured on page 70)

*This is the most elegant dessert I make, and all who try it love it.
These cute little puffs filled with ice cream are perfect for any special occasion.*
— *Debbie Krygeris, Downers Grove, Illinois*

1/2 cup water
1/4 cup plus 1 tablespoon butter
  (no substitutes), *divided*
1/2 cup all-purpose flour
  2 eggs
  3 cups vanilla ice cream, *divided*
  1 package (10 ounces) frozen
    sweetened raspberries,
    thawed
  2 squares (1 ounce *each*)
    semisweet chocolate
  2 tablespoons milk
1/4 cup chopped pistachios

In a small saucepan, bring water and 1/4 cup butter to a boil. Add flour all at once and stir until a smooth ball forms. Remove from the heat; let stand for 5 minutes. Add eggs, one at a time, beating well after each addition. Continue beating until mixture is smooth and shiny.

Drop by rounded teaspoonfuls 2 in. apart onto greased baking sheets. Bake at 400° for 22-25 minutes or until golden brown. Remove to wire racks. Immediately split puffs open; remove tops and set aside. Discard soft dough from inside. Cool puffs. Fill puffs with 2-3/4 cups ice cream; replace tops. Cover tightly and freeze.

For sauce, place the raspberries in a blender or food processor; cover and process until smooth. Strain seeds. Stir in the remaining ice cream until melted. In a small saucepan, heat the chocolate, milk and remaining butter over low heat until melted, stirring constantly.

To serve, spoon 2 tablespoons raspberry sauce on each dessert plate; top with filled cream puffs. Drizzle with chocolate sauce; sprinkle with pistachios. **Yield:** 1-1/2 dozen.

ORGANIZING AN ORNAMENT EXCHANGE

WHETHER you host the event for close friends, co-workers or acquaintances, an ornament exchange is one of the easiest parties to organize. All you need to do is purchase an ornament and make a little food…a good time is guaranteed when the gift opening begins! Here's how an ornament exchange works:
• Ask each guest (the number depends on you) to bring one wrapped ornament. Specify a price range (often between $5 and $10).

• As the guests arrive, assign a number to each package and give the guests a number, making sure it's not the number attached to their gift. (For a fun way to attach the numbers and to display the lovely pile of presents, see the Pretty Packages Centerpiece on page 83.)
• In turn, each person opens the package corresponding to their number. For a little added fun, see if folks can guess who purchased each ornament.

Partridge in a Pear Tree Pie

(Pictured at right)

*Delight guests and have
a partridge in a pear tree make an
appearance on your holiday table!
The crimson cranberry filling
makes this a fitting Christmas pie.*
—Jill Rens, Champlin, Minnesota

1 can (8 ounces) crushed
  pineapple
1 can (15 ounces) pear halves,
  drained
1 package (12 ounces) fresh *or*
  frozen cranberries
1-1/2 cups sugar
3 tablespoons all-purpose flour
1/4 teaspoon ground cinnamon
1/4 teaspoon salt
Pastry for double-crust pie
  (9 inches)
Additional sugar, optional

Drain pineapple, reserving 1/4 cup juice. Set aside five pear halves; chop remaining pears. In a saucepan, combine the pineapple, chopped pears, cranberries, sugar and reserved pineapple juice. Bring to a boil; cook and stir for 4-5 minutes or until some cranberries have popped. Cool for 30 minutes, stirring several times. In a bowl, combine the flour, cinnamon and salt. Stir in cooled cranberry mixture.

Line a 9-in. pie plate with bottom pastry; trim and flute edges. Spoon cranberry mixture into pastry shell; arrange pear halves on top. Bake at 400° for 35-40 minutes or until bubbly and crust is golden brown (cover edges with foil for last 15 minutes of baking if necessary). Cool on a wire rack.

Roll out remaining pastry. Using cookie cutters, cut out small leaves, small pears and a partridge. Place on an ungreased baking sheet; sprinkle with sugar if desired. Bake at 400° for 6-8 minutes or until golden brown. Place partridge in center of pie with leaves and pears around it. **Yield:** 6-8 servings.

Layered Coffee Ice Cream Dessert

(Pictured on page 71)

*Family and friends won't believe it when you tell them this attractive layered dessert
has only four ingredients. Our Test Kitchen home economists created this
make-ahead recipe with your busy days in mind.*

27 cream-filled chocolate
    sandwich cookies, crushed
    (about 2-1/2 cups)
6 tablespoons butter *or*
    margarine, melted
5 cups coffee ice cream,
    softened
1 cup prepared chocolate
    frosting
Chocolate-covered coffee beans,
    mint leaves and warm caramel ice
    cream topping, optional

Line the bottom and sides of a 9-in. x 5-in. x 3-in. loaf pan with heavy-duty foil. In a bowl, combine the crushed cookies and butter. Press half of the cookie mixture into the prepared pan. Gently spread half of the ice cream over the crumbs. Freeze for 15 minutes. Spread frosting over the ice cream, then carefully spread remaining ice cream over the top. Sprinkle with remaining crumb mixture and press down lightly. Cover and freeze overnight.

Remove from the freezer 5 minutes before serving. Invert dessert onto a serving platter. Discard foil. Garnish with coffee beans and mint if desired. Cut into slices. Serve with caramel topping if desired. **Yield:** 10 servings.

Celebration Cranberry Cake

*After I've served this cake, guests never leave my house without requesting the recipe.
The sweetness of the butter cream sauce balances beautifully with the cake's tart cranberries.*
—Jeri Clayton, Sandy, Utah

3 tablespoons butter (no
    substitutes), softened
1 cup sugar
1 cup evaporated milk
2 cups all-purpose flour
3 teaspoons baking powder
1 teaspoon salt
2 cups fresh *or* frozen
    cranberries, halved
BUTTER CREAM SAUCE:
1/2 cup butter
1 cup sugar
1 cup heavy whipping cream
1 teaspoon vanilla extract

In a mixing bowl, cream butter and sugar; beat in milk. Combine the flour, baking powder and salt; gradually add to creamed mixture. Stir in cranberries. Pour into a greased 9-in. square baking pan. Bake at 350° for 40-45 minutes or until a toothpick inserted near the center comes out clean. Cool on a wire rack.

For sauce, melt butter in a saucepan. Stir in the sugar and cream; bring to a boil, stirring often. Boil for 8-10 minutes or until slightly thickened. Remove from the heat; stir in vanilla. Serve warm with cake. **Yield:** 9 servings.

Raspberry Sponge Torte

(Pictured at right)

This lovely three-layer cake is moist, tender and light. It rivals any cake from the finest bakery. I use black walnuts to add a more distinctive flavor.
—Janet Zoz, Alvo, Nebraska

1/2 cup butter *or* margarine, softened
1/2 cup shortening
2 cups sugar
5 eggs, *separated*
1-1/2 teaspoons vanilla extract
2 cups all-purpose flour
1 teaspoon baking soda
1 cup buttermilk
1 cup finely chopped walnuts, toasted
1/2 cup flaked coconut
1/2 teaspoon cream of tartar
FILLING/FROSTING:
1 cup raspberry preserves, warmed
2 packages (one 8 ounces, one 3 ounces) cream cheese, softened
3/4 cup butter *or* margarine, softened
6-1/2 cups confectioners' sugar
2 teaspoons vanilla extract
1/2 cup chopped walnuts

In a large mixing bowl, cream butter, shortening and sugar. Add egg yolks, one at a time, beating well after each addition. Beat in vanilla. Combine the flour and baking soda; add to creamed mixture alternately with buttermilk. Stir in nuts and coconut.

In another mixing bowl, beat egg whites and cream of tartar until stiff peaks form. Fold into cake batter. Pour into three greased and floured 9-in. round baking pans. Bake at 350° for 28-30 minutes or until a toothpick inserted near the center comes out clean. Cool for 10 minutes before removing from pans to wire racks to cool completely.

Spread raspberry preserves over the top of two cake layers. Refrigerate for 30 minutes. Meanwhile, in a mixing bowl, beat the cream cheese, butter and confectioners' sugar until fluffy. Beat in vanilla. Spread between layers and over the top and sides of cake. Sprinkle with nuts. Store in the refrigerator. **Yield:** 12-16 servings.

KEEPING A CAKE PLATE PRETTY

TO HELP KEEP the serving plate clean when frosting a cake, try this trick. Tuck several 3-inch strips of waxed paper slightly under the cake, covering the plate's edge. Frost as desired, then carefully remove the waxed paper.

Orange Coconut Custard

These pretty parfaits are perfect for weekend guests as well as for the family during the week. I sometimes add banana slices for more tropical flavor.
—*Suzanne Cleveland, Lyons, Georgia*

1/4 cup sugar
1 tablespoon all-purpose flour
Dash salt
1 cup milk
4 egg yolks, beaten
1 teaspoon vanilla extract
1/4 teaspoon orange extract
1 cup heavy whipping cream, whipped
Fresh orange sections
1/4 cup flaked coconut, toasted

In a saucepan, combine the sugar, flour and salt. Gradually add the milk; stir until smooth. Bring to a boil; cook and stir for 2 minutes or until thickened. Remove from the heat. Stir a small amount of hot filling into egg yolks; return all to the pan, stirring constantly. Bring to a gentle boil; cook and stir for 1-2 minutes. Remove from the heat; cool slightly. Stir in extracts.

In four individual dessert glasses or bowls, layer the custard, whipped cream, orange sections and coconut. Refrigerate until serving. **Yield:** 4 servings.

Double-Crust Creamy Raisin Pie

Old-fashioned pudding pie never goes out of fashion. I got the recipe from a boyfriend's mother when I was 16 years old. One pie never lasts long around my house.
—*Janene Curtis, West Valley City, Utah*

2 cups all-purpose flour
3/4 teaspoon salt
3/4 cup butter-flavored shortening
1/4 cup cold water
FILLING:
1-1/2 cups water
1 cup raisins
3/4 cup sugar
3 tablespoons cornstarch
1/4 teaspoon salt
1-1/2 cups heavy whipping cream
1 teaspoon vanilla extract

In a bowl, combine flour and salt; cut in shortening until crumbly. Gradually add water, tossing with a fork until dough forms a ball. Divide dough in half. Roll out one portion to fit a 9-in. pie plate; place pastry in pie plate and trim even with edge of plate.

In a large saucepan, bring water and raisins to a boil. Reduce heat; simmer, uncovered, for 10 minutes. In a small bowl, combine the sugar, cornstarch and salt; stir in cream until smooth. Add to raisin mixture. Bring to a boil; cook and stir for 2 minutes or until thickened. Remove from the heat; stir in vanilla. Pour into pastry shell.

Roll out remaining pastry to fit top of pie. Place over filling; trim, seal and flute edges. Cut slits in top. Bake at 350° for 35-40 minutes or until crust is golden brown. Cool completely on a wire rack. Store in the refrigerator. **Yield:** 6-8 servings.

Mocha Meringue Cups

(Pictured at right)

No one can resist a rich mocha filling sitting on top of a crisp, chewy meringue cup. My clan expects me to make these treats for many special occasions throughout the year.
— *Helen Davis, Waterbury, Vermont*

   3 egg whites
1/4 teaspoon cream of tartar
Dash salt
   1 cup sugar
CHOCOLATE FILLING:
   2 cups milk chocolate chips
   1 cup heavy whipping cream
   1 teaspoon instant coffee
     granules
   1 teaspoon vanilla extract

In a small mixing bowl, beat the egg whites, cream of tartar and salt on medium speed until soft peaks form. Gradually beat in sugar, 1 tablespoon at a time, on high until stiff peaks form. Spoon meringue into eight mounds on parchment-lined baking sheets. Shape into 3-in. cups with the back of a spoon. Bake at 275° for 45-50 minutes. Turn oven off; leave meringues in oven for 1 hour. Remove from the oven and cool on baking sheet. When completely cooled, remove meringues from the paper and store in an airtight container at room temperature.

For filling, in a heavy saucepan, melt the chocolate chips, cream and coffee granules; stir until smooth. Remove from the heat; stir in vanilla. Transfer to a small mixing bowl; refrigerate until chilled. Beat until stiff peaks form. Immediately spoon into a pastry bag or plastic bag with a #20 star tip. Pipe filling into meringue cups. Refrigerate until serving. **Yield:** 8 servings.

Cream Cheese Cherry Dessert

When I'm anticipating a busy day, I make this pretty dessert the night before.
You don't need a very big piece to satisfy a sweet tooth.
—Jeanne Krab, Paxton, Nebraska

3 cups Rice Chex, crushed
3/4 cup packed brown sugar
1 cup chopped walnuts
1/2 cup flaked coconut
1/2 cup butter *or* margarine, melted
2 packages (8 ounces *each*) cream cheese, softened
1 cup sugar
1 teaspoon vanilla extract
2 eggs
2 cans (21 ounces *each*) cherry pie filling
1 carton (8 ounces) frozen whipped topping, thawed

In a large bowl, combine the cereal, brown sugar, walnuts, coconut and butter; set aside 1 cup for topping. Press remaining crumb mixture into a greased 13-in. x 9-in. x 2-in. baking dish; set aside.

In a mixing bowl, beat the cream cheese, sugar and vanilla. Add eggs, one at a time, beating well after each addition. Pour over the crust. Bake at 350° for 25-30 minutes or until center is almost set. Cool completely on a wire rack.

Spread pie filling over cream cheese layer; top with whipped topping. Sprinkle with reserved crumb mixture. Refrigerate for at least 1 hour before serving. **Yield:** 18-20 servings.

Mini Pineapple Upside-Down Cakes

These individual pineapple upside-down cakes are an eye-catching addition to my
holiday dessert table. A boxed cake mix makes them easy to bake anytime.
—Cindy Colley, Othello, Washington

2/3 cup packed brown sugar
1/3 cup butter *or* margarine, melted
2 cans (20 ounces *each*) sliced pineapple
1 package (18-1/4 ounces) yellow cake mix
3 eggs
1/3 cup vegetable oil
12 maraschino cherries, halved

In a bowl, combine the brown sugar and butter; mix well. Spoon into 24 greased muffin cups. Drain pineapple, reserving the juice. Trim pineapple to fit the muffin cups; place one ring in each cup.

In a mixing bowl, combine the cake mix, eggs, oil and 1-1/4 cups of the reserved pineapple juice; mix well. Spoon over pineapple, filling each cup two-thirds full. Bake at 350° for 20-25 minutes or until a toothpick inserted near the center comes out clean. Immediately invert onto wire racks to cool. Place a cherry in the center of each pineapple ring. **Yield:** 2 dozen.

Frosty Ginger Pumpkin Squares

(Pictured at right)

My family loves getting together to sample good food. While pumpkin makes it perfect for the holidays, this ice cream dessert is requested year-round.
—Kathryn Reeger, Shelocta, Pennsylvania

1/4 cup butter *or* margarine, melted
  1 cup crushed graham crackers (about 16 squares)
  1 cup crushed gingersnaps (about 18 cookies)
  2 cups canned pumpkin
  1 cup sugar
1/2 to 1 teaspoon ground cinnamon
1/2 teaspoon salt
1/2 teaspoon ground ginger
1/4 teaspoon ground nutmeg
  1 cup chopped walnuts
  2 quarts vanilla ice cream, softened slightly

In a bowl, combine the butter and crushed graham crackers and gingersnaps. Press half of the crumb mixture into an ungreased 13-in. x 9-in. x 2-in. dish. In a bowl, combine the pumpkin, sugar, cinnamon, salt, ginger and nutmeg.

Pumpkin Pecan Bites

This recipe makes a lot, so I like sharing the bite-size treats at potlucks. To easily frost them,
try putting the frosting in a pastry bag and piping it on top of the cupcakes.
—Carol Beyerl, Ellensburg, Washington

1 package (18-1/4 ounces) spice cake mix
1 can (15 ounces) solid-pack pumpkin
3 eggs
1/2 cup vegetable oil
1 tablespoon ground cinnamon
1 teaspoon baking soda
1/4 teaspoon ground cloves
36 pecan halves, cut into halves
CREAM CHEESE FROSTING:
1/2 cup butter *or* margarine, softened
4 ounces cream cheese, softened
1 teaspoon vanilla extract
3-3/4 cups confectioners' sugar
2 to 3 tablespoons milk
Ground cinnamon

In a large mixing bowl, combine the cake mix, pumpkin, eggs, oil, cinnamon, baking soda and cloves. Beat on medium speed for 2 minutes. Fill paper-lined miniature muffin cups two-thirds full. Press a pecan piece into each. Bake at 350° for 17-20 minutes or until a toothpick inserted near the center comes out clean. Cool for 5 minutes before removing from pans to wire racks to cool completely.

In a small mixing bowl, cream the butter, cream cheese and vanilla. Gradually add confectioners' sugar. Add enough milk to achieve spreading consistency. Frost cupcakes. Sprinkle with cinnamon. **Yield:** about 6 dozen.

Editor's Note: This recipe can be prepared in 2 dozen regular-size muffin cups. Bake for 22-26 minutes.

Coconut Trifle

The friend who shared this recipe is a great cook who never fails to come up with terrific dishes.
The fast-to-fix dessert tastes like coconut cream pie.
—Betty Claycomb, Alverton, Pennsylvania

1 prepared angel food cake (8 inches), cut into 1-inch cubes
2 cups cold milk
2 packages (3.4 ounces *each*) instant coconut cream pudding mix
1 quart vanilla ice cream, softened
1 carton (8 ounces) frozen whipped topping, thawed
1/4 cup flaked coconut, toasted

Place cake cubes in a large bowl. In a bowl, whisk milk and pudding mixes for 2 minutes. Let stand for 2 minutes or until soft-set. Stir in ice cream until well mixed. Pour over cake cubes; stir just until combined. Transfer to a 5-qt. trifle bowl. Spread with whipped topping and sprinkle with coconut. Cover and refrigerate for at least 30 minutes before serving. **Yield:** 20 servings.

Pretty Packages Centerpiece

(Pictured above)

WHEN HOSTING an ornament exchange, let the wrapped boxes and gift bags brought by guests serve as your centerpiece. The various shapes of boxes and bags and the variety of wrapping paper will add visual appeal and color in an instant.

Because most of the boxes brought to the party will likely be small, you may want to wrap a large empty box to serve as the anchor for the display.

Before the party, cut a long ribbon for each guest you're expecting. Then attach a number to each of the ribbons. Put the same amount of numbers on a separate piece of paper in a container and set aside.

As guests arrive, tie a numbered ribbon to each of the packages. Have guests select a number from the container (be sure it's not the same number you just assigned to their gift!). Set the boxes and bags around your large wrapped box. Position the ribbons so the numbers are visible.

When you're ready to begin the ornament exchange, have each guest look for their number and follow the ribbon to their gift. Have each person take a turn to unwrap their new ornament.

'Tis the Season

Festive Cookies & Candies

THE IRRESISTIBLE aroma of confections coming from the kitchen…a brightly colored tin bursting with delectable candy …a festive platter piled high with pretty cookies.

The young and young at heart agree that Christmas is the best time of year to indulge an insatiable sweet tooth.

Herald the arrival of the holidays with such goodies as Peppermint Biscotti, Grandma's Star Cookies, Chewy Almond Nougat and Hard Candy Peppermint Twists. (All recipes are shown at right.)

Your little "elves" (and even Santa himself) will be sweet on these tasty treats!

SWEET TREATS
(Clockwise from top)

Peppermint Biscotti (p. 90)

Grandma's Star Cookies (p. 86)

Chewy Almond Nougat (p. 88)

Hard Candy Peppermint Twists (p. 87)

Grandma's Star Cookies

(Pictured on page 85)

*My husband's grandma would only make these butter cutouts with a star cookie cutter.
I use various shapes for celebrations throughout the year.*
—*Jeannie Brown, Carmel, Indiana*

1-1/2 cups butter (no substitutes),
    softened
  1/2 cup shortening
    1 cup sugar
    1 cup packed brown sugar
    2 eggs
  1/4 cup orange juice concentrate,
    undiluted
    1 teaspoon vanilla extract
    5 cups all-purpose flour
    1 teaspoon baking soda
    1 teaspoon salt
FROSTING:
    3 cups confectioners' sugar
  1/4 cup butter, melted
1-1/2 teaspoons orange juice
    concentrate, undiluted
    1 teaspoon vanilla extract

    3 to 4 tablespoons milk
Food coloring and colored sugar, optional

In a large mixing bowl, cream butter, shortening and sugars. Add eggs, one at a time, beating well after each addition. Beat in orange juice concentrate and vanilla. Combine the flour, baking soda and salt; gradually add to creamed mixture. Cover and refrigerate for 2 hours or until easy to handle.

On a lightly floured surface, roll out dough to 1/4-in. thickness. Cut with a 3-in. star-shaped cookie cutter dipped in flour. Place 1 in. apart on ungreased baking sheets. Bake at 350° for 7-8 minutes or until edges are firm. Remove to wire racks to cool.

For frosting, combine confectioners' sugar, butter, orange juice concentrate, vanilla and enough milk to achieve spreading consistency. Tint with food coloring if desired. Frost cookies; sprinkle with colored sugar if desired. **Yield:** about 7 dozen.

Butter Wafers

*These crisp drop cookies are great for folks who don't like their treats too
sweet and who don't want to fuss with rolling out the dough.*
—*Evelyn Starr, Raymond, Washington*

    1 cup butter (no substitutes),
    softened
  1/3 cup confectioners' sugar
    1 cup all-purpose flour
  2/3 cup cornstarch
Colored sugar, optional

In a mixing bowl, cream butter and confectioners' sugar. Combine flour and cornstarch; add to creamed mixture and mix well. Drop by rounded tablespoonfuls 3 in. apart onto ungreased baking sheets (cookies will spread). Sprinkle with colored sugar if desired. Bake at 325° for 12-15 minutes or until edges are lightly browned and tops are set. Cool for 2 minutes before carefully removing to wire racks. **Yield:** about 2-1/2 dozen.

Hard Candy Peppermint Twists

(Pictured at right and on page 84)

It's fun to tuck a few of these twists onto a platter of Christmas cookies. The holidays in our home wouldn't be the same without peppermint candies.
—Sue Jent, Golconda, Illinois

1 **cup water**
1 **tablespoon white vinegar**
2 **cups sugar**
1-1/2 **teaspoons peppermint extract**
1/8 **teaspoon red food coloring**

Coat two 9-in. square baking pans with nonstick cooking spray; set aside. (Do not use butter or foil to prepare pans.)

In a heavy saucepan over medium heat, combine water and vinegar. Add sugar. Cook and stir until sugar is dissolved and mixture comes to a boil, about 8 minutes. (If sugar crystals are present, cover saucepan for 1-1/2 to 2 minutes to allow steam to wash crystals down.) Cook, without stirring, until a candy thermometer reads 300° (hard-crack stage), about 26 minutes.

Combine peppermint extract and food coloring. Remove syrup from the heat; stir in peppermint mixture until well blended (mixture will bubble up slightly). Keep face away from mixture as odor is strong. Immediately and carefully pour into prepared pans (do not scrape saucepan or tilt pans to spread mixture evenly). Cool for 1-1/2 to 2 minutes.

Using a sharp knife, score candy into 1/2-in.- to 3/4-in.- wide pieces, about 3 in. long. Place both pans in a warm oven (150° or your oven's lowest temperature) for about 5 minutes or until candy is warm enough to cut but cool enough to handle.

Using a heavy-duty kitchen scissors, cut along scored lines, one piece at a time. Immediately wrap each piece around the handle of a wooden spoon; remove candy and place on waxed paper to harden. Continue cutting and wrapping until mixture in pan begins to harden. Return pan to oven for at least 5 minutes. Meanwhile, remove second pan from the oven. Cut and wrap as before until mixture begins to harden. Return to oven and repeat with the first pan. Repeat until all mixture is cut and formed into twists. **Yield:** about 1/2 pound.

Chewy Almond Nougat

(Pictured on page 84)

*We've been making this candy for years. It continues to be a tradition
for when the kids and grandkids come home for the holidays.
I've substituted pistachios for the almonds with wonderful results.*
— Vera Kramer, Jenera, Ohio

3 egg whites
1-1/2 cups sugar
1-1/4 cups light corn syrup
1/4 cup water
ALMOND MIXTURE:
   3 cups sugar
   3 cups light corn syrup
   1/2 cup butter (no substitutes),
     melted
   4 teaspoons vanilla extract
   3 cups slivered almonds,
     toasted
   1 teaspoon salt

Heavily butter a 15-in. x 10-in. x 1-in. pan; set aside. Heavily butter a large bowl; set aside. In a stand mixer, beat egg whites until stiff peaks form. In a heavy saucepan over medium heat, combine the sugar, corn syrup and water. Cook and stir until sugar is dissolved and mixture comes to a boil, about 10 minutes. (If sugar crystals are present, cover and boil for 1-2 minutes to allow steam to wash crystals down.) Cook, without stirring, until a candy thermometer reads 238° (soft-ball stage), about 6-8 minutes.

With mixer running, carefully and slowly add hot liquid in a steady stream over egg whites. Beat 10 minutes longer or until mixture holds its shape and is lukewarm. (Mixture will be beginning to lose its gloss.) Transfer to prepared bowl.

For almond mixture, in a large heavy saucepan over medium heat, combine sugar and corn syrup. Cook and stir until sugar is dissolved and mixture comes to a boil, about 15 minutes. (If sugar crystals are present, cover and boil for 1-2 minutes to allow steam to wash crystals down.) With a clean spoon, cook and stir over medium-high heat until a candy thermometer reads 275° (soft-crack stage), about 15 minutes longer.

Pour over mixture in bowl (do not scrape saucepan). With a large wooden spoon, stir until blended. Combine butter and vanilla; gradually add to almond mixture until blended, stirring after each addition. Stir in almonds and salt until blended. Transfer to prepared pan. Let stand at room temperature for several hours or until firm. Cut into squares. Wrap in plastic wrap or waxed paper if desired. **Yield:** about 5-1/2 pounds.

Editor's Note: A heavy-duty stand mixer is needed for this recipe. Egg whites were beaten with a whisk attachment and hot liquid was added using a paddle.

Frosted Ginger Creams

(Pictured at right)

I have many recipes featuring ginger, but these soft cookies are real gems. The hint of lemon in the cream cheese frosting is a nice complement.
—Shirley Clark, Columbia, Missouri

1/4 cup shortening
1/2 cup sugar
1 egg
1/3 cup molasses
2 cups all-purpose flour
1 teaspoon ground ginger
1/2 teaspoon baking soda
1/2 teaspoon salt
1/2 teaspoon ground cinnamon
1/2 teaspoon ground cloves
1/3 cup water
FROSTING:
1-1/2 ounces cream cheese, softened
3 tablespoons butter *or* margarine, softened
1 cup plus 3 tablespoons confectioners' sugar
1/2 teaspoon vanilla extract
1 to 2 teaspoons lemon juice

In a large mixing bowl, cream shortening and sugar. Beat in egg and molasses. Combine the flour, ginger, baking soda, salt, cinnamon and cloves; gradually add to creamed mixture alternately with water (dough will be soft). Drop by heaping teaspoonfuls 2 in. apart onto greased baking sheets. Bake at 400° for 7-8 minutes or until tops are cracked. Remove to wire racks to cool.

In a small mixing bowl, beat cream cheese, butter and confectioners' sugar until light and fluffy. Beat in vanilla and enough lemon juice to achieve spreading consistency. Frost cookies. Store in the refrigerator. **Yield:** about 4 dozen.

GINGER FOLKLORE

DURING the Middle Ages, ginger was often used as a preservative. Because baked goods made with ginger did not spoil as quickly, they were thought to be magical.

Peppermint Biscotti

(Pictured on page 85)

Dipped in melted chocolate and rolled in crushed peppermint candy, this flavorful biscotti is a favorite. It's one of the many sweets I make for Christmas.
—Paula Marchesi, Lenhartsville, Pennsylvania

3/4 cup butter (no substitutes), softened
3/4 cup sugar
3 eggs
2 teaspoons peppermint extract
3-1/4 cups all-purpose flour
1 teaspoon baking powder
1/4 teaspoon salt
1 cup crushed peppermint candy
FROSTING:
2 cups (12 ounces) semisweet chocolate chips
2 tablespoons shortening
1/2 cup crushed peppermint candy

In a large mixing bowl, cream butter and sugar. Add eggs, one at a time, beating well after each addition. Beat in extract. Combine the flour, baking powder and salt; stir in peppermint candy. Gradually add to creamed mixture, beating until blended (dough will be stiff).

Divide dough in half. On an ungreased baking sheet, roll each portion into a 12-in. x 2-1/2-in. rectangle. Bake at 350° for 25-30 minutes or until golden brown. Carefully remove to wire racks; cool for 15 minutes. Transfer to a cutting board; cut diagonally with a sharp knife into 1/2-in. slices. Place cut side down on ungreased baking sheets. Bake for 12-15 minutes or until firm. Remove to wire racks to cool.

In a microwave-safe bowl, melt chocolate chips and shortening; stir until smooth. Dip one end of each cookie in chocolate; roll in candy. Place on waxed paper until set. Store in an airtight container. **Yield:** about 3-1/2 dozen.

Fudge Drops

This is my most-requested holiday recipe. Not a Christmas goes by that I don't make several batches for my family to enjoy and for friends as gifts.
—Linda Lundmark, Martinton, Illinois

1-2/3 cups sugar
1 can (5 ounces) evaporated milk
2 tablespoons butter *or* margarine
1/2 teaspoon salt
2-3/4 cups miniature marshmallows
2 cups (12 ounces) semisweet chocolate chips
1/2 cup coarsely chopped walnuts
1/2 cup raisins
1/2 cup coarsely chopped maraschino cherries
1 teaspoon vanilla extract

In a heavy saucepan, combine the sugar, milk, butter and salt. Bring to a boil over medium heat, stirring constantly. Boil and stir for 5 minutes. Remove from the heat; stir in remaining ingredients. Stir vigorously for 1 minute or until marshmallows are partially melted. Drop by tablespoonfuls onto waxed paper-lined baking sheets. Let stand at room temperature until cool. Store in airtight containers in a cool dry place. **Yield:** about 2-1/4 pounds.

Cherry-Pecan Icebox Cookies

(Pictured at right)

During the holiday season, I keep a roll of dough for these crisp cookies in the freezer. It's nice to offer unexpected company a home-baked treat.
—Betye Dalton, Tupelo, Oklahoma

1 cup butter (no substitutes), softened
1-1/4 cups sugar
1 egg
2-1/2 cups all-purpose flour
1-1/2 teaspoons baking soda
1/8 teaspoon salt
1 cup chopped pecans
3/4 cup chopped red *and/or* green candied cherries

In a large mixing bowl, cream butter and sugar. Add egg; mix well. Combine the flour, baking soda and salt; add to creamed mixture and mix well. Stir in pecans and candied cherries. Shape into four 8-in. rolls; wrap in plastic wrap. Refrigerate for at least 4 hours or until firm.

Unwrap and cut into 1/8- to 1/4-in. slices. Place 2 in. apart on ungreased baking sheets. Bake at 350° for 7-8 minutes or until lightly browned and edges are set. Cool for 1-2 minutes before removing to wire racks. **Yield:** 13 dozen.

Editor's Note: Dough may be frozen for up to 6 months. Remove from the freezer 1-1/2 hours before baking. Unwrap and cut into 1/8- to 1/4-in. slices. Place 2 in. apart on ungreased baking sheets. Bake at 350° for 8-9 minutes or until lightly browned and edges are set. Cool for 1-2 minutes before removing to wire racks.

Frosted Nutmeg Logs

*Every bite of these cookies tastes like a sip of eggnog, so it's no wonder we make them
each Christmas. Other cookie recipes come and go, but this is a timeless classic.*
—Sarah Miller, Wauconda, Washington

1 cup butter (no substitutes),
    softened
3/4 cup sugar
1 egg
2 teaspoons vanilla extract
1/2 to 1 teaspoon rum extract
3 cups all-purpose flour
1 teaspoon ground nutmeg
1/4 teaspoon salt
FROSTING:
1/3 cup butter, softened
2 cups confectioners' sugar
1 teaspoon vanilla extract
1/2 to 1 teaspoon rum extract
1 to 2 tablespoons half-and-half
    cream

In a large mixing bowl, cream butter and sugar. Add egg and extracts; mix well. Combine the flour, nutmeg and salt; gradually add to the creamed mixture. On a lightly floured surface, shape dough into 1/2-in.-wide logs. Cut into 2-in. pieces. Place 2 in. apart on ungreased baking sheets. Bake at 350° for 11-14 minutes or until center is set and edges are lightly browned. Cool for 2 minutes before removing from pans to wire racks.

For frosting, in a mixing bowl, combine the butter, confectioners' sugar, extracts and enough cream to achieve a spreading consistency. Frost cooled cookies. **Yield:** about 4-1/2 dozen.

Chocolate Billionaires

*I received this recipe from a friend while living in Texas. When we moved, I was sure
to take the recipe with me. Everyone raves about these chocolate and caramel candies.*
—June Humphrey, Strongsville, Ohio

1 package (14 ounces)
    caramels*
3 tablespoons water
1-1/2 cups chopped pecans
1 cup crisp rice cereal
3 cups milk chocolate chips
1-1/2 teaspoons shortening

Line two baking sheets with waxed paper; grease the paper and set aside. In a heavy saucepan, cook and stir the caramels over low heat until smooth. Stir in the pecans and cereal until coated. Drop by rounded teaspoonfuls onto prepared pans. Refrigerate for 10 minutes or until firm.

Meanwhile, in another heavy saucepan, melt the chocolate chips and shortening over low heat; stir until smooth. Dip candy into chocolate, coating all sides; place on prepared pans. Refrigerate until set. **Yield:** about 2 pounds.

*Editor's Note: This recipe was tested with Hershey caramels.

Double Delights

(Pictured at right)

These treats are perfect for folks who like both chocolate and vanilla cookies because it gives them the best of both worlds! They're an appealing addition to any cookie tray, and they're usually the first to disappear.
—Ruth Ann Stelfox, Raymond, Alberta

CHOCOLATE DOUGH:
- 1 cup butter (no substitutes), softened
- 1-1/2 cups sugar
- 2 eggs
- 2 teaspoons vanilla extract
- 2 cups all-purpose flour
- 2/3 cup baking cocoa
- 3/4 teaspoon baking soda
- 1/2 teaspoon salt
- 1 cup coarsely chopped pecans
- 5 squares (1 ounce *each*) white baking chocolate, cut into chunks

VANILLA DOUGH:
- 1 cup butter, softened
- 1-1/2 cups sugar
- 2 eggs
- 2 teaspoons vanilla extract
- 2-3/4 cups all-purpose flour
- 2 teaspoons cream of tartar
- 1 teaspoon baking soda
- 1/2 teaspoon salt
- 1 cup coarsely chopped pecans
- 1 package (4 ounces) German sweet chocolate, cut into chunks

For chocolate dough, in a large mixing bowl, cream butter and sugar. Beat in eggs and vanilla. Combine the flour, cocoa, baking soda and salt; gradually add to creamed mixture. Stir in pecans and white chocolate.

For vanilla dough, in another large mixing bowl, cream butter and sugar. Beat in eggs and vanilla. Combine the flour, cream of tartar, baking soda and salt; gradually add to creamed mixture. Stir in pecans and German chocolate.

Cover and refrigerate both doughs for 2 hours. Divide both doughs in half. Shape each portion into a 12-in. roll; wrap in plastic wrap. Refrigerate for 3 hours or until firm.

Unwrap and cut each roll in half lengthwise. Place a chocolate half and vanilla half together, pressing to form a log; wrap in plastic wrap. Refrigerate for 1 hour or until the dough holds together when cut. Use a serrated knife to cut into 1/4-in. slices.

Place 2 in. apart on greased baking sheets. Bake at 350° for 8-10 minutes or until set. Remove to wire racks to cool. **Yield:** about 15 dozen.

Nutty Chocolate Fudge

Some 17 years ago, when I was dating the man who is now my husband, his mother gave me this recipe for his favorite fudge. It's a tasty treat that's so simple to make.
—Maureen Drees, Manning, Iowa

3 tablespoons butter (no substitutes), *divided*
3 packages (4 ounces *each*) German sweet chocolate
2 cups (12 ounces) semisweet chocolate chips
1 jar (7 ounces) marshmallow creme
4-1/2 cups sugar
1 can (12 ounces) evaporated milk
2 cups pecans *or* walnuts, chopped

Line a 13-in. x 9-in. x 2-in. pan with foil; butter the foil with 1 tablespoon butter and set aside. Break German chocolate into 1-in. pieces; place in a bowl. Add the chocolate chips and marshmallow creme; set aside.

In a large saucepan, bring the sugar, milk and remaining butter to a boil over medium heat, stirring often. Reduce heat; simmer, uncovered, for 6 minutes, stirring occasionally. Slowly pour over the chocolate mixture; stir until chocolate is melted and smooth. Stir in nuts.

Pour into prepared pan. Let stand at room temperature until cool. Cut into squares. Store in an airtight container in the refrigerator. **Yield:** 2-1/4 pounds.

Lemon-Cream Sandwich Cookies

A light lemon filling sandwiched between flaky butter cookies makes these a perfect accompaniment to hot tea or coffee.
—Carol Steiner, Arrowwood, Alberta

3/4 cup butter (no substitutes), softened
1/2 cup confectioners' sugar
2 teaspoons lemon extract
1-1/2 cups all-purpose flour
1/4 cup cornstarch
LEMON FILLING:
1/4 cup butter, softened
1-1/2 cups confectioners' sugar
2 tablespoons lemon juice
2 teaspoons grated lemon peel

In a mixing bowl, cream butter and confectioners' sugar. Beat in extract. Combine flour and cornstarch; beat into creamed mixture. Divide into two balls; wrap in plastic wrap and refrigerate for 1 hour.

On a lightly floured surface, roll each portion of dough to 1/8-in. thickness. Cut into 2-in. rounds. Place on ungreased baking sheets. Bake at 350° for 10-12 minutes or until edges are lightly browned. Remove to wire racks to cool.

For filling, in a small mixing bowl, cream butter and confectioners' sugar. Beat in lemon juice and peel. Spread over the bottoms of half of the cookies; top with remaining cookies. **Yield:** 2 dozen.

Editor's Note: This recipe does not include eggs.

Minty Meringue Drops

(Pictured at right)

*These pretty mint green drops are
dotted with chocolate chips.
My kids don't consider it the
Christmas season until I make them.*
—Karen Wissing, Vashon, Washington

- 2 egg whites
- 1/4 teaspoon cream of tartar
- 3/4 cup sugar
- 1/8 teaspoon vanilla extract
- 2 to 6 drops green food coloring, optional
- 1 package (10 ounces) mint chocolate chips*

Lightly grease baking sheets or line with parchment paper; set aside. In a mixing bowl, beat egg whites until foamy. Add cream of tartar, beating until soft peaks form. Gradually beat in sugar, 1 tablespoon at a time, until stiff peaks form. Beat in vanilla and food coloring if desired. Fold in the chocolate chips.

Drop by rounded tablespoonfuls 2 in. apart onto prepared baking sheets. Bake at 250° for 30-35 minutes or until dry to the touch. Remove to wire racks to cool. Store in an airtight container. **Yield:** about 2-1/2 dozen.

*Editor's Note: If mint chocolate chips are not available, place 2 cups semisweet chocolate chips and 1/4 teaspoon peppermint extract in a resealable plastic bag; seal and toss to coat. Let stand at room temperature for 24-48 hours.

Coconut Bars

When I need a dessert that everyone will enjoy, this fits the bill.
Every bite of these gooey bars is finger-licking-good! I often keep the ingredients on hand.
— Patricia Hills, South Dayton, New York

2 cups graham cracker crumbs
(about 32 squares)
1/2 cup sugar
1/2 cup butter *or* margarine,
melted
1 package (14 ounces) flaked
coconut
1 can (14 ounces) sweetened
condensed milk

2 cups (12 ounces) semisweet chocolate chips
1 tablespoon peanut butter

In a bowl, combine the cracker crumbs, sugar and butter; press into an ungreased 13-in. x 9-in. x 2-in. baking pan. Bake at 350° for 10 minutes. Combine coconut and milk; spread over crust. Bake 15 minutes longer. Melt chocolate chips and peanut butter; spread over top. Cool completely on a wire rack before cutting. **Yield:** 3 dozen.

Chocolate-Covered Cherry Cookies

My five brothers and I lost our mother when we were young, so we started cooking at an early age.
Being successful in the kitchen is easy with tried-and-true recipes like this.
— Barbara Hart, Hickory, North Carolina

1/2 cup butter (no substitutes),
softened
1 cup sugar
1 egg
1-1/2 teaspoons vanilla extract
1-1/2 cups all-purpose flour
1/2 cup baking cocoa
1/2 teaspoon salt, *divided*
1/4 teaspoon baking powder
1/4 teaspoon baking soda
1 jar (10 ounces) maraschino
cherries
1 cup (6 ounces) semisweet
chocolate chips
1/2 cup sweetened condensed
milk

In a mixing bowl, cream the butter and sugar. Add egg and vanilla; mix well. Combine the flour, cocoa, 1/4 teaspoon salt, baking powder and baking soda; gradually add to the creamed mixture.

Drain cherries, reserving 1-1/2 teaspoons juice. Pat cherries dry. Shape 1 tablespoon of dough around each cherry. Place 2 in. apart on ungreased baking sheets. Bake at 350° for 8-10 minutes or until set. Cool on wire racks.

For frosting, in a saucepan, heat chocolate chips and milk until chips are melted; stir until smooth. Remove from the heat. Add reserved cherry juice and remaining salt. Frost cookies. **Yield:** about 2-1/2 dozen.

Double-Decker Fudge

(Pictured at right)

My younger brother and I share a passion for candy making. This smooth and creamy fudge from a co-worker of mine features the classic combination of peanut butter and chocolate.
—Peg Kipp, Lewisburg, Pennsylvania

1-1/2 **teaspoons butter (no substitutes), softened**
2-2/3 **cups milk chocolate chips**
   1 **cup creamy peanut butter,** *divided*
   2 **tablespoons shortening,** *divided*
2-2/3 **cups vanilla *or* white chips**

Line a 13-in. x 9-in. x 2-in. pan with foil and grease the foil with butter; set aside. In a heavy saucepan, melt the milk chocolate chips, 1/2 cup peanut butter and 1 tablespoon shortening over low heat; cook and stir constantly until smooth. Pour into prepared pan. Refrigerate for 10 minutes or until firm.

Meanwhile, in a heavy saucepan, melt the vanilla chips and the remaining peanut butter and shortening over low heat; cook and stir until smooth. Spread evenly over the chocolate layer. Refrigerate for 30 minutes or until firm. Using the foil, lift fudge out of pan. Gently peel off the foil; cut into 1-in. squares. **Yield:** about 2-1/2 pounds.

Family Traditions

I work full-time, and nothing relaxes me more than heading to the kitchen after a hectic day. So early in December every year, I take off of work for a week so I can do my holiday baking. I keep my two ovens busy from early morning to dinnertime. My hard work is rewarded with *mmmany* smiles!
—*Paula Marchesi, Lenhartsville, Pennsylvania*

Bavarian Mint Fudge

My sister-in-law sent this chocolate candy to us one Christmas, and it's been a traditional holiday treat in our home ever since. With just six ingredients, it couldn't be any easier to make.
—Sue Tucker, Edgemoor, South Carolina

1-1/2 teaspoons plus 1 tablespoon butter (no substitutes), *divided*
2 cups (12 ounces) semisweet chocolate chips
1 package (11-1/2 ounces) milk chocolate chips
1 can (14 ounces) sweetened condensed milk
1 teaspoon peppermint extract
1 teaspoon vanilla extract

Line an 11-in. x 7-in. x 2-in. pan with foil and grease the foil with 1-1/2 teaspoons butter; set aside. In a heavy saucepan, heat the chocolate chips and remaining butter over low heat until melted; stir until smooth. Remove from the heat; stir in the milk and extracts until well blended. Spread into prepared pan. Refrigerate until set.

Using the foil, lift fudge out of the pan. Discard the foil; cut fudge into 1-in. squares. Store in the refrigerator. **Yield:** about 2-1/2 pounds.

Holiday Peanut Bars

Oats, peanut butter and M&M's give this bar mass appeal. When I have free time, I often bake a pan and pop it in the freezer to take to a future potluck or bake sale.
—Peg Woitel, Fairbanks, Alaska

2 cups quick-cooking oats
1-1/2 cups all-purpose flour
3/4 cup packed brown sugar
1-1/2 teaspoons baking soda
1/2 teaspoon salt
3/4 cup butter *or* margarine, melted
1 package (14 ounces) peanut M&M's
1 can (14 ounces) sweetened condensed milk
1/2 cup chunky peanut butter
1 tablespoon vanilla extract

In a mixing bowl, combine the oats, flour, brown sugar, baking soda and salt. Add butter; mix until crumbly. Set aside 1 cup. Press the remaining crumb mixture into a greased 13-in. x 9-in. x 2-in. baking pan. Bake at 350° for 9-11 minutes or until edges are lightly browned (bars will puff up slightly).

Meanwhile, set aside 1 cup M&M's; chop remaining M&M's. In a mixing bowl, combine the milk, peanut butter and vanilla; mix well. Stir in chopped M&M's. Pour over crust; carefully spread evenly. Sprinkle with reserved M&M's; gently press into peanut butter mixture. Sprinkle with reserved crumb mixture. Bake 18-22 minutes longer or until edges are lightly browned. Cool on a wire rack before cutting. **Yield:** 3 dozen.

Aloha Brittle

(Pictured at right)

A vacation to Hawaii inspired me to create this mouth-watering brittle. Coconuts, macadamia nuts and pecans make my tropical-tasting recipe deliciously different.
—Marylyn Richardson
Windermere, British Columbia

1/2 cup flaked coconut
1 cup sugar
1/2 cup light corn syrup
1 jar (3-1/4 ounces) macadamia nuts
1/2 cup chopped pecans
1 teaspoon butter (no substitutes)
1 teaspoon baking soda
1 teaspoon water
1 teaspoon vanilla extract

Sprinkle coconut in a 12-in. circle on a large greased baking sheet. In a heavy saucepan, combine the sugar and corn syrup. Cook over medium heat, stirring constantly, until a candy thermometer reads 240° (soft-ball stage). Stir in the macadamia nuts, pecans and butter; cook and stir until the mixture reaches 300° (hard-crack stage).

Combine the baking soda, water and vanilla. Remove saucepan from the heat; stir in the baking soda mixture. Quickly pour over the coconut. Cool for 30 minutes; break into pieces. Store in an airtight container with waxed paper between layers. **Yield:** 1 pound.

KEEPING HOMEMADE CANDY FRESH

AFTER you've gone to the trouble of making candy from scratch, be sure to store it properly so it stays fresh longer.

- Stored in an airtight container in a cool dry place, most homemade candy will keep for about 2 to 3 weeks. Fudge and caramels can be wrapped tightly and frozen for up to 1 year.

- To prevent candies from exchanging flavors, always store different types of candy in separate containers, using waxed paper between layers.

  Also keep hard candy and soft candy in different containers; otherwise, the moisture from the soft candy will cause the hard candy to become sticky.

Raspberry 'n' Vanilla Chip Cookies

Many holiday cookies are fancy and time-consuming. So I appreciate this basic recipe
featuring raspberry chocolate chips. I know your family will like them, too.
—DeAnn Alleva, Hudson, Wisconsin

  1/2 cup butter (no substitutes),
     softened
  1 cup sugar
  2 eggs
  3 teaspoons vanilla extract
  2 cups all-purpose flour
  1 teaspoon baking soda
  1/2 teaspoon salt
1-1/2 cups raspberry chocolate chips
  1/2 cup vanilla *or* white chips

In a large mixing bowl, cream butter and sugar. Add eggs, one at a time, beating well after each addition. Beat in vanilla. Combine the flour, baking soda and salt; gradually add to the creamed mixture. Stir in chips. Roll into 1-1/2-in. balls. Place 2 in. apart onto lightly greased baking sheets. Bake at 350° for 12-15 minutes or until lightly browned. Remove to wire racks to cool. **Yield:** about 3-1/2 dozen.

Chewy German Chocolate Cookies

When I want a cookie that's as chewy as a brownie, this is the recipe I reach for.
Coffee granules add just the right amount of mocha flavor.
—Darlene Brenden, Salem, Oregon

  3 packages (4 ounces *each*)
     German sweet chocolate,
     chopped
  2 tablespoons shortening
  1 teaspoon instant coffe
     granules
  3 eggs
1-1/4 cups sugar
  1 teaspoon vanilla extract
  1 cup all-purpose flour
  1/2 teaspoon baking powder
  1/2 teaspoon salt
  1/2 cup chopped pecans
 55 to 60 pecan halves

In a heavy saucepan, melt chocolate and shortening over low heat; stir until smooth. Remove from the heat; stir in coffee granules. Set aside to cool.

In a mixing bowl, beat eggs and sugar until light and lemon-colored. Beat in the cooled chocolate and vanilla. Combine the flour, baking powder and salt; add to chocolate mixture (dough will be soft). Stir in chopped pecans. Cover and refrigerate for 30 minutes or until easy to handle.

Drop by rounded teaspoonfuls 2 in. apart onto greased baking sheets. Place a pecan half in the center of each. Bake at 350° for 9-10 minutes or until set. Cool for 1 minute before removing to wire racks. **Yield:** about 5 dozen.

Crunchy Pecan Drops

(Pictured at right)

My family looks forward to Christmas each year because that's the only time I make this candy. For a chocolate treat, I like to use chocolate kisses in place of the vanilla chips.
—Glenda Gibson, Columbia, Missouri

5 cups sugar
1 can (12 ounces) evaporated milk
1/2 cup butter (no substitutes), cubed
2 packages (10 to 12 ounces *each*) vanilla *or* white chips
1 jar (7 ounces) marshmallow creme
3 teaspoons vanilla extract
6 cups chopped pecans

In a large heavy saucepan, bring the sugar, milk and butter to a boil over medium-low heat, stirring constantly. Boil and stir for 8 minutes. Add the remaining ingredients; stir until combined. Cool for 10 minutes.

Quickly drop by tablespoonfuls onto waxed paper-lined baking sheets. If mixture becomes too thick, reheat slightly. Refrigerate for 20 minutes or until firm. Store in an airtight container in the refrigerator. **Yield:** about 14 dozen.

'Tis the Season

A Tree Trimming Get-Together

WONDERING how to make the joyful job of decorating your evergreen even merrier? Go out on a limb and enlist the help of family and friends!

They won't need much needling to accept the invitation when you promise to reward them with some festive fare.

As your guests string the lights, hang the ornaments and drape the garland, they can nibble on Italian Meatball Hoagies and Confetti Tortellini Salad.

For sweets that appeal to the kid in everyone, set out a platter of Snowflake and Icicle Cookies (which also serve as edible ornaments) and Gingerbread Teddies. (All recipes shown at right.)

Italian Meatball Hoagies

(Pictured on page 102)

My sister and I often prepare the meals for our busy family of eight. We like recipes that are easy to prepare yet filling. Served with a salad, these sandwiches are satisfying.
—Anna Collom, Hewitt, Minnesota

4 eggs
1/2 cup milk
1 cup grated Parmesan cheese
2 garlic cloves, minced
2 tablespoons dried parsley flakes
1-1/2 teaspoons dried basil
1-1/2 teaspoons dried oregano
1/4 teaspoon pepper
2 pounds ground beef
2 cups crushed saltines (about 60 crackers)
SAUCE:
2 cans (15 ounces *each*) tomato sauce
1/2 cup grated Parmesan cheese
1-1/2 teaspoons dried oregano

1 teaspoon dried basil
1 teaspoon dried parsley flakes
1/2 teaspoon salt
12 submarine sandwich buns (about 6 inches), split
Sliced mozzarella cheese, optional

In a large bowl, combine the first eight ingredients. Crumble beef over mixture and sprinkle with cracker crumbs; mix gently. Shape into 1-in. balls. Place in ungreased 15-in. x 10-in. x 1-in. baking pans. Bake at 350° for 20-25 minutes or until meat is no longer pink. Drain on paper towels.

In a large saucepan, combine the tomato sauce, Parmesan cheese, oregano, basil, parsley and salt. Bring to a boil over medium heat; add meatballs. Reduce heat; cover and simmer for 20 minutes or until heated through. Serve meatballs and sauce on buns. Top with mozzarella cheese if desired. **Yield:** 12 servings.

Barley Turkey Soup

Instead of using chicken broth, I frequently make homemade stock using the leftover holiday turkey. A steaming bowl of soup takes the chill out of winter.
—Mrs. Warren Constans, Fruitland, Idaho

2 quarts chicken broth
1-1/2 cups diced celery
1 cup medium pearl barley
1 medium onion, diced
3/4 cup diced carrots
1/4 teaspoon salt
1/2 teaspoon dried thyme
1 bay leaf
1/8 teaspoon ground allspice
1/8 teaspoon pepper

Dash cayenne pepper
2 cups cubed cooked turkey
1/4 cup minced fresh parsley, optional

In a Dutch oven or soup kettle, combine the first 11 ingredients. Bring to a boil. Reduce heat; simmer, uncovered, for 30-40 minutes or until vegetables and barley are tender. Stir in turkey and parsley if desired; heat through. Discard bay leaf before serving. **Yield:** 9 servings.

Gingerbread Teddies

(Pictured at right and on page 103)

Kids of all ages will be delighted to see these roly-poly teddy bears adorning your holiday table! I've been using this gingerbread recipe for as long as I can remember.
—Judith Scholovich
Waukesha, Wisconsin

4-1/2 cups all-purpose flour, *divided*
   2 cups packed brown sugar
1-1/2 cups shortening
  1/2 cup molasses
   2 eggs
   2 teaspoons baking soda
   2 teaspoons ground cinnamon
   2 teaspoons ground ginger
   1 teaspoon ground cloves
Semisweet chocolate chips

In a large mixing bowl, combine 2-1/4 cups flour, brown sugar, shortening, molasses, eggs, baking soda, cinnamon, ginger and cloves. Beat on high speed until combined. Beat in remaining flour. Cover and refrigerate for at least 2 hours.

Shape dough into 12 balls, 1-3/4 in. each; 12 balls, 1-1/4 in. each; 72 balls, 1/2 in. each; and 60 balls, 3/8 in. each. Place the 1-3/4-in. balls on three foil-lined baking sheets for the body of 12 bears; flatten to 1/2-in. thickness. Position 1-1/4-in. balls for heads; flatten to 1/2-in. thickness.

Attach six 1/2-in. balls to each bear for arms, legs and ears. Attach four 3/8-in. balls for paws. Attach one 3/8-in. ball for nose. Add chocolate chips for eyes and belly buttons. Make three cuts halfway through the dough on the end of each paw; make an indendation in each ear with a wooden spoon handle.

Bake at 350° for 12-16 minutes or until set. Cool for 10 minutes before carefully removing from pans to wire racks to cool completely (cookies will be fragile while warm). **Yield:** 1 dozen.

Editor's Note: Any remaining dough may be shaped into balls and baked for 8-10 minutes.

Confetti Tortellini Salad

(Pictured on page 103)

After sampling a similar pasta salad at a market in Florida, I came home to develop my own version. This recipe is as close to the original as anything I've ever tried.
—*Suzanne Zick, Lincolnton, North Carolina*

1-1/2 cups refrigerated *or* frozen
    cheese tortellini
  1 cup cauliflowerets
  1 cup broccoli florets
  2 medium carrots, cut into
    1/4-inch slices
  2 tablespoons thinly sliced
    green onions
  1 garlic clove, minced
1/4 cup grated Parmesan cheese
1/2 cup Italian salad dressing
1/4 teaspoon hot pepper sauce

In a large saucepan, cook tortellini according to package directions; drain. In a bowl, combine the tortellini, vegetables and garlic. Sprinkle with cheese. Combine the salad dressing and hot pepper sauce; pour over salad and toss gently. Cover and refrigerate until serving. **Yield:** 6 servings.

TREE DECORATING TIPS

A BEAUTIFULLY decorated Christmas tree adds to the magical memories of the holidays. So spruce up your evergreen like a pro with these helpful hints:

- Instead of simply wrapping the lights around your tree, string the lights around the branches, starting at the trunk and working out.

  As you come to the end of each strand, turn on the lights, stand back and move the lights to fill in any holes. Plan on a strand of 100 lights for every foot your tree is tall.

- When hanging ornaments, the general rule of thumb is to have the larger ornaments near the bottom of the tree and the smaller ones on top.

  Add depth by placing some ornaments near the trunk and some closer to the branch tip. Use approximately 40 ornaments for every tree foot.

- The last thing to do is add the garland. String less garland near the top and add more as you work your way down. Thin garlands look best when draped from branch to branch, while thick garlands are more appealing when loosely wrapped around the tree. For every tree foot, you'll need about two strands of garland.

Snowflake and Icicle Cookies

(Pictured at right and on page 103)

Our Test Kitchen home economists bring some of winter's wonder indoors with shaped butter cookies that get their sparkle from edible glitter. These cookie ornaments are great favors for your trim-a-tree party guests.

1 cup butter (no substitutes),
    softened
1 cup confectioners' sugar
1 egg
1 teaspoon vanilla extract
1/2 to 1 teaspoon almond extract
2-1/2 cups all-purpose flour
1/2 teaspoon salt
GLAZE:
1-1/2 cups confectioners' sugar
   1 tablespoon light corn syrup
1/4 teaspoon vanilla extract
   2 to 3 tablespoons water
White edible glitter *or* coarse sugar
Ribbon

In a large mixing bowl, cream butter and sugar. Beat in egg and extracts until light and fluffy. Combine flour and salt; gradually add to the creamed mixture. Divide dough in half. Place one portion in a bowl; shape the other portion into a 5-in. log. Cover both and refrigerate for 1-2 hours or until easy to handle.

For snowflakes: Divide dough from bowl in half. On a lightly floured surface, roll out one portion to 1/8-in. thickness. (Refrigerate other portion until ready to use.) Cut nine medium snowflakes and six large snowflakes with cookie cutters. Carefully place 1 in. apart on ungreased baking sheets. Using small decorating cutters, cut out desired shapes to create designs in snowflakes. Use a toothpick to help remove the cutouts. Cut six small snowflakes and place 1 in. apart on another baking sheet. With a plastic straw, poke a hole in the top of each cookie. Bake medium and large snowflakes at 375° for 6-1/2 to 7 minutes and small snowflakes for 6 minutes or until bottoms are lightly browned. Remove to wire racks to cool.

For icicles: Cut log into 1/4-in. slices; roll each into a 9-in. rope, tapering from the center to each end. Fold each rope in half; twist, pinching the ends to a point. Place 2 in. apart on ungreased baking sheets. Bake at 375° for 8-10 minutes or until lightly browned. Immediately poke a hole in the top of each icicle with a plastic straw. Remove to wire racks to cool.

For glaze, combine the sugar, corn syrup and vanilla in a bowl. Gradually add enough water to make a thin glaze. Brush over icicles and snowflakes; sprinkle with glitter or sugar. Let stand for at least 5 minutes or until set. Thread ribbon through the hole in the icicles and small snowflakes and through a cutout in the medium and large snowflakes. **Yield:** about 20 icicles and 21 snowflakes.

Editor's Note: Snowflake cookie cutters and decorating tools can be ordered from Sweet Celebrations, Inc. Call 1-800/328-6722 or visit *www.sweetc.com*. Edible glitter can be found at cake decorating specialty stores.

Focaccia Sandwich

My family believes that nothing satisfies hunger like a sandwich, so I make them often for lunch, dinner and late-night snacking. They request this version often.
— Tina Miller, Sun Valley, Nevada

1 loaf (1 pound) focaccia bread
1/2 cup spinach dip *or* chive and
    onion cream cheese spread
2 tablespoons Dijon mustard
8 ounces thinly sliced deli
    smoked turkey
4 ounces sliced Swiss cheese
1 medium tomato, thinly sliced

Cut bread in half horizontally. Spread 1/4 cup spinach dip on each half; spread with mustard. Layer the turkey, cheese and tomato on bottom half; replace top half. Cut into wedges. **Yield:** 10-12 servings.

Peppermint Ice Cream Dessert

With pudding, ice cream and whipped topping, this cool and creamy dessert is the perfect complement to a rich holiday meal. You'll appreciate its make-ahead convenience.
— Cindy Cyr, Fowler, Indiana

2 cups graham cracker crumbs
    (about 32 squares)
3/4 cup butter *or* margarine,
    softened
3 tablespoons sugar
FILLING:
1-1/2 cups cold milk
2 packages (3.9 ounces *each*)
    instant chocolate pudding mix
1 quart peppermint ice cream,
    softened
1 carton (8 ounces) frozen
    whipped topping, thawed

In a bowl, combine the cracker crumbs, butter and sugar. Set aside 3/4 cup for topping. Press remaining crumb mixture into an ungreased 13-in. x 9-in. x 2-in. dish. In a bowl, whisk milk and pudding mix for 2 minutes. Let stand for 2 minutes or until soft-set. Stir in ice cream until smooth. Pour over crust. Chill for at least 1 hour.

    Spread with whipped topping and sprinkle with reserved crumbs. Cover and refrigerate for 6-8 hours or overnight. **Yield:** 12-15 servings.

MAKING COOKIE AND CRACKER CRUMBS

PLACE cookies or crackers in a heavy-duty resealable plastic bag. Seal bag, pushing out as much air as possible. Press a rolling pin over the bag, crushing the crackers to fine crumbs. Crumbs also can be made in a blender or food processor.

Special Hot Chocolate Treats

(Pictured at right)

Dropping a whipped cream-filled chocolate cup into hot chocolate makes for an extra-special beverage. I make the chocolate cups ahead, chill them, then fill just before serving.
—Iola Egle, Bella Vista, Arkansas

HOT CHOCOLATE MIX:
- 8 cups nonfat dry milk powder
- 1 package (15 ounces) instant chocolate drink mix
- 1-1/2 cups powdered nondairy creamer
- 1-1/4 cups confectioners' sugar
- 3 tablespoons instant coffee granules
- 1/4 teaspoon ground cinnamon
- 1 envelope unsweetened orange *or* raspberry soft drink mix

CHOCOLATE CUPS:
- 1/2 cup semisweet chocolate chips
- 1 teaspoon shortening

Whipped cream in a can

In a large bowl, combine the first seven ingredients; mix well. Store in an airtight container for up to 6 months.

For chocolate cups, in a microwave, melt chips and shortening; stir until smooth. With a small pastry brush or 1/2 teaspoon measure, spread chocolate mixture on the inside of 1-in. foil or paper candy cups. Place on a baking sheet. Refrigerate for 45 minutes or until firm. Just before serving, remove foil or paper cups and add whipped cream. **Yield:** 11 cups hot chocolate mix and 16 chocolate cups.

To prepare hot chocolate: For each serving, combine 1/3 cup mix and 1 cup boiling water; stir to dissolve. Place one filled chocolate cup in each mug; stir until melted.

Thick 'n' Chewy Pizza

*This crowd-pleasing pizza is topped with a zippy sauce and family-favorite
ingredients. A co-worker shared the recipe with me.*
—Linda Pasbrig, West Bend, Wisconsin

1 package (1/4 ounce) active
  dry yeast
1/4 cup warm water (110° to
  115°)
1 egg
1 can (8 ounces) tomato sauce,
  divided
3 tablespoons vegetable oil
1 tablespoon sugar
1 teaspoon salt
1/4 teaspoon chili powder
1/4 to 1/2 teaspoon hot pepper
  sauce, *divided*
2-1/4 to 2-1/2 cups all-purpose flour
1 pound ground beef
3/4 cup chopped onion
1 can (4 ounces) mushroom
  stems and pieces, drained
1/3 cup chopped stuffed olives
1/4 cup chopped green pepper

1 tablespoon butter *or* margarine, melted
2 cups (8 ounces) shredded mozzarella cheese

In a mixing bowl, dissolve yeast in warm water. Add egg, 1/4 cup tomato sauce, oil, sugar, salt, chili powder and 1/8 to 1/4 teaspoon hot pepper sauce; beat until smooth. Add 1 cup flour; beat for 1 minute. Stir in enough remaining flour to form a soft dough. Turn onto a floured surface; knead until smooth and elastic, about 6-8 minutes. Place in a greased bowl, turning once to grease top. Cover and let rise in a warm place until doubled, about 1 hour.

Meanwhile, in a skillet, cook beef over medium heat until no longer pink; drain. Remove from the heat; stir in onion, mushrooms, olives, green pepper and remaining tomato sauce and hot pepper sauce.

Punch dough down; turn onto a lightly floured surface. Roll into a 14-in. x 9-in. rectangle. Place in a greased 15-in. x 10-in. x 1-in. baking pan. Brush with butter. Top with meat mixture; sprinkle with cheese. Bake at 425° for 15 minutes or until crust is lightly browned and cheese is melted. **Yield:** 8-10 slices.

Snowball Eggnog Punch

*Our grandchildren are thrilled when this ice cream punch appears on my brunch menu.
The tang from orange juice blends beautifully with the rich eggnog.*
—Joann Johnson, Mountain View, Arkansas

2 quarts eggnog,* chilled
1 quart orange juice, chilled
1 quart vanilla ice cream

Just before serving, combine the eggnog and orange juice in a punch bowl. Add scoops of ice cream. **Yield:** 3 quarts.
  *Editor's Note: This recipe was tested with commercially prepared eggnog.

Christmas Tree Sweet Rolls

(Pictured at right)

Every Christmas Eve, I make a special bread to enjoy the next morning while opening gifts. I often share one of the "trees" with a neighbor.
—Lori Daniels, Beverly, West Virginia

 2 packages (1/4 ounce *each*)
   active dry yeast
2-1/2 cups warm water (110° to
   115°), *divided*
 1/2 cup nonfat dry milk powder
 1/2 cup vegetable oil
   2 tablespoons sugar
   2 teaspoons salt
   7 to 8 cups all-purpose flour
FILLING:
   1 package (8 ounces) cream
   cheese, softened
 1/3 cup sugar
   1 teaspoon vanilla extract
 1/4 teaspoon ground cinnamon
   1 can (8 ounces) crushed
   pineapple, well drained
 1/2 cup chopped red and green
   candied cherries
 1/4 cup chopped pecans
GLAZE:
   2 cups confectioners' sugar
   2 tablespoons milk
   1 tablespoon butter *or*
   margarine, softened
   1 teaspoon vanilla extract
Red candied cherries and green
   colored sugar

In a large mixing bowl, dissolve yeast in 1/2 cup warm water. Add milk powder, oil, sugar, salt, remaining water and 2 cups flour. Beat on medium speed for 2 minutes. Stir in enough remaining flour to form a soft dough. Turn onto a floured surface; knead until smooth and elastic, about 6-8 minutes. Place in a greased bowl, turning once to grease top. Cover and let rise in a warm place until doubled, about 1 hour.

Meanwhile, in a small mixing bowl, combine the cream cheese, sugar, vanilla and cinnamon. Stir in the pineapple, cherries and pecans; set aside. Punch dough down. Turn onto a lightly floured surface; divide in half. Roll each portion into an 11-in. x 9-in. rectangle. Spread filling to within 1/2 in. of edges. Roll up each rectangle jelly-roll style, starting with a long side; pinch seam to seal.

To form a tree, cut each log into 11 slices, 1 in. each. Cover two baking sheets with foil and grease well. Center one slice near the top of each prepared baking sheet for tree-top. Arrange slices with sides touching in three more rows, adding one slice for each row, forming a tree. Center the remaining slice below the tree for trunk. Cover and let rise until doubled, about 30 minutes.

Bake at 350° for 20-25 minutes or until golden brown. Transfer foil with trees to wire racks; cool for 20 minutes. For glaze, in a bowl, combine the confectioners' sugar, milk, butter and vanilla until smooth. Transfer to a small pastry or plastic bag; cut a small hole in a corner of the bag. Pipe garlands on trees. Decorate with cherries and colored sugar. **Yield:** 2 trees (11 rolls each).

Three-Layer Gelatin Salad

My love of cooking started in high school. Now I get to try out recipes at church, where my husband is the pastor. My mother-in-law gave me the recipe for this pretty layered salad.
—Christine Fletcher, Bronx, New York

RASPBERRY LAYER:
  1 **package (3 ounces) raspberry gelatin**
  1 **cup boiling water**
  1 **package (10 ounces) frozen sweetened raspberries**
ORANGE LAYER:
  1 **can (11 ounces) mandarin oranges**
  1 **package (3 ounces) orange gelatin**
  1 **cup boiling water**
  1 **package (8 ounces) cream cheese, softened**
LIME LAYER:
  1 **package (3 ounces) lime gelatin**
  1 **cup boiling water**
  1 **can (8-1/2 ounces) crushed pineapple, undrained**

In a bowl, dissolve raspberry gelatin in boiling water. Stir in raspberries until thawed. Pour into an 8-in. square dish; refrigerate until set.

Drain oranges, reserving juice. In a mixing bowl, dissolve orange gelatin in boiling water. Beat in cream cheese and reserved juice; mix well. Fold in oranges. Pour over raspberry layer; refrigerate until set.

In a bowl, dissolve lime gelatin in boiling water. Stir in pineapple; cool for 10 minutes. Carefully spoon over orange layer. Refrigerate until set. **Yield:** 12-16 servings.

MAKING TABLETOP TREES

1. Wrap each cone with parchment paper, using straight pins to secure.

2. Wrap jute string and raffia around cone in a spiral pattern until desired look is achieved. Let dry.

3. With a table knife, remove parchment paper from the cone. Carefully separate the parchment paper from the jute and raffia.

Tabletop Trees

(Pictured above and on page 102)

For a country-style centerpiece, try your hand at these jute string and raffia Christmas trees. Tuck in a few branches from your evergreen, then add a little garland or some ornaments for a tabletop "forest" in a flash!

Styrofoam cones in assorted sizes
Parchment paper
Three-ply natural jute string
Green raffia
Commercial stiffener
Large, medium and small
    1/8-inch-thick natural wooden
    star cutouts
Gold metallic acrylic craft paint
Small flat paintbrush
Craft glue

Wrap each cone shape with parchment paper, using straight pins to secure paper to cone. Soak jute string and raffia in stiffener as directed by manufacturer. Wrap jute string around cone shape in a spiral pattern. Add raffia in the same way. Continue to add jute and raffia alternately until desired look is achieved, making sure the bottom of the cone is level. Secure any loose ends with straight pins. Let dry.

Carefully insert a table knife between the cone and parchment paper; move the cone around to loosen. Carefully remove parchment paper from the jute and raffia. Paint all sides of each star gold; let dry. Glue a star to the top of each tree.

GIVING
Thanks

Instead of hosting a formal Thanksgiving dinner,
why not put away the china, polished silverware
and fine linens? Then plan a down-home menu
reminiscent of meals at Grandma's, featuring
roasted turkey and all the fixings. You'll harvest a
bushel of compliments when you set out a succulent
spread of side dishes that captures the best flavors of fall.
And guests will eagerly gather around to sample
wonderful wedges of pleasing pies.

GIVING *Thanks*

On-the-Farm Thanksgiving

IF YOU'RE looking for a way to enjoy some simpler times this holiday season, forgo the fine table linens, polished silverware and fancy china.

Then stoke the fire in a rustic retreat and serve your family a country-style Thanksgiving supper.

Let the flavorful aroma of Herb-Glazed Turkey roasting in the oven take you back to Grandma's cozy farmhouse kitchen.

Then round out the down-home dinner with such hearty sides as Wild Rice Stuffed Squash, Cherry Cranberry Sauce, Citrus Spinach Salad and Mini Butter Biscuits. (All recipes shown at right.)

MEMORABLE AUTUMN MEAL
(Clockwise from top left)

Mini Butter Biscuits (p. 120)

Herb-Glazed Turkey (p. 120)

Wild Rice Stuffed Squash (p. 119)

Cherry Cranberry Sauce (p. 118)

Citrus Spinach Salad (p. 122)

Cherry Cranberry Sauce

(Pictured on page 116)

My mother-in-law makes this super-easy sauce every Thanksgiving. Cherries give tart cranberries a slightly sweet flavor. I serve it alongside turkey, pork and ham.
—*Merry Jo Orr, Iowa City, Iowa*

1-1/2 **cups sugar**
1-1/2 **cups water**
  4 **cups fresh *or* frozen cranberries (1 pound)**
  1 **can (14-1/2 ounces) pitted tart cherries, drained**

In a large saucepan, cook sugar and water over medium heat until sugar is dissolved. Add cranberries and cherries. Bring to a boil. Cook, uncovered, until cranberries begin to pop, about 6 minutes. Reduce heat; cook 20 minutes longer or until thickened. Pour into a serving dish. Cover and chill for at least 2 hours. **Yield:** 3-1/2 cups.

THANKSGIVING DAY TIMETABLE

A Few Weeks Before:
- Prepare two grocery lists—one for non-perishable items to purchase now and one for perishable items to purchase a few days before Thanksgiving.
- Order a fresh turkey or buy and freeze a frozen turkey
- Make Bittersweet Bouquet (page 123).

Four to Five Days Before:
- Thaw the frozen turkey in a pan in the refrigerator. (Allow 24 hours of thawing for every 5 pounds.)

Two to Three Days Before:
- Buy remaining grocery items, including the fresh turkey if you ordered one.

The Day Before:
- Set the table.
- Make the rice mixture for Wild Rice Stuffed Squash; cover and refrigerate.
- For the Citrus Spinach Salad, make the dressing; cover and chill. Wash and dry the spinach; refrigerate in a resealable plastic bag. Section the oranges and julienne the onion; store in separate resealable plastic bags and chill. Toast the almonds and sesame seeds; cover and keep at room temperature.
- Prepare the Cherry Cranberry Sauce; cover and refrigerate.
- Bake Pecan Pumpkin Torte; chill.
- Wash the broccoli for Herbed Broccoli Spears and cut into spears. Refrigerate in a resealable plastic bag.

Thanksgiving Day:
- Roast the Herb-Glazed Turkey.
- Assemble Wild Rice Stuffed Squash; bake.
- Remove salad dressing from the refrigerator 30 minutes before dinner; combine all salad ingredients. Just before serving, drizzle dressing over the salad and toss.
- Bake the Mini Butter Biscuits.
- Cover the cooked turkey and let stand for 15 minutes; carve.
- Make the Herbed Broccoli Spears.
- Set out the Cherry Cranberry Sauce.
- Serve Pecan Pumpkin Torte.

Wild Rice Stuffed Squash

(Pictured at right and on page 117)

I made this recipe when we invited both families to celebrate our first Thanksgiving in our new home. There were 37 of us, and those who tried this dish raved about it.
—Robin Thompson, Roseville, California

  1 package (6 ounces) long grain and wild rice mix
2-1/3 cups vegetable *or* chicken broth
  1 teaspoon rubbed sage
  1 teaspoon dried thyme
  2 celery ribs, chopped
  1 medium onion, chopped
  1 tablespoon olive *or* vegetable oil
3/4 cup dried cranberries
1/2 cup coarsely chopped pecan halves, toasted
  2 tablespoons minced fresh parsley
  4 medium acorn squash (about 22 ounces *each*)
3/4 cup water

In a large saucepan, combine the rice with contents of seasoning mix, broth, sage and thyme. Bring to a boil. Reduce heat; cover and simmer for 23-25 minutes or until rice is tender and liquid is almost absorbed. Meanwhile, in a large skillet, saute celery and onion in oil until tender. Stir in cranberries, pecans and parsley. Remove from the heat. Stir in rice mixture.

Cut squash in half widthwise. Remove and discard seeds and membranes. With a sharp knife, cut a thin slice from the bottom of each half so squash sits flat. Fill squash halves with about 1/2 cup rice mixture. Place in a greased 15-in. x 10-in. x 1-in. baking pan. Pour water into pan.

Coat one side of a large piece of heavy-duty foil with nonstick cooking spray. Cover pan tightly with foil, coated side down. Bake at 350° for 50-60 minutes or until squash is tender. **Yield:** 8 servings.

Herb-Glazed Turkey

(Pictured on page 116)

Honey and corn syrup blend with savory herbs and seasonings to give turkey a slightly sweet flavor. This tried-and-true recipe never fails to win me compliments.
—*Charlene Melenka, Vegreville, Alberta*

1 turkey (16 to 18 pounds)
1/4 cup olive *or* vegetables oil
2 teaspoons dried thyme
1-1/2 teaspoons salt, *divided*
1-1/4 teaspoons pepper, *divided*
1 cup honey
1 cup corn syrup
1/4 cup butter *or* margarine, melted
2 teaspoons dried rosemary, crushed
1 teaspoon rubbed sage
1 teaspoon dried basil

Brush turkey with oil; tie the drumsticks together. Place turkey breast side up on a rack in a roasting pan. Combine the thyme, 1 teaspoon salt and 1 teaspoon pepper; sprinkle evenly over turkey. Bake, uncovered, at 325° for 2 hours.

In a small bowl, combine the honey, corn syrup, butter, rosemary, sage, basil and remaining salt and pepper. Brush over turkey. Bake 2 hours longer or until a meat thermometer reads 180°, basting frequently with pan drippings. Cover loosely with foil if turkey browns too quickly. Cover and let stand for 15 minutes before carving. **Yield:** 16-18 servings.

Mini Butter Biscuits

(Pictured on page 116)

When my mom dropped her homemade rolls while on the way to my house one Thanksgiving, I improvised and whipped up a batch of these buttery bite-size biscuits. Since then they've been part of our traditional Thanksgiving meal.
—*Beverly Raleigh, Tulsa, Oklahoma*

2 cups self-rising flour*
1 cup cold butter *or* margarine
1 cup (8 ounces) sour cream

Place flour in a bowl; cut in butter until mixture resembles coarse crumbs. Stir in sour cream until mixture holds together. Drop by rounded tablespoonfuls into ungreased miniature muffin cups. Bake at 450° for 11-15 minutes or until lightly browned. Cool for 5 minutes before removing from pans to wire racks. **Yield:** about 3-1/2 dozen.

*Editor's Note: As a substitute for *each* cup of self-rising flour, place 1-1/2 teaspoons baking powder and 1/2 teaspoon salt in a measuring cup. Add all-purpose flour to measure 1 cup.

Pecan Pumpkin Torte

(Pictured at right)

Times were lean when I was younger, so we would tend a big vegetable garden packed with tomatoes, beans, zucchini and pumpkin. I've been relying on the recipe for this pretty pumpkin cake for years.
—*Linda Svercauski*
San Diego, California

2 cups all-purpose flour
2-1/2 teaspoons ground cinnamon
2 teaspoons baking soda
2 teaspoons baking powder
1/2 teaspoon salt
4 eggs
3 cups canned pumpkin
2 cups sugar
1-1/2 cups vegetable oil
1/2 cup chopped pecans
FROSTING:
2/3 cup whipped cream cheese
3-3/4 cups confectioners' sugar
1 teaspoon vanilla extract
3 to 4 teaspoons milk
Pecan halves, optional

In a large mixing bowl, combine the first five ingredients. In another bowl, whisk the eggs, pumpkin, sugar and oil. Add to the dry ingredients and mix well. Stir in chopped pecans. Pour into three greased 9-in. round baking pans. Bake at 350° for 40-50 minutes or until a toothpick inserted near the center comes out clean. Cool for 10 minutes before removing from pans to wire racks to cool completely.

For frosting, in a small mixing bowl, beat the cream cheese and confectioners' sugar until smooth. Beat in the vanilla and enough milk to achieve a spreading consistency. Place one cake layer on a serving platter; spread with a third of the frosting. Repeat layers twice. Garnish with pecan halves if desired. **Yield:** 12-16 servings.

Citrus Spinach Salad

(Pictured on page 116)

This simple green salad is the perfect partner for meals throughout the year.
Every bite is bursting with spinach, raisins and oranges.
— Bernice Knutson, Soldier, Iowa

2 tablespoons vegetable oil
2 tablespoons red wine vinegar
  or cider vinegar
1-1/2 teaspoons sugar
1/2 teaspoon grated orange peel
1/4 teaspoon dried tarragon
1/8 teaspoon salt
Dash pepper
Dash ground nutmeg
6 cups torn fresh spinach
3 medium navel oranges, peeled
  and sectioned
1 medium ripe avocado, peeled
  and sliced
1/2 cup raisins
1/2 cup julienned red onion
1/2 cup slivered almonds, toasted
1 tablespoon sesame seeds,
  toasted

In a small bowl, whisk the oil, vinegar, sugar, orange peel, tarragon, salt, pepper and nutmeg. In a serving bowl, combine the spinach, oranges, avocado, raisins and onion. Sprinkle with almonds and sesame seeds. Drizzle with dressing and toss to coat. Serve immediately. **Yield:** 6-8 servings.

BUYING AND STORING ORANGES

CHOOSE oranges that are heavy for their size and that feel firm. Avoid any with mold or spongy spots. Buying a big bag of oranges may be a bargain, but keep in mind that you can't see all areas on each orange. One pound equals about 3 medium oranges.

You can store oranges at a cool room temperature for a few days, but they'll keep for up to 2 weeks in the refrigerator.

Herbed Broccoli Spears

Our Test Kitchen shows that chopped tomato and a few simple seasonings are all you need
to make broccoli a taste sensation for special-occasion suppers.

1 pound fresh broccoli, cut into
  spears
1 medium tomato, chopped
1 garlic clove, minced
1/2 teaspoon onion salt
1/4 teaspoon dried basil
1/4 teaspoon dried oregano
1 tablespoon olive *or*
  vegetable oil

Place 1 in. of water and broccoli in a saucepan. Bring to a boil. Reduce heat; cover and simmer for 5-8 minutes or until crisp-tender. In a skillet, saute the tomato, garlic, onion salt, basil and oregano in oil for 1 minute or until heated through. Drain broccoli; top with tomato mixture and stir gently. **Yield:** 6 servings.

Bittersweet Bouquet

(Pictured at right and on page 117)

IF YOU'RE planning an informal, country-style Thanksgiving dinner, select a rustic table topper to match the mood.

With brightly colored orange and yellow berries, bittersweet is a natural choice for your autumn table.

You'll likely discover bittersweet blooming in abundance in autumn. But if you can't find it growing wild, order some from your local florist.

To make the bittersweet arrangement shown at right, cut floral foam to fit a crock or vase. Then carefully add the bittersweet branches one at a time. (The more dried out the branches, the easier the berries will fall off, so handle them as little as possible.)

One of the great things about using bittersweet is that because the branches are wiry and unmanageable, there's no pressure on you to make a perfect-looking arrangement. So even folks who avoid having to arrange flowers can make this easy, beautiful bouquet.

When set on a table in an entryway or on a sideboard in the dining room, this simply spectacular arrangement will generate many compliments.

A note of caution: Bittersweet berries are poisonous and should not come into contact with food. Also keep away from children and pets.

Side Dishes Suit the Season

WHEN the succulent golden turkey is set on the Thanksgiving table, a bounty of satisfying side dishes perfectly rounds out the year's memorable meal.

Whether you offer a delectable dressing, refreshing salad, vegetable casserole, classic chowder or colorful condiment, you'll harvest *mmm*any thanks (and recipe requests!) from delighted dinner guests.

Pineapple Sweet Potato Bake, Cranberry Spinach Salad and Wild Rice 'n' Bread Dressing (shown at right) are just a few palate-pleasing accompaniments that family and friends will fall for this Thanksgiving season.

THE FLAVORS OF FALL
(Clockwise from top right)

Pineapple Sweet Potato Bake (p. 128)

Cranberry Spinach Salad (p. 127)

Wild Rice 'n' Bread Dressing (p. 126)

Wild Rice 'n' Bread Dressing
(Pictured on page 124)

*Hearty wild rice is an appealing addition to traditional
bread stuffing, while chopped carrot adds pretty color.*
—*Marilyn Paradis, Woodburn, Oregon*

3/4 cup chopped celery
2/3 cup chopped onion
2/3 cup chopped carrot
1/3 cup vegetable oil
  3 tablespoons dried parsley
    flakes
  4 teaspoons chicken bouillon
    granules
  1 teaspoon garlic powder
  1 teaspoon dried marjoram
  1 teaspoon dried rosemary,
    crushed
  1 teaspoon rubbed sage
1/2 teaspoon pepper
1/4 teaspoon poultry seasoning
  2 cups chicken broth
  8 cups day-old bread cubes
  3 cups cooked wild rice

In a large skillet, saute the celery, onion and carrot in oil until tender. Stir in the parsley, bouillon, garlic powder, marjoram, rosemary, sage, pepper and poultry seasoning. Add the broth; heat through.

In a large bowl, combine bread cubes and wild rice. Stir in broth mixture; toss to coat. Transfer to a greased shallow 2-1/2-qt. baking dish. Cover and bake at 350° for 30 minutes. Uncover; bake 10-15 minutes longer or until heated through. **Yield:** 8-10 servings.

Cheesy Zucchini Casserole

*Whether I'm preparing a sit-down dinner at home or attending a potluck buffet,
family and friends have come to expect my signature vegetable dish.*
—*Effie Wanzer, McDonough, Georgia*

  5 medium zucchini (about 2
    pounds), diced
  2 tablespoons all-purpose flour
  2 teaspoons baking powder
  1 teaspoon salt
1/2 cup milk
  4 eggs, lightly beaten
  1 can (4 ounces) chopped green
    chilies
  4 cups (16 ounces) shredded
    Colby/Monterey Jack cheese
1/2 cup dry bread crumbs
  2 tablespoons butter *or*
    margarine, melted

In a large saucepan, cook zucchini in boiling water until crisp-tender, about 4 minutes; drain. Cool for 10 minutes. In a large bowl, combine the flour, baking powder and salt; whisk in milk until smooth. Beat in eggs and chilies. Stir in cheese and zucchini.

Transfer to a greased 13-in. x 9-in. x 2-in. baking dish. Toss bread crumbs and butter; sprinkle over zucchini mixture. Bake, uncovered, at 325° for 40-45 minutes or until a knife inserted near the center comes out clean and edges are lightly browned. Let stand for 5 minutes before cutting. **Yield:** 12-16 servings.

Cranberry Spinach Salad

(Pictured at right and on page 125)

This recipe started out as a summer salad with raspberries. I came up with this holiday version when I was putting together the menu for my first Thanksgiving dinner. I sometimes serve it on individual salad plates instead of in a big bowl.
—Garnet Amari, Fairfield, California

1 package (6 ounces) fresh baby spinach
1/2 to 3/4 cup chopped pecans, toasted
1/2 to 3/4 cup dried cranberries
1/3 cup olive *or* vegetable oil
3 tablespoons sugar
2 tablespoons balsamic vinegar *or* red wine vinegar
1 tablespoon sour cream
1/2 teaspoon Dijon mustard

In a bowl, combine the spinach, pecans and cranberries. In a jar with a tight-fitting lid, combine the remaining ingredients; shake well. Drizzle over salad and toss to coat; serve immediately. **Yield:** 6-8 servings.

TIPS FOR TOASTING NUTS

TOASTING nuts before using them in a recipe intensifies their flavor. Spread the nuts on a baking sheet and bake at 350° for 5 to 10 minutes or until lightly toasted. Be sure to watch them carefully so they don't burn.

Pineapple Sweet Potato Bake

(Pictured on page 125)

*Thanksgiving just wouldn't be the same without this fruity casserole.
I think you'll agree it's an attractive addition to any autumn meal.*
—Sue Howell, Tupelo, Mississippi

6 large sweet potatoes (about
  4-1/2 pounds)
1 can (20 ounces) pineapple
  chunks
1 cup sugar
2 tablespoons cornstarch
1/2 cup butter *or* margarine,
  cubed
16 maraschino cherries
Ground cinnamon

Place sweet potatoes in a Dutch oven or large kettle and cover with water. Bring to a boil. Reduce heat; cover and simmer for 30-45 minutes or until tender. Drain; cool slightly. Peel and cut each potato lengthwise into quarters; cut each quarter into two or three wedges. Place in a greased 13-in. x 9-in. x 2-in. baking dish.

Drain pineapple, reserving juice. Sprinkle pineapple over potatoes. In a saucepan, combine sugar and cornstarch. Stir in the reserved pineapple juice until blended. Add butter. Bring to a boil; cook and stir for 2 minutes or until thickened. Pour over potatoes and pineapple. Top with cherries; sprinkle with cinnamon. Bake, uncovered, at 350° for 30-35 minutes or until heated through. **Yield:** 8 servings.

Corn Chowder

*Chowder is a classic comfort food here in the Northeast, especially during cooler weather.
Whenever I make a trip home to Pittsburgh, Mom has this simmering on the stove for me.*
—Kristy Knight, Bayside, New York

1 large onion, chopped
1/2 cup butter *or* margarine
2-1/2 cups hot water
2 cans (14-3/4 ounces *each*)
  cream-style corn
4 medium potatoes, peeled and
  cut into 1/2-inch cubes
2 cups milk
1-1/2 teaspoons salt
3/4 teaspoon pepper
Minced fresh parsley

In a soup kettle or large saucepan, saute onion in butter until tender. Add the water, corn and potatoes; bring to a boil. Reduce heat; cover and simmer for 16-20 minutes or until potatoes are tender. Reduce heat to low. Stir in the milk, salt and pepper. Cook for 5-10 minutes or until heated through, stirring occasionally. Sprinkle with parsley. **Yield:** 8 servings (about 2 quarts).

Molded Peach Gelatin

(Pictured at right)

For folks who don't care for cranberry sauce, consider serving this pleasant peach mold at your Thanksgiving dinner. It's a convenient do-ahead dish when preparing for a busy day.
— Betty Howard, Wheeler, Texas

1 can (15-1/4 ounces) sliced peaches
1/2 cup sugar
1/4 to 1/2 teaspoon ground nutmeg
1 package (3 ounces) peach gelatin

Drain peaches, reserving the juice; add enough water to juice to measure 1 cup. Place peaches in a blender. Cover and process until smooth; set aside. In a saucepan, combine the sugar, nutmeg and reserved juice mixture. Bring to a boil over medium heat; cook and stir for 1 minute or until sugar is dissolved. Remove from the heat; stir in gelatin until dissolved. Stir in the peach puree. Pour into a 3-cup mold coated with nonstick cooking spray. Refrigerate until set. Just before serving, unmold onto a serving plate. **Yield:** 4-6 servings.

Harvest Potato Casserole

Sour cream and cream of chicken soup lend to the creamy texture of this
tried-and-true casserole. My family prefers this to traditional mashed potatoes.
—Mrs. Robert Cody, Dallas, Texas

    8 large potatoes
    2 bay leaves
1/4 cup butter *or* margarine,
       melted
1/2 teaspoon salt
1/4 teaspoon pepper
    2 cups (16 ounces) sour cream
    1 can (10-3/4 ounces)
       condensed cream of chicken
       soup, undiluted
    2 cups (8 ounces) shredded
       cheddar cheese, *divided*
    1 jar (2 ounces) diced
       pimientos, drained
    4 green onions, chopped
1/2 cup crushed cornflakes

Place potatoes and bay leaves in a Dutch oven or large kettle; cover with water. Bring to a boil. Reduce heat; cover and simmer for 25-30 minutes or until tender. Remove from the heat; cool to room temperature. Place in the freezer (still covered by the cooking water) for 1 hour.

Drain potatoes; peel and grate. Place in a greased 13-in. x 9-in. x 2-in. baking dish. Drizzle with butter. Sprinkle with salt and pepper; toss to coat. Combine the sour cream, soup, 1 cup cheese, pimientos and onions; spread over potatoes. Sprinkle with the remaining cheese; top with cornflakes (dish will be full). Bake, uncovered, at 350° for 45-50 minutes or until bubbly. **Yield:** 12-15 servings.

Buttermilk Corn Bread

The tattered recipe card for this corn bread proves it's been a family favorite for years.
Although my daughters enjoy it anytime, they mostly request it at Thanksgiving.
—Judy Sellgren, Grand Rapids, Michigan

1-1/4 cups cornmeal
    1 cup all-purpose flour
2/3 cup packed brown sugar
1/3 cup sugar
    1 teaspoon baking soda
1/2 teaspoon salt
    1 egg
    1 cup buttermilk
3/4 cup vegetable oil

In a mixing bowl, combine cornmeal, flour, sugars, baking soda and salt. In another bowl, beat the egg, buttermilk and oil; stir into dry ingredients just until moistened. Pour into a greased 9-in. round or square baking pan (pan will be full). Bake at 425° for 20-25 minutes or until a toothpick inserted near the center comes out clean. Cool on a wire rack for 5 minutes. Serve warm. **Yield:** 8-9 servings.

Sweet Potato Cranberry Relish

(Pictured at right)

Sweet potatoes are a tasty surprise in this slightly tart relish. It's lovely served alongside turkey, ham or pork.
—*Andrea O'Neal, Blaine, Tennessee*

1 **small sweet potato, peeled and diced**
2 **cups fresh *or* frozen cranberries, thawed**
1 **medium navel orange, peeled and sectioned**
1/2 **cup sugar**
1 **jalapeno pepper, seeded,* optional**
1/2 **cup chopped pecans, toasted**
3 **tablespoons chopped fresh cilantro *or* parsley**
1/8 **teaspoon salt**
1/8 **teaspoon ground cinnamon**

Place sweet potato in a saucepan and cover with water. Bring to a boil. Reduce heat; cover and cook for 10-15 minutes or just until tender. Drain; set aside.

In a food processor, combine the cranberries, orange, sugar and jalapeno if desired; cover and process until finely chopped. Transfer to a bowl; stir in the sweet potato, pecans, cilantro, salt and cinnamon. Cover and refrigerate for at least 1 hour before serving. **Yield:** 2 cups.

*Editor's Note: When cutting or seeding hot peppers, use rubber or plastic gloves to protect your hands. Avoid touching your face.

REMOVING ZEST FROM CITRUS FRUITS

ZEST is the colorful outer portion of citrus fruit peel (the bitter white portion underneath is called pith). The zest can be used to flavor a variety of foods, so it's great to have on hand.

Before peeling or juicing any citrus fruit, remove the zest with a small grater or citrus zester or stripper, avoiding the pith.

If the zest has been removed in strips, chop it into fine pieces. Then place in a resealable plastic bag and freeze for up to 6 months. When needed for a recipe, measure only as much zest as needed and return the rest to the freezer.

Cranberry Horseradish Sauce

With its fluffy texture and crimson color, this condiment could be mistaken for a dessert!
Be sure to tell folks the zippy taste pairs perfectly with turkey and ham.
—Bev Hescock, Baker City, Oregon

1 package (12 ounces) fresh
   cranberries
1/2 cup sugar
1/4 cup chopped onion
2 cups (16 ounces) sour cream
1 tablespoon prepared
   horseradish

Place the cranberries, sugar and onion in a blender or food processor; cover and process until coarsely chopped. Add sour cream and horseradish; process until smooth. Refrigerate until serving. **Yield:** 4 cups.

Blue Cheese Green Beans

I was a little hesitant when I first tried this recipe. My sons usually don't care
for green beans, and I thought they wouldn't be fond of the blue cheese.
To my pleasant surprise, they loved every bite.
—Martina Davis, Broken Arrow, Oklahoma

4 teaspoons half-and-half cream
1 tablespoon white wine
   vinegar *or* cider vinegar
1 tablespoon crumbed blue
   cheese
1-1/2 teaspoons grated Parmesan
   cheese
1/4 teaspoon dried oregano
1/8 teaspoon salt
1/8 teaspoon pepper
Pinch sugar
2 tablespoons olive *or*
   vegetable oil
1 pound fresh green beans,
   trimmed
4 bacon strips, cooked and
   crumbled

Place the first eight ingredients in a blender; cover and process until combined. Gradually add oil in a steady stream, processing until smooth; set aside. Place the beans in a large saucepan and cover with water; bring to a boil. Cook, uncovered, for 8-10 minutes or until crisp-tender. Drain and place in a serving bowl. Drizzle with the blue cheese mixture and sprinkle with bacon. **Yield:** 4 servings.

GREEN BEAN BASICS

BUY fresh green beans with slender green pods that are free of bruises or brown spots.

Store unwashed fresh green beans in a resealable plastic bag for up to 4 days. Wash just before using, removing strings and ends if necessary.

Shrimp Corn Bread Dressing

(Pictured at right)

A co-worker from Louisiana shared hearty helpings of this delightful dressing (and copies of the recipe!) more than 20 years ago. It's been a "must" on my Thanksgiving menu ever since.
—Cheryl McIntosh, Orange, Texas

7 cups water, *divided*
1 tablespoon seafood seasoning
1 pound uncooked medium shrimp, peeled and deveined
1 large onion, chopped
1 celery rib, chopped
1/2 cup chopped green pepper
3 green onions, chopped
1/2 cup butter *or* margarine
1 package (14 ounces) seasoned stuffing cubes *or* crushed seasoned stuffing
3 cups crumbled corn bread
1 teaspoon seasoned salt
1/8 teaspoon garlic powder
1/8 teaspoon *each* black, white and cayenne pepper
Celery leaves, optional

In a large saucepan, bring 5 cups of water and seafood seasoning to a boil. Add shrimp; return to a boil. Reduce heat; simmer, uncovered, for 2 minutes or until shrimp turn pink. Drain; set aside three shrimp for garnish. Chop the remaining shrimp.

In a large skillet, saute the onion, celery, green pepper and green onions in butter until tender. In a large bowl, combine the stuffing, corn bread, chopped shrimp, sauteed vegetables and seasonings. Stir in the remaining water. Transfer to a greased 13-in. x 9-in. x 2-in. baking dish. Cover and bake at 350° for 30 minutes. Uncover; bake 10-15 minutes longer or until lightly browned. Garnish with celery leaves if desired and reserved shrimp. **Yield:** 12-14 servings.

GIVING *Thanks*

Pleasing Thanksgiving Pies

EVEN AFTER a big turkey dinner with all the fixin's, who can resist a slice of pie?

From fruit-filled favorites and creamy custard creations to cool refrigerator treats and magnificent meringues, an assortment of homemade pies provides the perfect finishing touch on Thanksgiving Day.

So gather your guests around the dessert table to sample a wonderful wedge of Spiced Pumpkin Pie, Rustic Pear Tart or Cherry Meringue Pie...or maybe even a sliver of each! (All recipes are shown at right.)

A SLICE OF HEAVEN
(Clockwise from top)

Cherry Meringue Pie (p. 138)

Spiced Pumpkin Pie (p. 137)

Rustic Pear Tart (p. 136)

Rustic Pear Tart

(Pictured on page 134)

In this delightful pie from our Test Kitchen, the pastry makes a
"pouch" for a pleasant pear filling. For even more flavor, top the tart with
a powdered sugar glaze and toasted slivered almonds.

1-1/3 cups all-purpose flour
   3 tablespoons sugar
  1/4 teaspoon salt
   7 tablespoons cold butter
     (no substitutes), cubed
   2 to 3 tablespoons cold water
FILLING:
  3/4 cup sugar
  1/4 cup slivered almonds, toasted
  1/4 cup all-purpose flour
1-1/2 teaspoons grated lemon peel
  1/2 to 3/4 teaspoon ground
     cinnamon
   4 medium ripe pears, peeled
     and sliced
   1 tablespoon butter

GLAZE (optional):
  1/4 cup confectioners' sugar
1-1/2 teaspoons milk
  1/4 teaspoon vanilla extract
  1/4 cup slivered almonds, toasted

In a bowl, combine the flour, sugar and salt; cut in butter until crumbly. Gradually add water, tossing with a fork until dough forms a ball. Roll out to a 14-in. circle. Transfer pastry to a 14-in. pizza pan. In a bowl, combine the sugar, almonds, flour, lemon peel and cinnamon. Add pears; toss to coat. Spoon over the pastry to within 2 in. of edges; dot with butter. Fold edges of pastry over pears. Bake at 375° for 45-50 minutes or until golden brown.

For glaze, combine the confectioners' sugar, milk and vanilla. Pour over warm tart. Sprinkle with almonds. Cool on a wire rack. **Yield:** 8-10 servings.

Sour Cream Raisin Pie

For my family, this pie is as essential for Thanksgiving dinner as turkey, dressing and
mashed potatoes! I've been told this recipe's been in the family since the 1860s.
— Trish Rempe, Superior, Nebraska

Pastry for double-crust pie
  (9 inches)
   2 eggs
   1 cup (8 ounces) sour cream
  3/4 cup sugar
   2 tablespoons cider vinegar
   1 teaspoon ground cinnamon
  1/2 teaspoon ground cloves
  1/8 teaspoon salt
   1 cup raisins

Line a 9-in. pie plate with bottom pastry; trim even with edge of plate. In a mixing bowl, beat eggs on medium speed for 1 minute. Add sour cream, sugar, vinegar, cinnamon, cloves and salt; mix well. Stir in raisins. Pour into pastry shell. Roll out remaining pastry to fit top of pie. Place over filling; trim, seal and flute edges. Cut slits in pastry.

Cover edges loosely with foil. Bake at 400° for 10 minutes. Reduce heat to 350° and remove foil. Bake 40-45 minutes longer or until golden brown. Cool on a wire rack. Refrigerate leftovers. **Yield:** 6-8 servings.

Spiced Pumpkin Pie

(Pictured at right and on page 135)

*What would Thanksgiving be without
a traditional pumpkin pie like this?
The smooth and creamy filling features
a wonderful blend of spices.*
—Pat Marken, Hansville, Washington

3 eggs
1 cup milk
1/2 cup sugar
1/2 cup packed brown sugar
1 teaspoon ground cinnamon
3/4 teaspoon ground nutmeg
1/2 teaspoon salt
1/2 teaspoon ground ginger
1/2 teaspoon ground cloves
1 can (15 ounces) solid-pack
   pumpkin
1 unbaked pastry shell (9 inches)
**Whipped topping and additional
ground cinnamon**

In a bowl, lightly beat eggs. Add the milk, sugars, cinnamon, nutmeg, salt, ginger and cloves; mix well. Stir in the pumpkin just until blended. Pour into pastry shell. Bake at 350° for 50-60 minutes or until a knife inserted near the center comes out clean. Cool on a wire rack. Chill until serving. Garnish with whipped topping sprinkled with cinnamon. Refrigerate leftovers. **Yield:** 6-8 servings.

DECORATING PIE WITH PASTRY CUTOUTS

PASTRY CUTOUTS (pictured above on the Spiced Pumpkin Pie) are a fast, festive way to dress up plain single-crust pies.

To make cutouts, roll out dough to 1/8-inch thickness. Cut out with 1/2- or 1-inch cookie cutters of desired shape. If desired, score designs on cutouts with sharp knife.

Bake cutouts on an ungreased baking sheet at 400° for 6-8 minutes or until golden brown. Remove to a wire rack to cool. Arrange cutouts over the cooled filling on the baked pie.

Cutouts can also be used on double-crust pies. Brush the bottom of each unbaked cutout with water and place on top of an unbaked pie. Press lightly to secure. Bake pie according to the recipe.

Cherry Meringue Pie

(Pictured on page 134)

People are surprised to hear this pie's meringue crust features saltines.
The cream cheese and cherry pie filling make this dessert extra special.
—*Susan Card, Franklin, New Jersey*

3 egg whites
1 teaspoon white vinegar
1 cup sugar
1/2 cup crushed saltines (about 12 crackers)
1/2 cup finely chopped pecans
1 teaspoon baking powder
1 teaspoon vanilla extract
TOPPING:
1 package (3 ounces) cream cheese, softened
1/2 cup confectioners' sugar
1 teaspoon vanilla extract
1/2 cup heavy whipping cream, whipped
1 can (21 ounces) cherry pie filling

In a mixing bowl, beat egg whites and vinegar on medium speed until soft peaks form. Gradually beat in sugar, 1 tablespoon at a time, on high until stiff glossy peaks form and sugar is dissolved. Fold in the cracker crumbs, pecans, baking powder and vanilla. Spread onto the bottom and up the sides of a greased deep-dish 9-in. pie plate. Bake at 350° for 14-18 minutes or until meringue is lightly browned. Cool on a wire rack (meringue shell will fall in center).

In a small mixing bowl, beat the cream cheese, confectioners' sugar and vanilla until fluffy. Fold in the whipped cream. Spoon into meringue shell. Top with pie filling. Chill for at least 2 hours before serving. **Yield:** 8-10 servings.

White Chocolate Banana Pie

I developed this recipe based on a popular pie served at an Atlanta restaurant.
Everyone looks forward to this dessert at the annual Christmas party we host on our farm.
Chocolate curls as a garnish are a nice contrast to the creamy white pie.
—*Mary Ann Morgan, Cedartown, Georgia*

2 cups heavy whipping cream
6 squares (1 ounce *each*) white baking chocolate
3 teaspoons vanilla extract
2 medium firm bananas, sliced
Lemon juice
1 pastry shell (9 inches), baked

In a saucepan, cook and stir the cream and chocolate over low heat until chocolate is melted. Remove from the heat; stir in vanilla. Transfer to a mixing bowl. Cover and refrigerate for 6 hours or until thickened, stirring occasionally.

Beat on high speed until light and fluffy, about 4 minutes (do not overbeat). Dip banana slices in lemon juice. Pour half of the cream mixture into pastry shell. Top with bananas. Cover with remaining cream mixture. Refrigerate until serving. **Yield:** 6-8 servings.

Citrus Cranberry Pie

(Pictured at right)

To showcase abundant fall cranberries, our home economists developed the recipe for this lattice-topped pie. A dollop of orange cream complements the slightly tart flavor.

Pastry for double-crust pie (9 inches)
3-1/2 cups fresh *or* frozen cranberries
1 small navel orange, peeled, sectioned and chopped
1 cup sugar
2 tablespoons butter *or* margarine, melted
4-1/2 teaspoons all-purpose flour
2 teaspoons grated lemon peel
1 teaspoon grated orange peel
1/4 teaspoon salt
1 egg, lightly beaten
Additional sugar
ORANGE CREAM:
1 cup heavy whipping cream
1 tablespoon sugar
2 teaspoons grated orange peel
1 teaspoon orange extract

Line a 9-in. pie plate with bottom pastry; trim pastry even with edge of plate. In a bowl, combine the cranberries, orange, sugar, butter, flour, lemon and orange peel and salt. Pour into pastry shell. Roll out remaining pastry; make a lattice crust. Trim, seal and flute edges. Brush lattice crust with egg. Sprinkle with additional sugar. Cover edges loosely with foil. Bake at 450° for 10 minutes. Reduce heat to 350° and remove foil. Bake 40-45 minutes longer or until golden brown.

Meanwhile, in a mixing bowl, beat cream until it begins to thicken. Add the sugar, orange peel and extract; beat until stiff peaks form. Cover and refrigerate. Serve with warm pie. **Yield:** 6-8 servings.

Family Traditions

The night before Thanksgiving, our church holds a pie fest, where those attending are asked to bring a presliced pie to share. After the service, we head to the hall and find tables laden with slices of scrumptious pie for all to sample. It's a wonderful social before the busy preparations for Thanksgiving Day begin. —*Sue Jurack, Mequon, Wisconsin*

Caramel Chocolate Mousse Pie

Busy cooks will love the make-ahead convenience of this no-bake pie.
I prepare it the night before I'm expecting company, then garnish just before serving.
—Carol Steig, Butte, North Dakota

1/2 cup chopped pecans, toasted
1 graham cracker crust
(9 inches)
7 ounces caramels* (about 25)
1/4 cup evaporated milk
1/2 cup milk
20 large marshmallows
1 cup (6 ounces) semisweet
chocolate chips
3 tablespoons butter *or*
margarine, cubed
1 teaspoon vanilla extract
1 carton (8 ounces) frozen
whipped topping, thawed
Additional whipped topping,
toasted pecan halves and
chocolate curls, optional

Place pecans in crust. In a heavy saucepan over medium heat, cook and stir caramels and evaporated milk until caramels are melted and mixture is smooth. Cool for 10 minutes, stirring several times. Pour over pecans; refrigerate.

In a heavy saucepan, combine the milk, marshmallows, chocolate chips and butter; cook and stir over low heat until marshmallows are melted and mixture is smooth. Remove from the heat; stir in vanilla. Cool to room temperature, stirring several times. Fold in whipped topping. Pour over caramel layer. Cover and refrigerate overnight. Garnish with additional whipped topping, pecans and chocolate curls if desired. **Yield:** 6-8 servings.

*Editor's Note:** This recipe was tested with Hershey caramels.

Apple Butter Pumpkin Pie

The addition of apple butter gives this pumpkin pie a slightly fruity flavor.
I'm always happy to share reliable recipes like this.
—Edna Hoffman, Hebron, Indiana

3 eggs
1 cup canned pumpkin
1 cup prepared apple butter*
3/4 cup packed brown sugar
1 can (5 ounces) evaporated
milk
1/3 cup milk
1 teaspoon vanilla extract
1/2 teaspoon salt
1/2 teaspoon ground cinnamon
1/8 teaspoon *each* ground ginger,
cloves and nutmeg

1 unbaked pastry shell (9 inches)
Whipped cream, optional

In a bowl, combine the first seven ingredients. Add the salt, cinnamon, ginger, cloves and nutmeg; whisk until well blended. Pour into pastry shell. Bake at 400° for 50-55 minutes or until a knife inserted near the center comes out clean. Cover edges loosely with foil during the last 20 minutes if necessary. Cool on a wire rack. Garnish with whipped cream if desired. Refrigerate leftovers. **Yield:** 6-8 servings.

*Editor's Note:** This recipe was tested with commercially prepared apple butter.

Creamy Apple Pie

(Pictured at right)

Like my mother, I have a reputation for making great pies...thanks to wonderfully unique recipes like this. After the pie is baked, a cream sauce is poured inside. It's irresistible!
—Wanda Stuart, Kapaa, Hawaii

2-1/4 cups all-purpose flour
  3/4 teaspoon salt
  3/4 cup cold butter *or* margarine
    6 tablespoons cold water
FILLING:
    6 cups sliced peeled tart apples
    1 tablespoon lemon juice
  3/4 cup sugar
    2 tablespoons all-purpose flour
    1 teaspoon grated lemon peel
  1/2 teaspoon ground cinnamon
  1/4 teaspoon salt
    2 tablespoons butter *or*
      margarine
CREAM SAUCE:
    1 egg
    2 tablespoons sugar
    1 tablespoon lemon juice
    3 tablespoons cream cheese,
      softened
  1/4 cup sour cream

In a bowl, combine flour and salt; cut in butter until mixture resembles course crumbs. Gradually add water, tossing with a fork until dough forms a ball. Divide dough in half. Roll out one portion. Line a 9-in. pie plate with bottom pastry; trim pastry even with edge of plate. Set aside.

In a large bowl, toss apples with lemon juice. Combine the sugar, flour, lemon peel, cinnamon and salt; add to apples and gently toss. Mound apples in pastry shell so center is higher than edges; dot with butter. Roll out remaining pastry to fit top of pie; cut a hole in the center about the size of a quarter. Place over filling; trim, seal and flute edges. Cut slits in pastry. Add decorative cutouts if desired.

Cover edges loosely with foil. Bake at 450° for 10 minutes. Reduce heat to 375° and remove foil. Bake 35-40 minutes longer or until crust is golden brown and filling is bubbly. Cool on a wire rack for 10 minutes.

Meanwhile, in a small saucepan, beat the egg, sugar and lemon juice. Cook and stir over low heat until mixture is thickened and reaches 160°. Remove from the heat; stir in cream cheese and sour cream until smooth. Slowly pour into center of pie. Cool on a wire rack for 1 hour. Cover and refrigerate until serving. **Yield:** 6-8 servings.

Pastry for Single-Crust Pie

If you want to try your hand at making pie pastry from scratch,
give this traditional recipe from our Test Kitchen a try.

1-1/4 cups all-purpose flour
1/2 teaspoon salt
1/3 cup shortening
4 to 5 tablespoons cold water

In a bowl, combine flour and salt; cut in shortening until crumbly. Gradually add water, tossing with a fork until dough forms a ball. Roll out to fit a 9-in. or 10-in. pie plate. Transfer pastry to pie plate. Trim pastry to 1/2 in. beyond edge of plate; flute edges. Fill or bake shell according to recipe directions. **Yield:** 1 pastry shell (9 or 10 inches).

Pastry for Double-Crust Pie

Use this recipe from our Test Kitchen when you need pastry
for a double-crust or lattice-topped pie.

2 cups all-purpose flour
3/4 teaspoon salt
2/3 cup shortening
6 to 7 tablespoons cold water

In a bowl, combine flour and salt; cut in shortening until crumbly. Gradually add water, tossing with a fork until dough forms a ball. Divide dough in half so one ball is slightly larger than the other.

Roll out the larger ball to fit a 9-in. or 10-in. pie plate. Transfer pastry to pie plate. Trim pastry even with edge of plate. Pour desired filling into crust.

Roll out second ball; cut slits in pastry. Position over filling. Trim pastry to 1 in. beyond edge of pie plate. Fold top crust over bottom crust. Flute edges. Bake according to recipe directions. **Yield:** pastry for 1 double-crust or lattice-topped pie (9 or 10 inches).

1. Combine flour and salt in a bowl. With a pastry blender or two knives, cut in shortening until the mixture is the size of small peas.

2. Sprinkle a tablespoon of cold water at a time over the mixture and gently mix with a fork. Repeat until all the dough is moist, using only as much water as necessary to moisten the flour.

3. Shape into a ball. (For a double-crust pie, divide dough in half so that one ball is slightly larger than the other.) On a floured surface or floured pastry cloth, flatten the ball (the larger one, if making a double-crust pie) into a circle, pressing together any cracks or breaks.

4. Roll with a floured rolling pin from the center of the dough to the edges, forming a circle 2 inches larger than the pie plate. The dough should be about 1/8 inch thick.

5. To move pastry to the pie plate, roll up onto the rolling pin. Position over the edge of pie plate and unroll, letting the pastry ease into the plate. Do not stretch the pastry to fit.

For a single-crust pie, trim pastry with a kitchen shears to 1/2 inch beyond plate edge; turn under and flute as in step 8.

For a double-crust pie, trim pastry even with plate edge. For a lattice-crust pie, trim pastry to 1 inch beyond plate edge. Either bake the shell or fill according to recipe directions.

6. For a double-crust pie, roll out second ball into a 12-inch circle about 1/8 inch thick. With a knife, cut slits in dough to allow steam to escape while baking. Roll up onto the rolling pin; position over filling.

7. With kitchen shears, trim top crust to 1 inch beyond plate edge. Fold top crust over bottom crust.

8. To flute the edge as shown above right, place your thumb on the inside of the crust and your other thumb and index finger on the outside of the crust. Press the dough to seal.

EASTER
Gatherings

Welcome the arrival of spring—and warmer weather—
and head outdoors on Easter to grill some moist and
tender lamb chops! A special spring menu awaits you
on the following pages. If you have a case of spring fever,
invite folks over for an old-fashioned Easter egg hunt.
The mouth-watering menu items will appeal to old
and young alike. There's even a chapter with Grade A
ideas for using leftover hard-cooked Easter eggs.

Inviting Easter Dinner

WHY PREPARE a traditional ham dinner at Easter when you can enjoy the warm weather as you barbecue in the backyard?

Lamb with Spinach and Onions stars moist and tender lamb chops, which are marinated, then grilled alongside onion wedges. This innovative entree also features a bed of sauteed spinach and a savory onion sauce.

(For folks who expect to see ham on the table, you'll find an on-the-grill version on page 151.)

Every "bunny" will love simply seasoned Chive Buttered Carrots.

For a light yet luscious ending to this special spring meal, serve slices of Lemon Ricotta Cheesecake. (All recipes shown at right.)

A SUPPER FOR SPRING
(Clockwise from top)

**Lemon Ricotta
Cheesecake** (p.149)

**Lamb with Spinach
And Onions** (p.150)

Chive Buttered Carrots (p.148)

EASTER DAY DINNER AGENDA

A Few Weeks Before:

- Prepare two grocery lists—one for non-perishable items to purchase now and one for perishable items to purchase a few days before Easter.

Two to Three Days Before:

- Buy remaining grocery items.

The Day Before:

- Set the table.
- Buy daffodils and assemble the Daffodil Topiary (see page 153).
- For Lamb with Spinach and Onions, marinate the lamb chops. Make the onion sauce; cover and chill.
- Wash and slice carrots for Chive Buttered Carrots. Refrigerate in a resealable plastic bag.
- Make the Savory Leek Soup up to the point of adding the cream, salt and pepper. Cover and refrigerate.
- Bake Whole Wheat Swirl Bread. Cool and store in an airtight container.
- Prepare the Lemon Ricotta Cheesecake; chill.

Easter Day:

- For Lamb with Spinach and Onions, grill the lamb and onion wedges. Saute the spinach. Reheat the onion sauce and serve with lamb, onions and spinach.
- Reheat the Savory Leek Soup; add the cream, salt and pepper until heated through.
- Prepare the Chive Buttered Carrots.
- Slice the Whole Wheat Swirl Bread and serve with butter.
- Serve Lemon Ricotta Cheesecake for dessert.

Chive Buttered Carrots

(Pictured on page 146)

It's nice to have a reliable side dish like this that pairs well with any entree.
A friend shared the recipe with me several years ago, and I use it often.
—Opal Snell, Jamestown, Ohio

2-1/2 pounds carrots, diagonally
   sliced 1/2 inch thick
   6 tablespoons butter *or*
   margarine
1/4 to 1/2 teaspoon seasoned salt
1/4 teaspoon pepper
4-1/2 teaspoons minced chives

Place 1 in. of water and carrots in a large saucepan. Bring to a boil. Reduce heat; cover and simmer for 4-5 minutes or until crisp-tender. Drain well. In a large skillet, melt butter. Add seasoned salt, pepper and carrots; cook and stir for 1-2 minutes or until carrots are tender. Sprinkle with chives. **Yield:** 6 servings.

Lemon Ricotta Cheesecake

(Pictured at right and on page 147)

I'm an avid recipe collector and can't recall where I found this one. I do know its delicate flavor is well received whenever I make it for a special occasion.
—Julie Nitschke, Stowe, Vermont

1-1/2 cups vanilla wafer crumbs
    (about 45 wafers)
  1/4 cup butter *or* margarine,
    melted
    1 teaspoon grated lemon peel
FILLING:
    2 packages (8 ounces *each*)
    cream cheese, softened
    1 carton (15 ounces) ricotta
    cheese
1-1/4 cups sugar
  1/4 cup cornstarch
    4 eggs
    2 cups half-and-half cream
  1/3 cup lemon juice
    3 teaspoons grated lemon peel
    2 teaspoons vanilla extract
Fresh mint and lemon slices,
  optional

In a bowl, combine wafer crumbs, butter and lemon peel. Press onto the bottom of a greased 9-in. springform pan. Bake at 325° for 12-14 minutes or until lightly browned. Cool.

In a large mixing bowl, beat cream cheese and ricotta until smooth. Combine sugar and cornstarch; add to cheese mixture and beat well. Add eggs and cream, beating on low speed just until combined. Beat in lemon juice, peel and vanilla just until blended. Pour into crust. Place pan on a baking sheet.

Bake at 325° for 70-80 minutes or until center is almost set. Cool on a wire rack for 10 minutes. Carefully run a knife around edge of pan to loosen; cool 1 hour longer. Refrigerate overnight. Remove sides of pan. Garnish with mint and lemon if desired. **Yield:** 12-14 servings.

Lamb with Spinach and Onions

(Pictured on page 146)

*Grilling is a wonderful way to prepare lamb. The marinade and on-the-side
onion sauce enhance the meat's naturally terrific taste.*
—*Sarah Vasques, Milford, New Hampshire*

1/2 cup lime juice
1/4 cup dry red wine *or* 1
   tablespoon red wine vinegar
1 small onion, chopped
2 tablespoons minced fresh
   rosemary *or* 2 teaspoons dried
   rosemary, crushed
2 tablespoons olive *or*
   vegetable oil
2 tablespoons Worcestershire
   sauce
3 garlic cloves, minced
1 tablespoon minced fresh
   thyme *or* 1 teaspoon dried
   thyme
1/4 teaspoon pepper
Dash liquid smoke, optional
12 rib lamb chops (1 inch thick)
ONION SAUCE:
   2 tablespoons finely chopped
      green onions
   1 teaspoon butter *or* margarine
   1 cup balsamic vinegar
   1 cup dry red wine *or* 1/2 cup
      beef broth and 1/2 cup grape
      juice
   1/2 cup loosely packed fresh mint
      leaves, chopped
   1 tablespoon sugar
   1 large sweet onion, cut into
      quarters
Olive *or* vegetable oil
Salt and pepper to taste

SPINACH:
   1/4 cup finely chopped green onions
   3 garlic cloves, minced
   3 tablespoons olive *or* vegetable oil
   3 tablespoons butter *or* margarine
   12 cups fresh baby spinach
Salt and pepper to taste

In a large resealable plastic bag, combine the first 10 ingredients; add lamb chops. Seal bag and turn to coat; refrigerate for 8 hours or overnight.

In a saucepan, saute green onions in butter until tender. Add vinegar and wine or broth and grape juice; bring to a boil. Add mint and sugar. Reduce heat; simmer, uncovered, for 30 minutes or until sauce is reduced to 3/4 cup. Strain; discard mint. Set sauce aside.

Thread onion wedges onto metal or soaked wooden skewers. Brush with oil; sprinkle with salt and pepper. Discard marinade from lamb. Grill chops, covered, over medium-hot heat for 5-6 minutes on each side or until meat reaches desired doneness (for medium, a meat thermometer should read 160°; well-done, 170°). Grill onion skewers for 2-3 minutes or until tender.

In a large skillet, saute green onions and garlic in oil and butter until tender. Add the spinach, salt and pepper; saute for 2-3 minutes or until spinach just begins to wilt and is heated through. Place on a serving platter. Remove onion from skewers; place onion and lamb chops over spinach. **Yield:** 6 servings.

Savory Leek Soup

(Pictured at right)

There's no mistaking that savory is the main herb seasoning this rich and creamy soup.
—Eleanor Davis
Pittsburgh, Pennsylvania

4 medium leeks (white portion only), chopped
1/2 cup minced chives
1/2 cup butter *or* margarine
4 cups chicken broth
2 cups mashed potatoes (prepared with milk and butter)
2 tablespoons minced fresh savory *or* 2 teaspoons dried savory
3 cups half-and-half cream
Salt and pepper to taste

In a large saucepan, saute leeks and chives in butter until tender. Add the broth, potatoes and savory; bring to a boil. Reduce heat; simmer, uncovered, for 8-10 minutes. Cool slightly. Process in batches in a blender or food processor until smooth; return to pan. Stir in the cream, salt and pepper; heat through. **Yield:** 8-10 servings.

Orange Barbecued Ham

This recipe decreases the amount of time I spend in the kitchen...
because my husband does the grilling!
—Lucy Kampstra, Bradenton, Florida

1/2 cup ketchup
1/3 cup orange marmalade
2 tablespoons finely chopped onion
2 tablespoons vegetable oil
1 tablespoon lemon juice
1 to 1-1/2 teaspoons ground mustard
3 to 5 drops hot pepper sauce

1 boneless fully cooked ham slice (1-1/2 pounds and 3/4 inch thick)

In a bowl, combine the first seven ingredients. Pour half of the sauce into a microwave-safe bowl; set aside. Grill ham, covered, over indirect low heat for 3 minutes on each side. Baste with the remaining sauce. Grill 6-8 minutes longer or until heated through, turning and basting occasionally. Cover and microwave reserved sauce on high for 30 seconds or until heated through. Serve with ham. **Yield:** 6 servings.

Daffodil Topiary

(Pictured at right and on page 147)

The sight of daffodils is one of the surest ways to know that spring is finally in full bloom. So make this topiary featuring those lovely yellow flowers and bring a ray of sunshine to your Easter table.

Floral foam
Small white ceramic flowerpot
   with saucer
About 1/2 cup marbles *or* floral
   stones
Straight-sided glass to fit inside
   flowerpot
About 36 daffodils
Wide rubber band
Natural raffia
Natural wood excelsior

Cut a piece of floral foam to fit into bottom of flowerpot. Place marbles or floral stones inside glass. Push glass into floral foam to secure and place inside the flowerpot.

Arrange the daffodils, keeping flower heads compact and uniform all around. Wrap a wide rubber band around the ends of the stems to secure. Trim stem ends so they are even. Wrap raffia around stems and tie ends in a large bow.

Place the assembled arrangement into the glass, making sure stems are straight. Carefully add water. Arrange excelsior around the base of the topiary to cover the glass and inside of the flowerpot.

1. Cut floral foam to fit bottom of flower-pot. Place marbles or stones inside glass. Push glass into foam and set inside pot.

2. Make a bouquet of daffodils; secure with a rubber band and raffia. Place bouquet in the glass; add water.

3. Arrange excelsior around the base of the topiary to cover the glass.

Whole Wheat Swirl Bread

I developed this pretty swirl bread by combining two different recipes.
—Estelle Hardin, Washington, Utah

2 packages (1/4 ounce *each*)
  active dry yeast
1 teaspoon sugar
3 cups warm water (110° to
  115°), *divided*
1 cup nonfat dry milk powder
1/3 cup vegetable oil
1/3 cup honey
3 teaspoons salt
7-1/2 to 8-1/2 cups all-purpose flour
WHOLE WHEAT DOUGH:
2 packages (1/4 ounce *each*)
  active dry yeast
1 teaspoon sugar
3 cups warm water (110° to
  115°), *divided*
1 cup nonfat dry milk powder
1/3 cup vegetable oil
1/3 cup honey
3 teaspoons salt
5 cups whole wheat flour
2-1/2 to 3-1/2 cups all-purpose flour

In a large mixing bowl, dissolve yeast and sugar in 1/2 cup warm water; let stand for 5 minutes. Add the milk powder, oil, honey, salt and remaining water. Beat for 1 minute. Add 4 cups flour; beat on medium for 3 minutes. Stir in enough remaining flour to form a soft dough. Turn onto a floured surface; knead until smooth and elastic, about 6 minutes. Place in a greased bowl, turning once to grease top. Cover and let rise in a warm place until doubled, about 1 hour.

Meanwhile, in a large mixing bowl, dissolve yeast and sugar in 1/2 cup warm water. Add the milk powder, oil, honey, salt and remaining water. Beat for 1 minute. Add whole wheat flour. Beat on medium for 3 minutes. Stir in enough all-purpose flour to form a soft dough. Turn onto a floured surface; knead until smooth and elastic, about 6 minutes. Place in a greased bowl, turning once to grease top. Cover and rise in a warm place until doubled, about 1 hour.

Punch each dough down; divide into fourths. Roll one white portion and one whole wheat portion into 14-in. x 10-in. rectangles. Place whole wheat dough on top of white dough; roll up jelly-roll style. Pinch ends to seal and tuck under. Repeat with remaining dough. Place in four greased 9-in. x 5-in. x 3-in. loaf pans. Cover and let rise until doubled, about 40 minutes. Bake at 350° for 40-45 minutes or until golden brown. Remove from pans to wire racks to cool. **Yield:** 4 loaves.

Old-Fashioned Easter Egg Hunt

THE THOUGHT of spring conjures up images of Easter bonnets, shiny new shoes, brightly colored clothes and most importantly …more time spent outdoors!

So if you have a case of spring fever, hatch a plan to host an old-fashioned Easter egg hunt.

Your brood will happily perch upon their seats to sample Bacon 'n' Egg Bundles.

Bring a bit of sunshine to the buffet table by serving a dish brimming with Marinated Fruit Salad.

For those youngsters who just can't sit still, French Toast Sticks and Meringue Bunnies are easy to eat on the fly. (All recipes are shown at right.)

A MEAL WITH KID APPEAL
(Clockwise from top)

Meringue Bunnies (p.157)

French Toast Sticks (p.156)

Bacon 'n' Egg Bundles (p.158)

Marinated Fruit Salad (p.157)

French Toast Sticks

(Pictured on page 155)

These French toast sticks from our Test Kitchen are handy to have in the freezer for a hearty breakfast in an instant. They're great for buffets because they can be eaten on the go.

6 slices day-old Texas Toast
4 eggs
1 cup milk
2 tablespoons sugar
1 teaspoon vanilla extract
1/4 to 1/2 teaspoon ground
　　cinnamon
1 cup crushed cornflakes,
　　optional
Confectioners' sugar, optional
Maple syrup

Cut each piece of bread into thirds; place in an ungreased 13-in. x 9-in. x 2-in. dish. In a large bowl, whisk the eggs, milk, sugar, vanilla and cinnamon. Pour over bread; soak for 2 minutes, turning once. If desired, coat bread with corn-flake crumbs on all sides. Place in a greased 15-in. x 10-in. x 1-in. baking pan. Freeze until firm, about 45 minutes. Transfer to an airtight container or resealable freezer bag and store in the freezer.

To bake, place desired number of frozen French toast sticks on a greased baking sheet. Bake at 425° for 8 minutes. Turn; bake 10-12 minutes longer or until golden brown. Sprinkle with confectioners' sugar if desired. Serve with syrup. **Yield:** 1-1/2 dozen.

Bird's Nests

To celebrate the arrival of spring, our Test Kitchen shaped chocolate-coated chow mein noodles into nests, then filled them with jelly bean "eggs".
You may want to make a double batch because they're bound to fly off your table!

1 package (11-1/2 ounces) milk
　　chocolate chips
1 tablespoon shortening
1 can (5 ounces) chow mein
　　noodles
2/3 cup flaked coconut
45 to 60 jelly beans

In a saucepan, melt the chocolate chips and shortening over low heat; stir until smooth. Remove from the heat. Stir in the chow mein noodles and coconut until well coated. Divide in-to 15 mounds on a waxed paper-lined baking sheet. Shape into nests; press an indentation in the center. Place three or four jelly beans in each nest. Cool. Store in an airtight container. **Yield:** 15 servings.

Meringue Bunnies

(Pictured at right and on page 154)

These cute cookies created by our home economists are a great addition to your table when entertaining at Easter. Enlist the kids to help shape the bunnies.

> 2 egg whites
> 1/8 teaspoon cream of tartar
> 1/2 cup sugar
> 1/4 cup pink candy coating disks
> 36 heart-shaped red decorating sprinkles

In a mixing bowl, beat the egg whites and cream of tartar on medium speed until soft peaks form. Gradually add sugar, 1 tablespoon at a time, beating on high until stiff peaks form. Transfer to a pastry or plastic bag; cut a small hole in a corner of the bag. On parchment-lined baking sheets, pipe the meringue into 4-3/4-in. bunny shapes. Bake at 225° for 1-1/2 hours or until firm. Remove to wire racks.

In a microwave, melt candy coating; stir until smooth. Place in a pastry or plastic bag; cut a small hole in a corner of the bag. Pipe ears, whiskers and mouths on bunnies. Attach hearts for eyes and nose with melted candy coating. **Yield:** 1 dozen.

Marinated Fruit Salad

(Pictured on page 154)

Juice adds refreshing flavor to this make-ahead fruit salad from our home economists. For added color, sprinkle some strawberries or raspberries on top just before serving.

> 2 cups cubed cantaloupe
> 2 cups cubed honeydew
> 2 medium kiwifruit, peeled, halved and sliced
> 1/4 cup orange peach mango juice concentrate *or* orange pineapple juice concentrate,* undiluted

In a bowl, combine the cantaloupe, honeydew and kiwi. Add juice concentrate; toss to coat. Refrigerate for at least 2 hours, stirring occasionally. Serve with a slotted spoon. **Yield:** 6-8 servings.

Editor's Note: This recipe was tested with Dole frozen juice concentrate.

Bacon 'n' Egg Bundles

(Pictured on page 154)

This is a fun way to serve bacon and eggs all in one bite!
The recipe can easily be doubled for a larger group.
—Edith Landinger, Longview, Texas

1 teaspoon butter *or* margarine
12 to 18 bacon strips
6 eggs
Fresh parsley sprigs

Lightly grease six muffin cups with the butter. In a large skillet, cook the bacon over medium heat until cooked but not crisp. Drain on paper towels.

Cut six bacon strips in half widthwise; line the bottom of each muffin cup with two bacon pieces. Line the sides of each muffin cup with one or two bacon strips. Break an egg into each cup. Bake, uncovered, at 325° for 12-18 minutes or until whites are completely set and yolks begin to thicken but are not firm. Transfer to a serving plate; surround with parsley. **Yield:** 6 servings.

BUYING AND STORING BACON

ALWAYS check the date stamp on packages of vacuum-sealed bacon to make sure it's fresh. The date reflects the last date of sale.

Once the package is opened, bacon should be used within a week. For long-term storage, freeze bacon for up to 1 month.

Springtime Strawberry Bars

Warmer weather calls for a lighter dessert like these fruity bars.
The recipe makes a big batch, so it's perfect for company.
—Marna Heitz, Farley, Iowa

1 cup butter *or* margarine, softened
1-1/2 cups sugar
2 eggs
1 teaspoon grated lemon peel
3-1/4 cups all-purpose flour, *divided*
3/4 cup slivered almonds, chopped
1 teaspoon baking powder
1/2 teaspoon salt
1 jar (12 ounces) strawberry preserves

In a large mixing bowl, cream the butter and sugar. Add eggs, one at a time, beating well after each addition. Beat in lemon peel. Combine 3 cups flour, almonds, baking powder and salt; gradually add to the creamed mixture until mixture resembles coarse crumbs (do not overmix).

Set aside 1 cup of dough. Press the remaining dough into a greased 15-in. x 10-in. x 1-in. baking pan. Spread preserves to within 1/4 in. of edges. Combine the reserved dough with the remaining flour; sprinkle over preserves. Bake at 350° for 25-30 minutes or until lightly browned. Cool on a wire rack. Cut into bars. **Yield:** about 3 dozen.

Ham 'n' Cheese Egg Bake

(Pictured at right)

This make-ahead egg casserole is just the thing when entertaining in the morning. It's loaded with ham, cheese and mushrooms.
—Susan Miller
North Andover, Massachusetts

1-1/2 cups (6 ounces) shredded
   cheddar cheese
1-1/2 cups (6 ounces) shredded
   mozzarella cheese
   1/2 pound fresh mushrooms,
   sliced
     6 green onions, sliced
     1 medium sweet red pepper,
   chopped
     2 tablespoons butter *or*
   margarine
1-3/4 cups cubed fully cooked ham
   1/4 cup all-purpose flour
     8 eggs
1-3/4 cups milk
Salt and pepper to taste

Combine the cheeses; sprinkle into a greased 13-in. x 9-in. x 2-in. baking dish. In a large skillet, saute the mushrooms, onions and red pepper in butter; stir in ham. Spoon over the cheese. In a bowl, combine the flour, eggs, milk, salt and pepper. Pour over ham mixture; cover and refrigerate overnight.

Remove from the refrigerator 30 minutes before baking. Bake, uncovered, at 350° for 35-45 minutes or until a knife inserted near the center comes out clean. Let stand for 5 minutes before serving. **Yield:** 8-10 servings.

Fast Fruit Punch

This family recipe is featured at all of our special events. The pink punch is so pretty on the table.
—Joanne Stark, Wabamun, Alberta

1/2 cup orange breakfast
    drink mix
4 cups water
1 can (12 ounces) frozen pink
    lemonade concentrate,
    thawed
1 can (12 ounces) frozen
    white grape raspberry juice
    concentrate, thawed
1 can (12 ounces) frozen orange
    juice concentrate, thawed

2 cups chilled cranberry juice
2 cups chilled pineapple juice
2 bottles (2 liters *each*) lemon-lime soda, chilled
Lemon, lime and orange slices

In a large container or punch bowl, dissolve drink mix in water. Stir in the next five ingredients. Add soda and sliced fruit. Serve immediately. **Yield:** 40 servings (7-3/4 quarts).

Buttermilk Potato Doughnut Holes

Having worked in a school cafeteria for more than 10 years, I've seen my share of recipes. Everyone loves the comforting flavor of these old-fashioned doughnuts.
—Linda Lam, Mt. Sidney, Virginia

2 cups sugar
3 eggs
1/3 cup shortening
1-1/2 cups hot mashed potatoes
    (prepared without milk and
    butter)
1 cup buttermilk
1 teaspoon vanilla extract
5-1/2 cups all-purpose flour
4 teaspoons baking powder
1 teaspoon salt
1 teaspoon ground nutmeg
Oil for deep-fat frying
Additional sugar

In a mixing bowl, beat sugar, eggs and shortening. Add the potatoes, buttermilk and vanilla. Combine the dry ingredients; add to potato mixture. Cover and refrigerate for 1 hour.

In an electric skillet or deep-fat fryer, heat oil to 375°. Drop rounded teaspoonfuls of batter, a few at a time, into hot oil. Fry for 1-1/2 minutes on each side or until golden brown. Drain on paper towels; roll in additional sugar while warm. **Yield:** about 9-1/2 dozen.

POTATO POINTERS

WHEN BUYING potatoes, look for those that are firm, well shaped and free of blemishes. Avoid potatoes that are wrinkled, cracked or sprouting.

If kept in a cool, dark, well-ventilated place, most potatoes will keep for up to 2 weeks. However, new potatoes should be used within 4 days of purchase.

One pound of russet potatoes—about 3 medium potatoes—equals approximately 3-1/2 cups chopped or 2 to 3 cups mashed.

Easter Egg Candies

(Pictured at right)

Our home economists prove that candy making can be easy! Have kids help roll the candies in sprinkles, colored sugar or jimmies.

1 package (10 to 12 ounces) vanilla *or* white chips
1 package (3 ounces) cream cheese, cubed
1 teaspoon water
1/2 teaspoon vanilla extract
Colored sprinkles, colored sugar *and/or* jimmies

In a microwave-safe bowl, melt the chips at 50% power. Add the cream cheese, water and vanilla; stir until blended. Chill for 1 hour or until easy to handle. Quickly shape into 1-1/4-in. eggs. Roll in sprinkles, colored sugar or jimmies. Store in an airtight container in the refrigerator. **Yield:** about 4 dozen (1-1/2 pounds).

Italian Veggie Turkey Pitas

One day I took the recipe for a favorite dip and added vegetables and turkey to create this flavorful sandwich filling. Pitas are a nice change from ordinary bread.
——Elaine Hollenbach, Milton, Wisconsin

1 cup mayonnaise
1/2 cup sour cream
1 envelope Italian salad dressing mix
1/2 teaspoon hot pepper sauce
2 cups diced cooked turkey
1 cup chopped cauliflowerets
1 cup chopped broccoli florets
1 cup shredded red cabbage
1 celery rib, julienned
1 small carrot, julienned
1/2 medium green pepper, julienned
1 green onion, chopped
5 pita breads (6 inches), halved
Lettuce leaves, optional

In a large bowl, combine the mayonnaise, sour cream, salad dressing mix and hot pepper sauce. Stir in the turkey, cauliflower, broccoli, cabbage, celery, carrot, green pepper and onion. Spoon into pita breads lined with lettuce if desired. **Yield:** 5 servings.

Blueberry-Rhubarb Refrigerator Jam

I think the best recipes come from good friends...that's where I got this jam recipe.
It's a great way to use an abundant supply of rhubarb.
—Arloia Lutz, Sebewaing, Michigan

5 cups chopped fresh *or* frozen rhubarb, thawed
1/2 cup water
5 cups sugar
1 can (21 ounces) blueberry pie filling
2 cups fresh *or* frozen blueberries
3 tablespoons lemon juice
2 packages (3 ounces *each*) raspberry gelatin

In a large kettle, cook rhubarb and water over medium-high heat for 3-5 minutes or until rhubarb is tender. Add sugar. Bring to a boil; boil for 2 minutes. Stir in pie filling, blueberries and lemon juice. Return to a boil. Reduce heat; cook and stir for 10 minutes. Remove from the heat; stir in gelatin until dissolved. Cool slightly. Pour into refrigerator containers. Cool to room temperature. Cover and refrigerate. **Yield:** 4-1/2 pints.

Asparagus Rice Salad

Fresh asparagus makes this salad special. It's one of my favorite salads to serve in spring.
—Adrene Schmidt, Waldersee, Manitoba

1 can (14-1/2 ounces) chicken broth
1/4 cup water
1 cup uncooked long grain rice
2 cups cut fresh asparagus (2-inch pieces)
3/4 cup frozen peas, thawed
3 green onions, sliced
1/3 cup pecan halves
2 to 4 tablespoons minced fresh cilantro *or* parsley
1/4 cup olive *or* vegetable oil
3 tablespoons lemon juice
3 tablespoons sour cream
1/2 teaspoon grated lemon peel
1/4 teaspoon salt
1/4 teaspoon white pepper
4 cups fresh spinach

In a saucepan, bring broth and water to a boil. Stir in rice. Reduce heat; cover and simmer for 15 minutes or until tender. Place 1 in. of water and asparagus in a skillet; bring to a boil. Reduce heat; cover and simmer for 2 minutes. Add peas; return to a boil. Reduce heat; cover and simmer for 2-3 minutes or until crisp-tender. Drain.

In a large bowl, combine the rice, asparagus mixture, onions, pecans and cilantro; mix well. In a bowl, whisk the oil, lemon juice, sour cream, lemon peel, salt and pepper. Pour over rice mixture; toss to coat. Cover and refrigerate for 1-2 hours.

Just before serving, line a serving platter with 1 cup of spinach. Tear remaining spinach; arrange over spinach leaves. Top with rice mixture. **Yield:** 6 servings.

Rabbit Rolls

(Pictured at right)

To create these cute rolls that depict the back view of a bunny, our home economists twisted a rope of dough to form the ears, then used a ball of dough for the tail.

    4 to 4-1/2 cups all-purpose flour
1/2 cup sugar
    2 packages (1/4 ounce *each*)
       active dry yeast
1-1/2 teaspoons salt
    1 cup plus 1/2 teaspoon water,
       divided
    6 tablespoons butter *or*
       margarine, cubed
    1 egg, *separated*
    1 egg

In a mixing bowl, combine 1 cup flour, sugar, yeast and salt. In a saucepan, heat 1 cup water and butter to 120°-130°. Add to dry ingredients; beat for 2 minutes. Cover and refrigerate egg white. Add egg yolk, egg and 1 cup flour to yeast mixture; beat until smooth. Stir in enough remaining flour to form a firm dough.

Turn onto a lightly floured surface; knead until smooth and elastic, about 6-8 minutes. Place in a greased bowl, turning once to grease top. Cover and let rise in a warm place until doubled, about 1 hour.

Turn dough onto a lightly floured surface; divide into 20 pieces. Shape 18 pieces into 10-in.-long ropes. Fold in half; twist top half twice to form ears. Place 2 in. apart on greased baking sheets. Shape remaining dough into 18 balls. Place one on the loop end of each roll to form tail; press into dough. Cover and let rise until doubled, about 30 minutes.

Whisk the reserved egg white with remaining water; brush over rolls. Bake at 375° for 12-15 minutes or until golden brown. Cool on wire racks. **Yield:** 1-1/2 dozen.

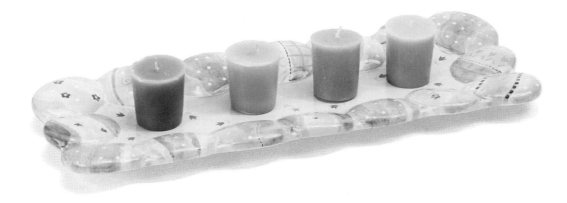

Chocolate Chip Coffee Cake

The irresistible aromas of chocolate, cinnamon and nutmeg waft through the house
as this tasty coffee cake bakes. Before long, my family is clamoring for a generous slice!
— Kathy Dunn, Yorktown, Virginia

1 cup butter *or* margarine,
   softened
1-1/4 cups sugar
2 eggs
1-1/4 cups sour cream
1 teaspoon vanilla extract
2-1/2 cups all-purpose flour
1 teaspoon baking powder
1 teaspoon ground nutmeg
1/2 teaspoon baking soda
FILLING/TOPPING:
3/4 cup chopped pecans
3/4 cup miniature semisweet
   chocolate chips
1/3 cup sugar

1/3 cup packed brown sugar
1-1/2 teaspoons ground cinnamon
1/2 teaspoon ground nutmeg

In a large mixing bowl, cream butter and sugar. Add eggs, one at a time, beating well after each addition. Add sour cream and vanilla; mix well. Combine the flour, baking powder, nutmeg and baking soda; add to creamed mixture just until combined (batter will be stiff). Place half of the batter in a greased 13-in. x 9-in. x 2-in. baking pan.

Combine the filling/topping ingredients. Sprinkle half over batter. Spread remaining batter over top. Sprinkle with remaining filling/topping. Bake at 325° for 40-45 minutes or until golden brown. Cool on a wire rack. **Yield:** 12-15 servings.

HOW YOUR EASTER EGG HUNT CAN BE A HIT

PLANNING an Easter egg hunt is a wonderful excuse to squelch spring fever. Throwing the party is a breeze if you keep these tips in mind:

- Since most folks have plans on Easter Sunday, schedule the party a week or two earlier on a Saturday or Sunday morning.
- If you don't want the expense of buying every guest an Easter basket, ask each child to bring a basket from home. You may want to have a few extra baskets (or some lunch bags) on hand the day of the party just in case someone forgot to bring their own.
- Keep the event casual by serving a buffet-style brunch and offer foods that appeal to old and young alike.
- There's no need to go all out on your decorating. Simply set out a vase brimming with tulips, fill an assortment of Easter baskets with decorated eggs or sprinkle colorful jelly beans on the buffet table.
- For food safety purposes, it's best not to use real eggs for the hunt. Instead, rely on colored plastic eggs, which can be found in a variety of stores. To be fair to all guests, plan on having each child look for the same number of eggs.
- In addition to filling the eggs with candy, surprise the children with stickers, Silly Putty, jacks or even a certificate for a book or puzzle that they can "cash in" with you.
- For the younger children, "hide" the eggs in open areas, but get a little more creative for the older kids. Before starting the hunt, instruct the children that they all need to look for the number of eggs you specify.

Easter Egg Invitation

(Pictured at right)

THINK outside the box when creating the invitations for your Easter egg hunt. Why not make your own invitations and send them off in a fun way?

Look in variety or craft stores for paper in the shape of a bunny, chick or egg. (We traced a chick cookie cutter onto yellow paper to make our invitation shown at right.)

Tuck the invitation inside a colored plastic egg. Then rest the egg on a bed of Easter grass in a small box. Close the box, secure with tape and adhere a mailing sticker. Take the boxed invitations to the post office for mailing.

Or if your guests live nearby, tuck the ends of a ribbon inside the plastic egg, then seal. Drive to your guests' homes and hang an egg invitation on their front door.

Deviled Egg Bunnies

These eggs are a must at our traditional Easter dinner. With nine grandchildren, there are never any leftovers.
—Bernice Martinoni, Petaluma, California

8 hard-cooked eggs
6 tablespoons mayonnaise
1 tablespoon sweet pickle relish
1/4 teaspoon salt
Dash pepper
8 baby carrots
32 dried currants
8 mini marshmallows, halved

Slice eggs in half lengthwise; remove yolks and set whites aside. In a small bowl, mash yolks. Add the mayonnaise, pickle relish, salt and pepper; mix well. Pipe into the egg whites, creating a mound at the pointed end of the white for the bunny's head. For the ears, cut each carrot lengthwise into four slices; place two slices upright on bunny's head. Press currants into eggs for eyes; add marshmallow pieces for tails. Cover and refrigerate until serving. **Yield:** 16 servings.

Exciting Ideas for Hard-Cooked Eggs!

EASTER just wouldn't be the same without colorful baskets brimming with beautifully decorated hard-cooked eggs.

But what do you do with all of those Grade A goodies after the Easter Bunny has hopped away?

If your family doesn't think dozens of leftover hard-cooked eggs are all they're cracked up to be, turn to this chapter, where fellow cooks—and our own home economists—shell out some "eggs-citing" new recipes.

Molded Egg Salad, Ham 'n' Potato Casserole and Three-Cheese Deviled Eggs (all recipes shown at right) are just a sample of the innovative ideas you'll find on the following pages.

LIVELY LEFTOVERS
(Clockwise from top left)

Molded Egg Salad (p.169)

Ham 'n' Potato Casserole (p.168)

Three-Cheese Deviled Eggs (p.170)

Hard-Cooked Eggs

Our home economists share this recipe for hard-cooked eggs that can be eaten plain or used in various recipes.

12 eggs
Cold water

Place eggs in a single layer in a large saucepan; add enough cold water to cover by 1 in. Cover and quickly bring to a boil. Remove from the heat. Let stand for 15 minutes for large eggs (18 minutes for extra-large eggs and 12 minutes for medium eggs). Rinse eggs in cold water and place in ice water until completely cooled. Drain; refrigerate. **Yield:** 12 servings.

Ham 'n' Potato Casserole

(Pictured on page 167)

Sour cream and cheese give this hearty casserole an irresistible richness. Paired with fresh fruit, it is a filling breakfast, lunch or dinner.
—*Rosetta Miller, Middlebury, Indiana*

1/4 cup butter *or* margarine
1/4 cup all-purpose flour
1 teaspoon salt
1/4 teaspoon pepper
1-1/2 cups (12 ounces) sour cream
4 ounces process cheese (Velveeta), cubed
1 cup (4 ounces) shredded Colby cheese
8 hard-cooked eggs, chopped
3 cups cubed cooked potatoes
2 cups cubed fully cooked ham
2 tablespoons dried minced onion
2 tablespoons minced fresh parsley

In a large saucepan over medium heat, melt butter. Stir in flour, salt and pepper until smooth. Cook and stir for 1-2 minutes. Remove from the heat; stir in sour cream and cheeses. Cook and stir over low heat just until cheese is melted (mixture will be thick). Remove from the heat. Stir in the eggs, potatoes, ham, onion and parsley.

Transfer to a greased 2-qt. baking dish. Bake, uncovered, at 350° for 30-35 minutes or until bubbly and edges are golden brown. **Yield:** 6 servings.

Family Traditions

When I was a youngster, we celebrated Easter by "eppering". These were contests to see who had the hardest egg. To play, you cupped your egg in your fist so that only a small portion of each end was showing. Your opponent would tap it with his egg, trying to crack yours. Then you got a chance to tap your opponent's egg. If you cracked your opponent's egg at both ends, you got to keep it.
—*Robert Braker, Boynton Beach, Florida*

Molded Egg Salad

(Pictured at right and on page 166)

This pretty mold is an attractive way to display egg salad. My family enjoys hearty helpings on crackers for a snack or on bread for lunch.
—Joann Erbe, Hobart, Indiana

12 hard-cooked eggs, finely chopped
2 cups mayonnaise
1-1/2 cups finely chopped celery
1/4 cup finely chopped green pepper
1/4 cup sweet pickle relish
2 tablespoons lemon juice
1/2 teaspoon salt
2 envelopes unflavored gelatin
1/2 cup cold water

In a bowl, combine the eggs, mayonnaise, celery, green pepper, pickle relish, lemon juice and salt; set aside. In a saucepan, sprinkle gelatin over water; let stand for 1 minute. Cook and stir over low heat until dissolved. Immediately drizzle over egg mixture; mix well. Quickly transfer to a 7-cup mold coated with nonstick cooking spray. Cover and refrigerate for 8 hours or overnight. Unmold; serve with crackers or bread. **Yield:** 6 cups.

GARNISHING SALAD MOLDS

MAKE YOUR salad mold the center of attention by adding some garnishes to the middle.

In the Molded Egg Salad picture (above), we rolled up thin slices of salami and tucked them in the center, along with a few celery leaves. Not only does it add interest and color, the garnishes are edible, too!

You can also roll up thin slices of ham or use bunches of red and green grapes.

(For another idea, see the Red Radish Rosettes used to garnish the Potato Salad Mold on page 211.)

Three-Cheese Deviled Eggs

(Pictured on page 166)

Our home economists enhanced ordinary deviled eggs by stirring in three different kinds of cheese.
A dash of paprika and sprinkle of chives on top add a little color.

6 hard-cooked eggs
3/4 cup mayonnaise
2 tablespoons finely shredded
   Monterey Jack cheese
2 tablespoons finely shredded
   Swiss cheese
2 tablespoons minced chives,
   divided
1/8 teaspoon ground mustard
1/8 teaspoon pepper

2 ounces process cheese (Velveeta), cubed
Dash paprika

Cut eggs in half lengthwise. Remove yolks; set whites aside. In a bowl, mash the yolks. Add the mayonnaise, shredded cheeses, 1 tablespoon chives, mustard and pepper. In a microwave-safe bowl, melt the process cheese on high for 1-2 minutes; stir until smooth. Stir into yolk mixture. Pipe or spoon into egg whites. Sprinkle with paprika and remaining chives. Refrigerate until serving. **Yield:** 1 dozen.

Egg Bake with Sausage Biscuits

When I want to treat my family to a delicious down-home breakfast,
this is the recipe I rely on. Sausage biscuits are a perfect partner for the egg and cheese casserole.
—Penny Bridge, Lebanon, Indiana

6 tablespoons butter *or*
   margarine, *divided*
1/4 cup all-purpose flour
1-1/2 cups milk
1 cup heavy whipping cream
1/4 cup minced fresh parsley
1/4 teaspoon *each* dried basil,
   marjoram and thyme
3 cups (12 ounces) shredded
   cheddar cheese
12 hard-cooked eggs, thinly
   sliced
1 pound sliced bacon, cooked
   and crumbled
1/2 cup dry bread crumbs
SAUSAGE BISCUITS:
2 cups biscuit/baking mix

2/3 cup milk
3/4 pound bulk pork sausage, cooked and crumbled

In a large saucepan, melt 4 tablespoons butter. Stir in flour until smooth. Gradually whisk in milk and cream. Add the parsley, basil, marjoram and thyme. Bring to a boil; cook and stir for 1-2 minutes or until thickened and bubbly. Remove from the heat; stir in cheese until melted.

In a greased shallow 2-1/2-qt. baking dish, layer a third of the egg slices, a third of the bacon and about 1 cup cheese sauce. Repeat layers twice. Melt remaining butter; toss with bread crumbs. Sprinkle over the top. Bake, uncovered, at 400° for 25-30 minutes or until bubbly and golden brown.

In a bowl, combine biscuit mix and milk. Stir in sausage. Shape into 1-1/2-in. balls. Place 2 in. apart on an ungreased baking sheet. Bake at 400° for 13-15 minutes or until lightly browned. Serve with casserole. **Yield:** 10-12 servings.

Swiss 'n' Asparagus Egg Salad

(Pictured at right)

Whether served alone or on bread, this egg salad from our Test Kitchen will satisfy your hunger. Asparagus, Swiss cheese and ham give ordinary egg salad a tasty twist.

8 fresh asparagus spears, cut into 1/4-inch pieces
6 hard-cooked eggs, chopped
1 cup (4 ounces) shredded Swiss cheese
1/2 cup cubed fully cooked ham
3/4 cup mayonnaise
1 teaspoon Dijon mustard
Salt to taste
10 slices rye bread

Place 1 in. of water and asparagus in a saucepan. Bring to a boil; simmer, uncovered, for 5 minutes or until crisp-tender. Drain and cool. In a bowl, combine the asparagus, eggs, cheese, ham, mayonnaise, mustard and salt. Spread on five slices of bread, about 1/2 cup on each; top with the remaining bread. **Yield:** 5 servings.

STORING HARD-COOKED EASTER EGGS

TO SAFELY enjoy leftover hard-cooked eggs in a variety of ways, keep these helpful hints in mind:

- After making hard-cooked eggs, refrigerate them as soon as the ice water has cooled them. Keep them refrigerated until you're ready for coloring, then chill as soon as you're done.
- Don't let hard-cooked eggs stand at room temperature for more than 2 hours. If you plan on using hard-cooked eggs as a centerpiece, cook extra eggs for eating and discard the eggs on display.
- Don't eat any colored eggs that have cracked. Either throw them out immediately or use them for display and then discard.
- Unpeeled hard-cooked eggs will stay fresh in the refrigerator for up to 1 week. Once shelled, the eggs should be used right away.

Egg and Spinach Side Dish

With four young children, I'm always on the lookout for fast and flavorful recipes.
This speedy side dish is a nice complement to chicken or steak dinners.
—Jeanne Prendergast, Clearwater, Florida

2 packages (10 ounces *each*)
   frozen chopped spinach,
   thawed and squeezed dry
1-1/2 cups mayonnaise
5 hard-cooked eggs, coarsely
   chopped
1/4 cup shredded Parmesan
   cheese
1/4 to 1/2 teaspoon crushed red
   pepper flakes
1/2 teaspoon garlic salt

In a large bowl, combine all of the ingredients. Spoon into a greased 1-1/2-qt. microwave-safe dish. Microwave, uncovered, on high for 3-4 minutes or until bubbly and heated through. **Yield:** 4-6 servings.

   Editor's Note: This recipe was tested in an 850-watt microwave. Reduced-fat or fat-free mayonnaise is not recommended for this recipe.

Breakfast Burritos

Instead of making breakfast burritos with scrambled eggs, our home economists
created this version as a way to use extra hard-cooked Easter eggs.
Green chilies and pepper Jack cheese add a little zip.

1/2 pound bulk pork sausage
1/4 cup chopped sweet red pepper
1/4 cup chopped green onions
1 package (3 ounces) cream
   cheese, cubed
1 can (4 ounces) chopped green
   chilies
3 hard-cooked eggs, chopped
1 cup (4 ounces) shredded
   pepper Jack cheese
4 flour tortillas (8 inches)
Salsa, sour cream and sliced ripe
   olives, optional

In a large skillet, cook the sausage, red pepper and onions over medium heat until meat is no longer pink; drain. Add the cream cheese; cook and stir until cheese is melted. Add the chilies, eggs and cheese. Spoon 1/2 cup filling off center on each tortilla; fold ends and sides over filling and roll up. Serve with salsa, sour cream and olives if desired. **Yield:** 4 servings.

German-Style Pickled Eggs

(Pictured at right)

I make these deviled eggs and refrigerate them in a glass gallon jar for my husband to sell at his tavern. The customers love them! I found the recipe in an old cookbook years ago.
—Marjorie Hennig, Seymour, Indiana

2 cups cider vinegar
1 cup sugar
1/2 cup water
2 tablespoons prepared mustard
1 tablespoon salt
1 tablespoon celery seed
1 tablespoon mustard seed
6 whole cloves
2 medium onions, thinly sliced
12 hard-cooked eggs, peeled

In a large saucepan, combine the first eight ingredients. Bring to a boil. Reduce heat; cover and simmer for 10 minutes. Cool completely. Place onions and eggs in a large jar; add enough vinegar mixture to completely cover. Cover and refrigerate for at least 8 hours or overnight. Use a clean spoon each time you remove eggs for serving. May be refrigerated for up to 1 week. **Yield:** 12 servings.

CHOPPING HARD-COOKED EGGS

MY MOM and I are always looking for ways to cut preparation time in the kitchen. A few years ago, I discovered a real time-saver for chopping hard-cooked eggs.

Instead of cutting each egg individually, I put the shelled eggs in a bowl and break them apart with my pastry cutter. It works perfectly!   *—Jory Stiffarm*
Fort Wayne, Indiana

SPECIAL
Celebrations

An informal, fun-filled fondue party is an easy way
to entertain in winter. To bring a little luck of the Irish
to your table on St. Patrick's Day, try our traditional
feast. You can add spark to your menus with a
Cinco de Mayo celebration, July Fourth Burger Bar
or Greek-style Olympic gathering. It's a snap to
host a 25th wedding anniversary celebration in
your home with some crowd-pleasing recipes.
And on Halloween, set out a scrumptiously spooky spread.

A Fun-Filled Fondue Feast

AFTER all the hustle of the holidays, are you looking for an extra-easy way to entertain? Then gather a group of friends for an informal fondue party.

Within this chapter you'll find tried-and-true classics like Marinated Tenderloin Fondue with Cranberry Orange Dipping Sauce, Chocolate Pecan Fondue and Swiss Cheese Fondue. (All shown at right.)

But you'll also discover twists on the traditional like Tomato Fondue, Apple Wonton Bundles and Citrus Fondue that will become newfound favorites.

So next time you're planning a special winter gathering, dip into fondue for a guaranteed good time!

DELICIOUS DIPPING
(Clockwise from top right)

Marinated Tenderloin Fondue (p. 178)

Cranberry Orange Dipping Sauce (p. 179)

Chocolate Pecan Fondue (p. 179)

Swiss Cheese Fondue (p. 180)

Marinated Tenderloin Fondue

(Pictured on page 177)

When I was a kid in the 1970s, Mom made fondue a lot. She served this meat version every New Year's Day. Now I carry on that fun tradition with my own family.
—Sue Gronholz, Beaver Dam, Wisconsin

1 cup soy sauce
1/2 cup packed brown sugar
1/2 cup cider vinegar
1/2 cup pineapple juice
2 teaspoons salt
1/2 teaspoon garlic powder
1 pound *each* pork and beef tenderloin, cut into 1-inch cubes
2 to 3 cups vegetable oil

In a bowl, combine the first six ingredients. Pour into two large resealable plastic bags; add pork to one bag and beef to the other. Seal bags and turn to coat; refrigerate for 2 hours, turning occasionally. Drain and discard marinade. Pat meat dry with paper towels. Heat oil in a fondue pot to 375°. Use fondue forks to cook meat in oil until pork juices run clear and beef reaches desired doneness. **Yield:** 8 servings.

HOSTING A FONDUE PARTY

THE BEST PART about hosting a fondue party is that you do the prep work in advance, then guests do their own cooking! Here are some helpful hints to make your fondue party go off without a hitch.

- Most fondue pots hold up to six fondue forks. Depending on your number of guests, you'll need several pots. Extra pots also are needed if you're cooking different types of fondue.

  Electric fondue pots are better for oil cooking because they allow you to maintain a higher temperature. For recipes where the fondue simply needs to be warmed, you could use a small slow cooker instead.

  Be on the lookout for discounted fondue pots on clearance racks at department stores and at rummage sales. Or ask friends and family if they have one you can borrow.
- If children will be attending the party, think twice about setting up the fondue on a cloth-covered table. To avoid the risk of little hands pulling the cloth and spilling the hot pots, consider placing things on a high, sturdy, easy-to-clean surface such as a kitchen island or breakfast bar.
- The day before the party, cut up meats and fruits (except fruits that may discolor), prepare the cheese, chocolate and any condiments. Store in airtight containers and refrigerate perishable items.

  Set out fondue pots, fondue forks and serving dishes. Also have salad plates, knives and forks available.
- A few hours before the party, cube bread and store in a resealable plastic bag. Place meats and fruits in serving containers, cover with plastic wrap and refrigerate.
- As guests arrive, heat the fondue ingredients and set out the items to be dipped.
- During the party, keep perishable items like meat chilled by placing the serving container on a plate of ice (as shown in the photo on page 177).

Cranberry Orange Dipping Sauce

(Pictured at right and on page 177)

If you want to make ordinary fondue extraordinary, whip up a batch of this flavorful sauce. It pairs well with pork, beef and chicken.
—Ruth Peterson, Jenison, Michigan

1-1/2 teaspoons cornstarch
1-1/2 teaspoons brown sugar
1/4 cup orange juice
1 can (8 ounces) whole-berry cranberry sauce
Dash ground cinnamon

In a heavy saucepan, combine the cornstarch, brown sugar and orange juice until smooth. Bring to a boil over medium heat; cook and stir for 1-2 minutes or until thickened. Remove from the heat; stir in the cranberry sauce and cinnamon until blended. Cover and refrigerate. Serve cold. **Yield:** about 1 cup.

Chocolate Pecan Fondue

(Pictured on page 176)

When our kids have friends sleep over, I like to surprise them with this chocolate treat.
Our favorite dippers include fruit, marshmallows, cookies and pound cake.
—Suzanne Cleveland, Lyons, Georgia

1/2 cup half-and-half cream
2 tablespoons honey
9 ounces semisweet chocolate, broken into small pieces
1/4 cup finely chopped pecans
1 teaspoon vanilla extract
Fresh fruit and shortbread cookies

In a heavy saucepan over low heat, combine cream and honey; heat until warm. Add chocolate; stir until melted. Stir in pecans and vanilla. Transfer to a warmed fondue pot or small slow cooker and keep warm. Serve with fruit and cookies. **Yield:** 1-1/3 cups.

Swiss Cheese Fondue

(Pictured on page 176)

As cold winter winds blow outside, our Test Kitchen home economists suggest warming up with this rich and creamy fondue. Don't be surprised when the pot is scraped clean!

1 garlic clove, halved
2 cups white wine, chicken broth *or* apple juice, *divided*
1/4 teaspoon ground nutmeg
7 cups (28 ounces) shredded Swiss cheese
2 tablespoons cornstarch
Cubed French bread

Rub garlic clove over the bottom and sides of a fondue pot; discard garlic and set fondue pot aside. In a large saucepan over medium-low heat, bring 1-3/4 cups wine and nutmeg to a simmer. Gradually add cheese, stirring after each addition until cheese is melted (cheese will separate from wine).

Combine cornstarch and remaining wine until smooth; gradually stir into cheese mixture. Cook and stir until mixture comes to a boil. Cook and stir for 1-2 minutes or until thickened and mixture is blended and smooth. Transfer to prepared fondue pot and keep warm. Serve with bread cubes. **Yield:** about 4 cups.

Citrus Fondue

This light and refreshing fondue is just right for warmer weather. It's the perfect way to showcase the naturally great flavor of fruit.
—*Wanda Whitfield, Eastanolle, Georgia*

1 cup sugar
3 tablespoons plus 1 teaspoon all-purpose flour
1 cup water
1/4 cup butter *or* margarine, cubed
1 tablespoon lemon juice
1 tablespoon orange juice
1/4 teaspoon grated lemon peel
1/4 teaspoon grated orange peel
1/8 teaspoon ground ginger
Fresh fruit

In a heavy saucepan, combine the sugar and flour. Stir in water until smooth. Bring to a boil over medium heat; cook and stir for 2 minutes or until thickened. Remove from the heat. Stir in the butter, lemon and orange juice and peel and ginger; cook until the butter is melted. Transfer to a fondue pot and keep warm. Serve with fruit. **Yield:** 1-3/4 cups.

Apple Wonton Bundles

(Pictured at right)

When preparing fondue for the main meal, don't forget to have a fondue dessert as well. These deliciously different treats taste just like caramel apples.
—Darlene Brenden, Salem, Oregon

  4 **medium tart apples, peeled**
64 **wonton wrappers**
  2 **to 3 cups vegetable oil**
  1 **jar (12 ounces) caramel ice cream topping, warmed**

Cut each apple into four wedges; cut wedges into four pieces. Place a piece of apple in the center of each wonton wrapper. Brush edges of wrapper with water and bring up around apple; pinch to seal. Cover with plastic wrap until ready to cook. Heat oil in a fondue pot to 375°. Use fondue forks to cook wonton bundles until golden brown (about 1 minute). Cool slightly. Serve with caramel topping. **Yield:** 64 bundles.

Tomato Fondue

Both the young and young at heart will gobble up this cheesy tomato fondue when served alongside hot dogs and bread cubes.
—Marlene Muckenhirn, Delano, Minnesota

   1 **garlic clove, halved**
1/2 **cup condensed tomato soup, undiluted**
1-1/2 **teaspoons ground mustard**
1-1/2 **teaspoons Worcestershire sauce**
 10 **slices process American cheese (Velveeta), cubed**
1/4 **to 1/3 cup milk**
   1 **package (16 ounces) miniature hot dogs *or* smoked sausage, warmed**
Cubed French bread

Rub garlic clove over the bottom and sides of a small fondue pot or slow cooker; discard garlic and set fondue pot aside. In a small saucepan, combine the tomato soup, mustard and Worcestershire sauce; heat through. Stir in cheese until melted. Stir in milk; heat through. Transfer to prepared fondue pot and keep warm. Serve with hot dogs and bread cubes. **Yield:** about 1 cup.

Beef Fondue with Sauces

When my husband was stationed in England in the mid-1960s, I traveled to Switzerland and purchased two copper fondue pots. I've used them countless times since then.
—*Margaret Inman, Fort Pierce, Florida*

CURRY SAUCE:
- 1/2 cup mayonnaise
- 2 to 3 tablespoons curry powder
- 2 to 3 tablespoons milk
- 1/2 teaspoon hot pepper sauce

MUSTARD SAUCE:
- 1/4 cup mayonnaise
- 1/4 cup Dijon mustard
- 1 teaspoon hot pepper sauce
- 1 garlic clove, minced

ONION-HORSERADISH SAUCE:
- 1/4 cup finely chopped onion
- 1/4 cup mayonnaise
- 1 tablespoon prepared horseradish
- 2 to 3 teaspoons water
- 1/4 teaspoon hot pepper sauce

FONDUE:
- 1-1/2 pounds beef tenderloin, cut into 3/4-inch cubes
- 3 to 4 cups vegetable oil

In three separate bowls, combine the curry sauce, mustard sauce and onion-horseradish sauce ingredients. Pat meat dry with paper towels. Heat oil in a fondue pot to 375°. Use fondue forks to cook meat in oil until it reaches desired doneness. Serve with sauces. **Yield:** 4-6 servings (1/2 cup of each sauce).

Family Traditions

At my family's fondue parties, we have a tradition that if the meat falls off your fork and into the pot, you must kiss the person to your right!
—*Margaret Inman, Fort Pierce, Florida*

Butterscotch Fondue

As a change from the more traditional chocolate fondue, try this rich, buttery version. You can make it in advance, refrigerate it and reheat when ready to serve.
—*Sharon Mensing, Greenfield, Iowa*

- 1/2 cup packed brown sugar
- 1/3 cup light corn syrup
- 1/4 cup heavy whipping cream
- 2 tablespoons butter *or* margarine
- 1/2 teaspoon vanilla extract
- Fresh fruit

In a small saucepan, combine the brown sugar, corn syrup, cream and butter. Bring to a boil over medium heat, stirring occasionally. Reduce heat to medium-low; cook for 5 minutes. Remove from the heat; stir in vanilla. Transfer to a fondue pot and keep warm. Serve with fruit. **Yield:** about 1 cup.

Mongolian Fondue

(Pictured above)

Mealtime is so much fun and filled with laughter and conversation when fondue is on the menu.
I created this recipe after tasting something similar in a restaurant. Family and friends request it often.
—Marion Lowery, Medford, Oregon

1/2 cup soy sauce
1/4 cup water
  1 teaspoon white wine vinegar
    or cider vinegar
1-1/2 teaspoons minced garlic,
    divided
  1 cup sliced carrots (1/4 inch
    thick)
  2 cans (14-1/2 ounces *each*) beef
    broth
1/4 teaspoon ground ginger *or* 1
    teaspoon minced fresh
    gingerroot
  2 pounds boneless beef sirloin
    steak, cut into 2-1/2-inch x
    1/4-inch strips
  1 pound turkey breast, cut into
    2-1/2-inch x 1/4-inch strips
  1 pound uncooked large
    shrimp, peeled and deveined

  3 small zucchini, cut into 1/2-inch slices
  1 *each* medium sweet red, yellow and green pepper,
    cut into 1-inch chunks
  1 to 2 cups whole fresh mushrooms
  1 cup cubed red onion (1-inch pieces)
  1 jar (7 ounces) hoisin sauce
  1 jar (4 ounces) Chinese hot mustard

In a saucepan, combine the soy sauce, water, vinegar and
1/2 teaspoon garlic; bring to a boil. Remove from the heat.
Cover and refrigerate for at least 1 hour.

  In a small saucepan, cook carrots in a small amount of water for 3 minutes or until crisp-tender; drain and pat dry.
In a saucepan, bring the broth, ginger and remaining garlic
to a boil. Transfer to a fondue pot and keep warm. Pat steak,
turkey and shrimp dry with paper towels.

  Use fondue forks to cook beef to desired doneness.
Cook turkey until juices run clear. Cook shrimp until pink.
Cook vegetables until they reach desired doneness. Serve
with hoisin sauce, mustard sauce and reserved garlic-soy
sauce. **Yield:** 6-8 servings.

St. Patrick's Day Celebration

YOU DON'T have to be Irish to join in the fun of St. Patrick's Day. (Plus, what better way to welcome the arrival of spring than by "The Wearing of the Green"?)

Bring a little luck of the Irish to your home…ask relatives and friends over to share in this flavorful feast.

Mint Tea Punch and Floating Four-Leaf Clovers will have leprechauns of every age leaping for joy.

Then dig in to the traditional tastes of Irish Soda Bread, Colcannon Potatoes and Spicy Corned Beef. (Recipes are shown at right.)

All eyes—whether they're Irish or not—will surely be smiling around your dinner table!

LUCK OF THE IRISH
(Clockwise from top right)

Irish Soda Bread (p. 186)

Colcannon Potatoes (p. 188)

Spicy Corned Beef (p. 190)

Mint Tea Punch and
Floating Four-Leaf Clovers (p. 187)

Irish Soda Bread

(*Pictured on page 185*)

Each St. Patrick's Day, I bake this bread for my neighbor, who is Irish. Then I make another loaf for my family to enjoy. Sweet raisins contrast nicely with the caraway.
—*Emma Dewees, Eagleville, Pennsylvania*

4 cups all-purpose flour
3 tablespoons sugar
3 teaspoons baking powder
1 teaspoon salt
3/4 teaspoon baking soda
6 tablespoons cold butter *or* margarine
1-1/2 cups raisins
1 tablespoon caraway seeds
2 eggs, beaten
1-1/2 cups buttermilk

In a large bowl, combine the first five ingredients. Cut in butter until mixture resembles coarse crumbs. Stir in the raisins and caraway seeds. Set aside 1 tablespoon beaten egg. In a bowl, combine buttermilk and remaining egg; stir into crumb mixture just until flour is moistened (dough will be sticky). Turn onto a well-floured surface; knead about 10 times. Shape into a ball.

Place in a greased 9-in. round baking pan. Cut a 4-in. X, 1/4 in. deep, in the center of the ball. Brush top with reserved egg. Bake at 350° for 1 hour and 20 minutes or until a toothpick inserted near the center comes out clean. Cover loosely with foil during the last 20 minutes if top browns too quickly. Cool for 10 minutes before removing from pan to a wire rack to cool completely. **Yield:** 1 loaf.

THE IRISH SODA BREAD STORY

THIS CLASSIC quick bread from Ireland is so named because it uses baking soda for leavening. Legend has it that the X is cut into the top of the bread before baking to ward off evil spirits.

Horseradish-Mustard Sauce for Corned Beef

When you have a strong Irish heritage and a son named Patrick, you can't help but make a big fuss on March 17! This zesty sauce is the perfect accompaniment to corned beef.
—*Denise Bender, Bayville, New York*

1 cup (8 ounces) sour cream
2 tablespoons prepared horseradish
2 tablespoons prepared mustard

In a small bowl, combine the sour cream, horseradish and mustard. Serve with corned beef. **Yield:** 10 servings.

Mint Tea Punch

(Pictured at right and on page 184)

This pretty punch prepared with green tea has a hint of mint, making it the highlight of any spring meal.
—Sandra McKenzie
Braham, Minnesota

10 cups water, *divided*
5 bags green tea with mint
1 cup sugar
1 cup pineapple juice
1/2 cup lemon juice
2-1/2 cups chilled ginger ale
4 to 5 drops green food coloring, optional
Floating Four-Leaf Clovers (recipe below)

In a large saucepan, bring 5 cups water to a boil; add tea bags and steep for 5 minutes. Remove and discard tea bags. Stir in sugar, pineapple juice, lemon juice and remaining water. Cover and refrigerate for 4 hours.

Just before serving, add ginger ale and food coloring if desired. Add Floating Four-Leaf Clovers. **Yield:** about 3-1/2 quarts.

Floating Four-Leaf Clovers

(Pictured above and on page 184)

Instead of using regular ice cubes in Mint Tea Punch, our home economists stayed in the spirit of St. Patrick's Day and prepared these cute clover cubes. They're made with soda so they won't dilute your beverage. They can be made weeks in advance and stored in the freezer.

4 cups plus 2 tablespoons chilled lemon-lime soda, *divided*
12 lime slices
1 strip lime peel (6 inches)

Pour 1/4 cup lemon-lime soda into 12 muffin cups; freeze until solid. On a work surface, cut lime slices into quarters. Rotate each quarter slice clockwise until one end of outer edge touches the center; place over frozen soda. To make a stem, cut the lime strip into 1/2-in. pieces. Place at one corner of clover. Freeze for 20 minutes. Slowly pour remaining soda into cups until lime is almost covered. Immediately freeze until solid. **Yield:** 12 clover cubes.

Colcannon Potatoes

(Pictured on page 185)

*Every Irish family has its own version of this classic side dish...my recipe comes from
my father's family in Ireland. It's part of my St. Pat's menu,
along with lamb chops, carrots and soda bread.*
—*Marilou Robinson, Portland, Oregon*

2 pounds cabbage, shredded
2 cups water
4 pounds potatoes, peeled and
    quartered
2 cups milk
1 cup chopped green onions
Salt and coarsely ground pepper
    to taste
1/4 cup butter *or* margarine,
    melted
Crumbled cooked bacon and
    minced fresh parsley

In a large saucepan, bring cabbage and water to a boil. Reduce heat; cover and simmer for 10-12 minutes or until tender. Drain, reserving cooking liquid. Keep cabbage warm. Place cooking liquid and potatoes in a large saucepan; add enough additional water to cover the potatoes. Bring to a boil. Reduce heat; cover and cook for 15-17 minutes or until tender. Drain and keep warm.

In a small saucepan, bring milk and onions to a boil; remove from the heat. In a large mixing bowl, mash potatoes. Add milk mixture; beat until blended. Add cabbage, salt and pepper; beat until blended. Top with melted butter, bacon and parsley. **Yield:** 12-16 servings.

DO YOU KNOW ABOUT COLCANNON?

COLCANNON—a combination of mashed potatoes and either cabbage or kale—is mostly associated with the harvest and is traditionally eaten in Ireland on Halloween.

Symbols of good fortune (a golden ring predicting marriage within a year, a sixpence for forthcoming wealth, a thimble for spinsterhood and a button for bachelorhood) are often hidden in the dish for folks to find.

Hot Pastrami Spread

(Pictured at right)

I first tasted this at a church party a few years ago. Everyone raves about it and the dish is always scraped clean. You can also serve the savory spread with bite-size bagel pieces.
—Arlene Wilson
Center Barnstead, New Hampshire

2 packages (8 ounces *each*) cream cheese, softened
1/2 cup sour cream
2 packages (2-1/2 ounces *each*) thinly sliced pastrami, chopped
1/2 cup finely chopped green pepper
1/3 cup chopped pecans *or* walnuts, optional
Thinly sliced pumpernickel and light rye bread

In a small mixing bowl, beat cream cheese and sour cream until smooth. Add pastrami and green pepper; mix well. Transfer to a greased 1-qt. baking dish. Sprinkle with pecans if desired. Bake, uncovered, at 350° for 25-30 minutes or until heated through and edges are bubbly. Cut out bread with a shamrock-shaped cookie cutter if desired. Serve with spread. **Yield:** about 3-1/2 cups.

Reuben Chicken

With just four ingredients and little preparation time, this rich and cheesy main dish couldn't be easier. My family prefers it to traditional Reuben sandwiches made with corned beef.
—Dana Chandler, Wilmington, Delaware

6 boneless skinless chicken breast halves
1 cup Thousand Island salad dressing
1 can (14 ounces) sauerkraut, rinsed and drained
6 slices Swiss cheese

Pound chicken between two pieces of waxed paper to flatten. Place in a greased 13-in. x 9-in. x 2-in. baking dish. Spoon salad dressing over chicken; cover with sauerkraut. Cover and bake 350° for 30 minutes. Uncover; top with cheese. Bake 20-30 minutes longer or until chicken juices run clear. **Yield:** 6 servings.

Spicy Corned Beef

(Pictured on page 184)

This corned beef recipe is so easy to fix because it can be simmered one day and baked the next.
—Jacqueline Clark, Eugene, Oregon

2 corned beef briskets (about 3 pounds *each*)
1 medium onion, halved
1 medium carrot, cut into chunks
1 celery rib with leaves
1 tablespoon mixed pickling spices
1/3 cup packed brown sugar
1 tablespoon prepared mustard
1/2 cup sweet pickle juice

Place corned beef in a large Dutch oven; cover with water. Add the onion, carrot, celery and pickling spices. Bring to a boil. Reduce heat; cover and simmer for 2-1/2 to 3 hours or until meat is tender.

Transfer corned beef to a 13-in. x 9-in. x 2-in. baking dish; discard broth and vegetables. Score the surface of meat with shallow diagonal cuts. Combine brown sugar and mustard; spread over meat. Pour pickle juice into dish. Bake, uncovered, at 325° for 1 hour, basting occasionally. **Yield:** 18-20 servings.

Potato Asparagus Bake

Many of my springtime menus include this dish,
which can be made ahead, refrigerated and baked when ready.
—Deborah Sears, Heathsville, Virginia

1 pound potatoes, peeled and quartered
1 pound fresh asparagus, trimmed
2 tablespoons butter *or* margarine, *divided*
1 tablespoon all-purpose flour
3/4 cup heavy whipping cream
1/2 teaspoon salt
1/4 teaspoon pepper
3 tablespoons dry bread crumbs
3 tablespoons grated Parmesan cheese

Place potatoes in a saucepan and cover with water. Bring to a boil. Reduce heat; cover and cook for 15-20 minutes or until tender. Meanwhile, cut the tips off asparagus spears; set aside for garnish. Cut stalks into 1-in. pieces; place in a saucepan and cover with water. Bring to a boil. Reduce heat; cover and cook for 8-10 minutes or until tender. Drain asparagus and place in a food processor or blender. Cover and process until pureed; set aside. Drain potatoes; mash and set aside.

In a large saucepan, melt 1 tablespoon butter; whisk in flour until smooth. Gradually stir in cream. Bring to a boil; cook and stir for 2 minutes or until thickened. Stir in asparagus pieces, mashed potatoes, salt and pepper. Transfer to a greased shallow 1-1/2-qt. baking dish. Top with reserved asparagus tips.

Melt remaining butter; lightly brush some over top. Toss bread crumbs, Parmesan cheese and remaining butter; sprinkle over casserole. Bake, uncovered, at 350° for 25-30 minutes or until lightly browned. **Yield:** 8-10 servings.

Three's-a-Charm Shamrock Soup

(Pictured at right)

There's no better way to use up leftover St. Patrick's Day corned beef, cabbage and potatoes than to make a hearty soup. This second-time-around soup is one of my best.
—Deborah McMurtrey
Estes Park, Colorado

  6 celery ribs, chopped
  4 medium carrots, sliced
  2 cups cubed peeled potatoes
  5 cups water
  3 cups cubed cooked
    corned beef
  2 cups chopped cooked cabbage
  1 teaspoon dill weed
  1 teaspoon salt
  1 teaspoon seasoned salt
1/2 teaspoon white pepper

In a large soup kettle, bring the celery, carrots, potatoes and water to a boil. Reduce heat; cover and simmer until vegetables are tender, about 20 minutes. Stir in the remaining ingredients. Cover and simmer for 15-20 minutes or until heated through. **Yield:** 10 servings (2-1/2 quarts).

Irish Beef 'n' Carrot Stew

My husband was born on St. Patrick's Day, and this is the special meal I make to celebrate that occasion. My family looks forward to it all year.
—Marie Biggs, Anacortes, Washington

1 pound carrots, peeled and cut into 2-1/2-inch pieces
2 medium onions, chopped
3 tablespoons vegetable oil
3 tablespoons all-purpose flour
Salt and pepper to taste
1-1/2 pounds boneless beef chuck steak, cut into 1-inch strips
1/2 teaspoon chopped fresh basil
2/3 cup Guinness, other dark beer *or* beef broth
1 teaspoon honey
2/3 cup additional beef broth
Mashed *or* boiled potatoes

Place carrots in a greased shallow 2-qt. baking dish. In a skillet, saute onions in oil for 5 minutes or until tender. Using a slotted spoon, transfer onions to dish.

In a resealable plastic bag, combine the flour, salt and pepper. Add beef, a few pieces at a time, and shake to coat; reserve flour mixture. In the same skillet, brown meat in oil on all sides. Transfer to baking dish.

Stir reserved flour mixture into oil; cook and stir over medium heat for 1 minute. Add basil and beer or broth. Bring to a boil; cook and stir for 1 minute or until thickened. Stir in honey and additional broth; return to a boil, stirring constantly. Pour over beef. Cover and bake at 325° for 1-1/2 hours or until beef is tender. Serve with potatoes. **Yield:** 4-6 servings.

Chocolate Lime Dessert

(Pictured on opposite page)

The pretty pale green color of this refreshing lime gelatin dessert is perfect for a St. Patrick's Day party, but don't be surprised when your family requests it year-round!
—Jane Lochowicz, Brookfield, Wisconsin

1 package (3 ounces) lime gelatin
1-3/4 cups boiling water
2 cups crushed chocolate wafers
6 tablespoons butter *or* margarine, melted
1/4 cup lime juice
2 teaspoons lemon juice
1 cup sugar
1 can (12 ounces) evaporated milk

Pots o' Gold (recipe on opposite page)

In a small mixing bowl, dissolve gelatin in boiling water. Refrigerate until partially set, about 1-1/2 hours. In a bowl, combine wafer crumbs and butter; press into a 13-in. x 9-in. x 2-in. dish. Set aside.

Beat gelatin with an electric mixer until foamy. Add the lime and lemon juices. Gradually add sugar, beating until dissolved. While beating, slowly add the milk; mix well. Pour over prepared crust. Refrigerate until set. Garnish with Pots o' Gold. **Yield:** 12-15 servings.

Pots o' Gold

(Pictured at right)

You won't find a real pot of gold at the end of a rainbow, but this chocolate garnish from our Test Kitchen will make any dessert look like a million bucks!

1/2 cup semisweet chocolate chips
1/4 teaspoon shortening
**1/2 cup light green candy coating
       disks**

Place a sheet of waxed paper on a baking sheet; draw a 1-in. pot with a 2-in. x 1-in. rainbow coming out of the pot. Place another sheet of waxed paper over the top. Secure both to a baking sheet with tape; set aside.

In a microwave, melt the chocolate chips and shortening; stir until smooth. Cut a hole in the corner of a pastry or plastic bag. Insert round tip #3 and add the melted chocolate. Pipe chocolate over outlines; chill.

In another microwave-safe bowl, melt candy coating. Cut a hole in another pastry bag. Insert round tip #3 and fill with candy coating. Fill in chocolate outline. Chill until set. Use as a garnish for desserts. **Yield:** 16 Pots o' Gold.

Editor's Note: Pots o' Gold can be made a week in advance. When set, use a spatula to remove them from the waxed paper and place in a single layer in an airtight container. Store in a cool dry place.

MAKING POTS O' GOLD

SPOON the melted chocolate into a pastry or plastic bag fitted with a #3 round tip. Pipe the chocolate onto the waxed paper, using the outline on the paper beneath as your guide. Chill, then fill with melted candy coating as directed.

Cinco de Mayo Fiesta

THE HOLIDAY of Cinco de Mayo (the fifth of May) commemorates the victory of a band of Mexicans over the French army at the battle of Puebla in 1862. (It is not Mexico's Independence Day, which is actually September 16.)

Celebrate this occasion in style with a scrumptious spread of food from south of the border.

Greet guests with a cool glass of Refreshing Lime Slush. Then turn up the heat and serve Southwest Rib Roast with Salsa.

Creamy Cheesy Green Chili Rice is an appropriate accompaniment to the spicy entree.

For dessert, scoop up Cinnamon Chocolate Chip Ice Cream and pass a bowl brimming with traditional Sopaipillas. (All recipes shown at right.)

Mmm-Mexican Meal

(Clockwise from top right)

Refreshing Lime Slush (p. 197)

Cheesy Green Chili Rice (p. 197)

Cinnamon Chocolate Chip Ice Cream (p. 198)

Sopaipillas (p. 198)

Southwest Rib Roast With Salsa (p. 196)

Southwest Rib Roast with Salsa

(Pictured on page 194)

After purchasing a steer at a local 4-H fair, we were looking for tasty new beef recipes.
A blend of seasonings makes this tender cut of meat even more succulent.
— Darlene King, Estevan, Saskatchewan

2 tablespoons chili powder
2 teaspoons salt
2 teaspoons ground cumin
1 teaspoon cayenne pepper
1 beef rib roast (8 to 10 pounds)
2 cans (15 ounces *each*) black beans, rinsed and drained
2 medium tomatoes, seeded and chopped
1 medium red onion, chopped
1/3 cup minced fresh cilantro *or* parsley

In a bowl, combine the chili powder, salt, cumin and cayenne. Set aside 2 teaspoons for salsa. Rub the remaining seasoning mixture over roast. Place roast fat side up in a shallow roasting pan. Bake, uncovered, at 325° for 2-1/2 to 3 hours or until meat reaches desired doneness (for rare, a meat thermometer should read 140°; medium, 160°; well-done, 170°). Transfer to serving platter. Let stand for 15 minutes before carving.

For salsa, combine the beans, tomatoes, onion, cilantro and reserved seasoning mixture in a bowl; mix well. Serve with roast. **Yield:** 12-16 servings.

Nana's Chilies Rellenos

This zesty dish is not for the faint of heart. My family has been enjoying it
for three generations…and will be doing so for years to come!
— Peta-Maree Lamb, Poulsbo, Washington

1 can (27 ounces) whole green chilies,* drained
4 cups (16 ounces) shredded sharp cheddar cheese
4 eggs
1 can (12 ounces) evaporated milk
1/4 cup all-purpose flour
1 can (29 ounces) tomato sauce
1 envelope taco seasoning
8 ounces sharp cheddar cheese, cut into 1-inch cubes

Slice chilies in half and remove seeds. Arrange half of the chilies in a greased 13-in. x 9-in. x 2-in. baking dish. Sprinkle with shredded cheese. Cover with remaining chilies. In a small mixing bowl, beat eggs, milk and flour until smooth; pour over cheese. Bake, uncovered, at 350° for 30 minutes.

Whisk tomato sauce and taco seasoning until blended; pour over casserole. Carefully place cheese cubes on top in a checkerboard pattern; bake 10-15 minutes longer or until top is set. Let stand for 10 minutes before serving. **Yield:** 8-10 servings.

*Editor's Note: When cutting or seeding hot peppers, use rubber or plastic gloves to protect your hands. Avoid touching your face.

Refreshing Lime Slush

(Pictured at right and on page 195)

Nothing quenches my thirst on a hot summer day quite like this slush with a subtle lime flavor. When warm weather arrives, a batch will be chilling in my freezer.
—Karen Bourne, Magrath, Alberta

11 cups water
3 cups sugar
3/4 cup limeade concentrate
2 liters lemon-lime soda, chilled
Lime slices, optional

In a 4-qt. freezer container, combine the water, sugar and limeade concentrate until sugar is dissolved; cover and freeze. Remove from the freezer several hours before serving. Chop mixture until slushy. Add soda just before serving. Garnish with lime slices if desired. **Yield:** 5-1/2 quarts (30 servings).

Cheesy Green Chili Rice

(Pictured on page 195)

This creamy rice dish is a nice addition to a spicy meal. When I first tried it at a church potluck, I knew I had to have the recipe.
—Laurie Fisher, Greeley, Colorado

1 large onion, chopped
2 tablespoons butter *or* margarine
4 cups hot cooked long grain rice
2 cups (16 ounces) sour cream
1 cup small-curd cottage cheese
1/2 teaspoon salt
1/8 teaspoon pepper
2 cans (4 ounces *each*) chopped green chilies, drained
2 cups (8 ounces) shredded cheddar cheese

In a large skillet, cook onion in butter until tender. Remove from the heat. Stir in the rice, sour cream, cottage cheese, salt and pepper. Spoon half of the mixture into a greased 11-in. x 7-in. x 2-in. baking dish. Top with half of the chilies and cheese. Repeat layers. Bake, uncovered, at 375° for 20-25 minutes or until heated through and bubbly. **Yield:** 6-8 servings.

Sopaipillas

(Pictured on page 194)

*These deep-fried breads were a hit when I made them for our
daughter's birthday party. They're a fun way to round out a Mexican-theme meal.*
—*Glenda Jarboe, Oroville, California*

1-3/4 cups all-purpose flour
   2 teaspoons baking powder
   1 teaspoon salt
   2 tablespoons shortening
  2/3 cup water
Oil for deep-fat frying
Honey

In a bowl, combine the dry ingredients; cut in shortening until crumbly. Gradually add water, tossing with a fork until mixture holds together. On a lightly floured surface, knead dough for 1-2 minutes or until smooth. Cover and let stand for 5 minutes. Roll out to 1/4-in. thickness. Cut with a 2-1/2-in. star cookie cutter or into 2-1/2-in. triangles.

In an electric skillet or deep-fat fryer, heat oil to 375°. Fry sopaipillas for 1-2 minutes on each side or until golden brown and puffed. Drain on paper towels. Serve immediately with honey. **Yield:** 1 dozen.

Cinnamon Chocolate Chip Ice Cream

(Pictured on page 195)

*I was first served this creamy, soft-set ice cream at a friend's house.
A hint of cinnamon is the secret ingredient.*
—*Gloria Heidner, Elk River, Minnesota*

  2 cups heavy whipping cream
  2 cups half-and-half cream
  1 cup sugar
1/2 cup chocolate syrup
1-1/2 teaspoons vanilla extract
  1/4 teaspoon ground cinnamon
Pinch salt
  1/2 cup miniature semisweet
    chocolate chips
Additional miniature semisweet
  chocolate chips

In a bowl, combine the first seven ingredients; stir until the sugar is dissolved. Fill cylinder of ice cream freezer two-thirds full; freeze according to manufacturer's directions. Stir in chocolate chips. Refrigerate remaining mixture until ready to freeze. Allow to ripen in ice cream freezer or firm up in your refrigerator freezer 2-4 hours before serving. Sprinkle with additional chips. **Yield:** about 2 quarts.

Black Bean Chicken Tacos

(Pictured at right)

While growing up, I developed a love of cooking from scratch. Friends and family are delighted when I present my homemade tortillas so they can assemble these tasty tacos.
— Teresa Obsnuk, Berwyn, Illinois

2 cups all-purpose flour
1 teaspoon baking powder
1-1/2 teaspoons ground cumin, *divided*
2 tablespoons shortening
1/2 cup plus 1 tablespoon warm water
1 pound boneless skinless chicken breasts, cubed
2 cups salsa
1 can (15 ounces) black beans, rinsed and drained
1 teaspoon onion powder
1/2 teaspoon chili powder

Shredded lettuce, shredded cheddar cheese, chopped ripe olives, sour cream and additional salsa, optional

In a bowl, combine the flour, baking powder and 1/2 teaspoon cumin. Cut in shortening until crumbly. Stir in enough water for mixture to form a ball. Knead on a floured surface for 1 minute. Cover and let rest for 20 minutes.

Meanwhile, in a large skillet, combine the chicken, salsa, beans, onion powder, chili powder and remaining cumin. Cover and simmer for 15-20 minutes or until chicken juices run clear.

For tortillas, divide dough into eight balls; roll each ball into an 8-in. circle. In an ungreased skillet, cook tortillas, one at a time, until lightly browned, about 30 seconds on each side. Layer between pieces of waxed paper or paper towel; keep warm. Spoon chicken mixture over half of each tortilla and fold over. Serve with lettuce, cheese, olives, sour cream and salsa if desired. **Yield:** 4-6 servings.

Making Homemade Tortillas

1. Roll out each ball of dough into an 8-inch circle (dough will be very thin).

2. Cook tortillas, one at a time, in an ungreased skillet for about 30 seconds on each side or until lightly browned.

Three Milk Cake

With a large Hispanic population here, I have found the best recipes for Mexican food.
This traditional Tres Leches Cake is a cross between cake and pudding.
—*Janice Montiverdi, Sugar Land, Texas*

6 eggs, *separated*
1-1/2 cups sugar
2 cups all-purpose flour
2 teaspoons baking powder
1/2 teaspoon baking soda
1/2 teaspoon salt
1-1/2 cups water
1 teaspoon almond extract
TOPPING:
   1 can (14 ounces) sweetened
     condensed milk
   2 cups heavy whipping cream
   1/2 cup light corn syrup
   7 tablespoons evaporated milk
   2 teaspoons vanilla extract
ICING:
   1/2 cup heavy whipping cream
   1/2 cup sugar
   1 teaspoon vanilla extract
   1 cup (8 ounces) sour cream

2 tablespoons confectioners' sugar
1 teaspoon almond extract

In a large mixing bowl, beat egg whites until soft peaks form. Gradually beat in sugar until stiff peaks form. Add yolks, one at a time, beating until combined. Combine the flour, baking powder, baking soda and salt; add to egg mixture alternately with water. Stir in extract. Pour into a greased 13-in. x 9-in. x 2-in. baking dish. Bake at 350° for 35-45 minutes or until a toothpick comes out clean. Cool on a wire rack. Poke holes in cake with a fork. Chill overnight.

In a saucepan, combine condensed milk, cream, corn syrup and evaporated milk. Bring to a boil over medium heat, stirring constantly; cook and stir for 2 minutes. Remove from the heat; stir in vanilla. Slowly pour over cold cake, letting milk absorb into cake. Cover and refrigerate.

In a mixing bowl, beat cream until soft peaks form. Gradually beat in sugar until stiff peaks form. Stir in vanilla. In a bowl, combine the sour cream, confectioners' sugar and extract. Fold in whipped cream. Spread over topping. Refrigerate until serving. **Yield:** 12-15 servings.

Creamy Chicken Enchiladas

I adapted the recipe for these rich and creamy enchiladas from a cooking class I had a while back.
—*Janice Montiverdi*

1 small onion, chopped
1 small green pepper, chopped
1 jalapeno pepper, seeded and
   chopped*
1 tablespoon vegetable oil
5-1/2 cups cubed cooked chicken
1/4 cup butter *or* margarine
1/4 cup all-purpose flour

3 cups chicken broth
1 to 2 tablespoons ground cumin
1 teaspoon garlic powder
1 teaspoon salt
1/2 teaspoon white pepper
1 cup (8 ounces) sour cream
12 flour tortillas (8 inches)
1-1/2 cups (12 ounces) shredded Monterey Jack cheese

In a large skillet, saute onion, green pepper and jalapeno in oil until onion is tender. Stir in chicken. Remove from the heat; set aside.

For sauce, melt butter in a saucepan. Stir in flour until smooth. Add broth, cumin, garlic powder, salt and pepper. Bring to a boil; cook and stir for 2 minutes or until thickened and bubbly. Remove from the heat; stir in sour cream.

Add 1 cup of the sauce to chicken mixture. Spoon 1/2 cup chicken mixture on each tortilla; roll up and place seam side down in a greased 13-in. x 9-in. x 2-in. baking dish. Pour remaining sauce over enchiladas.

Bake, uncovered, at 350° for 15 minutes or until sauce is bubbly. Sprinkle with cheese. Bake 5-10 minutes longer. **Yield:** 6 servings.

*Editor's Note: When cutting or seeding hot peppers, use rubber or plastic gloves to protect your hands. Avoid touching your face.

Cheese-Stuffed Jalapenos

(Pictured at right)

A few years ago, I saw a man in the grocery store buying a big bag full of jalapeno peppers. I asked him what he intended to do with them, and he shared this recipe with me right there in the store!
—Janice Montiverdi

25 medium fresh jalapeno
    peppers*
 1 package (8 ounces) cream
    cheese, softened
 3 cups (12 ounces) finely
    shredded cheddar cheese
1-1/2 teaspoons Worcestershire
    sauce
 4 bacon strips, cooked and
    crumbled

Cut jalapenos in half lengthwise; remove seeds and membranes. In a large saucepan, boil peppers in water for 5-10 minutes (the longer you boil the peppers, the milder they become). Drain and rinse in cold water; set aside.

In a small mixing bowl, beat the cream cheese, cheddar cheese and Worcestershire sauce. Spoon 2 teaspoonfuls into each jalapeno half; sprinkle with bacon. Place on a greased baking sheet. Bake at 400° for 5-10 minutes or until cheese is melted. Serve warm. **Yield:** about 4 dozen.

*Editor's Note: When cutting or seeding hot peppers, use rubber or plastic gloves to protect your hands. Avoid touching your face.

Chicken Tortilla Soup

This soup is as good as (if not better than) any kind I've had in a restaurant.
I get so many compliments…I know you will, too!
—Laura Johnson, Largo, Florida

1 large onion, chopped
2 tablespoons olive *or*
   vegetable oil
1 can (4 ounces) chopped green
   chilies
2 garlic cloves, minced
1 jalapeno pepper, seeded and
   chopped*
1 teaspoon ground cumin
5 cups chicken broth
1 can (15 ounces) tomato sauce
1 can (14-1/2 ounces) diced
   tomatoes with garlic and
   onion, undrained
3 cans (5 ounces *each*) white
   chicken, drained
1/4 cup minced fresh cilantro
   or parsley
2 teaspoons lime juice
Salt and pepper to taste
Crushed tortilla chips
Shredded Monterey Jack *or*
   cheddar cheese

In a large saucepan, saute onion in oil; add the chilies, garlic, jalapeno and cumin. Stir in the broth, tomato sauce and tomatoes. Bring to a boil. Reduce heat; stir in chicken. Simmer, uncovered, for 10 minutes. Add the cilantro, lime juice, salt and pepper. Top with chips and cheese. **Yield:** 7 servings.

   *Editor's Note: When cutting or seeding hot peppers, use rubber or plastic gloves to protect your hands. Avoid touching your face.

LEARN ABOUT CILANTRO

WITH its slightly sharp flavor, cilantro—also known as Chinese parsley—gives a distinctive taste to Mexican, Latin American and Oriental dishes. (The spice coriander comes from the seed of the cilantro plant.)

   Like all other fresh herbs, cilantro should be used as soon as possible. For short-term storage, immerse the freshly cut stems in water about 2 inches deep. Cover leaves loosely with a plastic bag and refrigerate for several days. Wash just before using.

Chili Pepper Place Card

(Pictured at right)

Pepper-shaped place cards add the perfect touch to a Mexican meal. You can make them a week in advance and store them in an airtight container. Attach the raffia and name tag just before using.

1 sun-dried tomato *or* spinach flour tortilla (8 to 10 inches)
Chili pepper cookie cutter (3-1/2 inches x 1-1/2 inches)
Nonstick cooking spray

Warm tortilla in the microwave for 10 seconds. With cookie cutter, cut out pepper shapes from tortilla. (The warmer the tortilla is, the easier it will be to cut.) If necessary, use a paring knife to assist with the cutting. Using the end of a straw, make a hole in the stem of the pepper. Place on a baking sheet; lightly coat with nonstick cooking spray. Bake at 350° for 7-8 minutes or until slightly crisp. Remove to a wire rack to cool.

Loop raffia or string through the hole; attach a name tag and tie. **Yield:** 6 to 7 place cards.

WATER GOBLET NAPKIN BOUQUET

BRING a burst of color to your table by taking two napkins in different colors and making this napkin bouquet.

1. Layer one napkin on top of the other so that each corner is offset a bit.

2. Grab the napkins in the center and pull up.

3. With the edges pointing up, place napkins in a water goblet and fluff.

Fourth of July Burger Bar

FOLKS from sea to shining sea agree that no food is more American than a juicy hamburger.

So when you and your family gather to salute the Stars and Stripes on the Fourth of July, fire up the grill and bring on the burgers!

Add a little spark to your patriotic picnic with meaty All-American Hamburgers and Tortilla Burgers.

Don't forget to include an appealing assortment of side dishes and desserts, like Old-Fashioned Lemonade and Sherbet Watermelon. (All recipes shown at right.)

Tortilla Burgers

(Pictured on page 205)

With pork instead of ground beef and tortillas in place of buns,
these Southwestern-style burgers stand out from all others.
—Katie Koziolek, Hartland, Minnesota

1 teaspoon ground cumin
1/2 teaspoon dried oregano
1/2 teaspoon crushed red pepper
    flakes
1/4 teaspoon seasoned salt
1 pound ground pork
4 flour or corn tortillas
    (6 inches), warmed
Salsa, sour cream and shredded
  cheese, optional

In a bowl, combine the first four ingredients. Crumble pork over seasonings and mix well. Shape into four oval patties. Grill, covered, over medium heat for 6-7 minutes on each side or until meat is no longer pink. Serve on tortillas with salsa, sour cream and cheese if desired. **Yield:** 4 servings.

HINTS FOR MAKING HAMBURGERS

HAMBURGERS are one of the easiest entrees to prepare. And with a few timeless tips, your burgers will turn out tasty every time!

- To keep hamburgers moist, first combine the filling ingredients, then add the meat and mix just until combined. Overmixing can cause the burgers to be dense and heavy.
- If you don't like getting your hands messy when mixing the meat mixture, put the ingredients in a large resealable plastic bag, then mix.

  Or if you do use your hands, first dampen them with water and nothing will stick.

- The leaner the ground beef, the drier the cooked burger will be. Ground sirloin makes the leanest burgers, then ground round, ground chuck and, lastly, ground beef.
- Keep in mind that the more fat there is in the meat, the more shrinkage there is during cooking. So if you're making burgers out of regular ground beef, shape the patties to be slightly larger than the bun.
- Don't use a metal spatula to flatten the burgers while cooking...you'll squeeze out all of the succulent juices.
- Always cook ground beef hamburgers until a meat thermometer reads 160°.

All-American Hamburgers

(Pictured at right and on page 204)

We do a lot of camping and outdoor cooking. Hamburgers are on our menu more than any other food.
— Diane Hixon, Niceville, Florida

2 tablespoons diced onion
2 tablespoons chili sauce
2 teaspoons Worcestershire sauce
2 teaspoons prepared mustard
1 pound ground beef
4 slices American *or* cheddar cheese, halved diagonally
2 slices Swiss cheese, halved diagonally
4 hamburger buns, split and toasted
Lettuce leaves, sliced tomato and onion, cooked bacon, ketchup and mustard, optional

In a bowl, combine the first four ingredients. Crumble beef over mixture and mix well. Shape into four patties. Grill, covered, over medium heat for 6 minutes on each side or until meat is no longer pink. During the last minute of cooking, top each patty with two triangles of American cheese and one triangle of Swiss cheese. Serve on buns with lettuce, tomato, onion, bacon, ketchup and mustard if desired. **Yield:** 4 servings.

Old-Fashioned Lemonade

(Pictured on page 204)

This sweet-tart lemonade is a traditional part of my Memorial Day and Fourth of July menus. Folks can't get enough of the fresh-squeezed flavor.
— Tammi Simpson, Greensburg, Kentucky

6 medium lemons
2 to 2-1/2 cups sugar
5 cups water, *divided*
1 tablespoon grated lemon peel

Squeeze juice from the lemons (juice should measure about 1-3/4 cups); set aside. In a large saucepan, combine the sugar, 1 cup water and lemon peel. Cook and stir over medium heat until sugar is dissolved, about 4 minutes. Remove from the heat. Stir in reserved lemon juice and remaining water. Pour into a pitcher and refrigerate until chilled. Serve over ice. **Yield:** 2 quarts.

Sherbet Watermelon

(Pictured on page 205)

I usually double this recipe so I can have one dessert on hand for family and friends who stop by unexpectedly in summer. Each refreshing wedge comes complete with chocolate chip "seeds".
—*Margaret Hanson-Maddox, Montpelier, Indiana*

About 1 pint lime sherbet, slightly softened
About 1 pint pineapple sherbet, slightly softened
About 1-1/2 pints raspberry sherbet, slightly softened
1/4 cup miniature semisweet chocolate chips

Line a 1-1/2-qt. round metal bowl with plastic wrap. Press a thin layer of lime sherbet against the bottom and sides of bowl. Freeze, uncovered, until firm. Spread a thin layer of pineapple sherbet evenly over lime sherbet layer. Freeze until firm. Pack raspberry sherbet into center of sherbet-lined bowl. Smooth the top to resemble a cut watermelon. Cover and freeze until firm, about 8 hours.

Just before serving, remove bowl from the freezer and uncover. Invert onto a serving plate. Remove bowl and plastic wrap. Cut into wedges; press a few chocolate chips into the raspberry sherbet section of each wedge to resemble watermelon seeds. **Yield:** 8 servings.

Dilly Turkey Burgers

This recipe originally called for ground lamb, but my family prefers turkey instead. Dill is a great herb to enhance the flavor of turkey.
—*Andrea Ros, Moon Township, Pennsylvania*

1 egg, lightly beaten
1/2 cup soft bread crumbs
2 tablespoons lemon juice
1 to 2 tablespoons snipped fresh dill *or* 1 to 2 teaspoons dill weed
1 garlic clove, minced
1/2 teaspoon salt
1/2 teaspoon dried oregano
1/4 teaspoon pepper
1 pound ground turkey
4 hamburger buns, split
Lettuce leaves
2 tablespoons mayonnaise, optional

In a large bowl, combine the first eight ingredients. Crumble turkey over mixture and mix well. Shape into four patties. Grill, covered, over medium heat or broil 4 in. from the heat for 4-5 minutes on each side or until a meat thermometer reads 165°. Serve on buns with lettuce and mayonnaise if desired. **Yield:** 4 servings.

Burger Bar Topping Tray

(Pictured above)

WHEN serving a burger bar at your barbecue, set out a large platter loaded with an assortment of condiments and toppings.

Traditional additions include lettuce (leaves or shredded), shredded and sliced cheese, dill pickles, pickle relish and tomato and onion slices.

Ketchup and mustard are reliable standbys, but don't forget mayonnaise, butter and even sour cream. For folks who want to add a little zip to their burger, you could also offer salsa, pickled jalapeno slices and guacamole.

Looking for a few hot additions? Consider sauteed mushrooms, warmed process cheese sauce (Mexican or plain) or a can of heated chili, with or without beans.

There's no limit to what you can use to top hot-off-the-grill burgers!

Chili Burgers

Here's our attempt at re-creating an open-faced burger we enjoyed in a restaurant.
The chili can also be served over hot dogs.
—Jesse and Anne Foust, Bluefield, West Virginia

CHILI:
  1 pound ground beef
  1 large onion, chopped
  1 can (16 ounces) kidney beans,
    rinsed and drained
  1 can (14-1/2 ounces) diced
    tomatoes, undrained
  1 can (14-1/2 ounces) beef broth
  1 can (8 ounces) tomato sauce
  1 tablespoon chili powder
  1/2 teaspoon garlic powder
  1/2 teaspoon dried basil
BURGERS:
  1 egg
  1/2 cup soft bread crumbs
  1 teaspoon salt

  1/2 teaspoon ground cumin
  1/4 teaspoon pepper
  1 pound ground beef
  4 hamburger buns
Chopped onion and shredded cheddar cheese

In a Dutch oven, cook beef and onion over medium heat until meat is no longer pink; drain. Stir in the remaining chili ingredients. Bring to a boil; reduce heat. Simmer, uncovered, for 1 hour.

In a large bowl, combine the egg, crumbs, salt, cumin and pepper. Crumble beef over mixture; mix well. Shape into four patties. Grill, covered, over medium heat for 4-5 minutes on each side or until meat is no longer pink. Serve on buns with chili. Top with onion and cheese. Refrigerate or freeze remaining chili. **Yield:** 4 servings.

Wagon Wheel Pasta Salad

Summertime gatherings aren't complete without a refreshing pasta salad.
This tasty version features a mayonnaise and picante dressing.
—Kathryn Donahey, Oil City, Pennsylvania

  3 cups uncooked wagon wheel
    pasta *or* elbow macaroni
  1 can (16 ounces) kidney beans,
    rinsed and drained
  1 cup cubed cheddar cheese
  1 cup halved cherry tomatoes
  1 small green pepper, julienned
  1 small sweet red pepper,
    julienned
  1/2 cup thinly sliced green onions

  2 cups mayonnaise
  1 cup picante sauce
  1 teaspoon salt
  1 teaspoon ground cumin

Cook pasta according to package directions; drain and rinse in cold water. In a large bowl, combine the pasta, beans, cheese, tomatoes, peppers and onions; mix well. Combine the mayonnaise, picante sauce, salt and cumin; pour over salad and toss to coat. Cover and refrigerate for 2 hours before serving. **Yield:** 16 servings.

Potato Salad Mold

(Pictured at right)

This potato salad is the result of my combining several recipes through the years. Using a mold makes for a pretty presentation.
—Linda Murray
Allenstown, New Hampshire

4 cups sliced peeled cooked red potatoes
1/4 cup chopped celery
1/4 cup sliced green onions
1/4 cup sliced radishes
1 cup (8 ounces) sour cream
2 tablespoons cider vinegar
1 envelope zesty Italian salad dressing mix
1/8 teaspoon pepper
Red Radish Rosettes, optional

In a large bowl, combine the potatoes, celery, onions and radishes. Combine the sour cream, vinegar, salad dressing mix and pepper; pour over potato mixture and toss gently. Press into a 5-cup ring mold coated with nonstick cooking spray. Cover with plastic wrap. Refrigerate for 2-3 hours.

Run a knife around edges of mold to loosen. Invert onto a serving plate. Garnish with Red Radish Rosettes if desired. **Yield:** 6 servings.

MAKING RED RADISH ROSETTES

1. With a small paring knife, slice off the stem so the radish rests on the cutting board with its root standing straight up. Cut a V into the top of the radish, removing the root. Cut two more V's into the top of the radish, positioning them like an X over the first V. You should end up with six pointed peaks.

2. Carefully cut an inverted V under each of the pointed peaks. Soak radishes in cold water for at least 8 hours, allowing petals to open.

Blue Cheese Burgers

*Instead of topping your burgers with the usual cheddar or Swiss cheeses,
stuff them with blue cheese. We've been serving these for many years.*
—*Jesse and Anne Foust, Bluefield, West Virginia*

1 pound ground beef
Salt and pepper to taste
   2 ounces crumbled blue cheese
   2 hamburger buns, split and
     toasted
   2 thin slices red onion
Tomato slices and lettuce leaves,
   optional

Shape beef into four thin patties. Grill, covered, over medium heat for 6 minutes on each side or until meat is no longer pink. Season with salt and pepper. Press blue cheese into the center of two patties; top with remaining patties. Serve on buns with onion, tomato and lettuce if desired. **Yield:** 2 servings.

Pepperoncini Firecrackers

*My youngest daughter and I enjoy time in the kitchen together making these attractive
appetizers. The "firecrackers" burst with chicken, cheese and pepperoncinis.*
—*Virginia Perkins, Columbiana, Ohio*

   1 jar (32 ounces) pepperoncinis
1/2 pound boneless skinless
     chicken breasts, cooked and
     cut into 24 pieces
  24 thin strips Monterey Jack *or*
     pepper Jack cheese (about
     1-1/2 inches x 1/4 inch x
     1/8 inch)
  24 sheets phyllo dough
Refrigerated butter-flavored spray
Melted butter
  48 fresh chives

Remove 24 pepperoncinis from jar; remove and discard stems and seeds. Drain peppers on paper towels. Stuff each with a piece of chicken and a cheese strip (cheese may need to be cut to fit in some peppers).

Place one sheet of phyllo dough on a work surface (keep remaining dough covered with waxed paper to avoid drying out). Spritz dough with butter-flavored spray. Repeat three times; stack sprayed phyllo dough. Cut stack into four pieces, about 6-1/2 in. x 4-1/4 in. each.

Center one stuffed pepper on one long side of each phyllo stack; roll up and twist the ends to seal. Repeat with remaining peppers and dough. Place on ungreased baking sheets. Drizzle butter over center of firecrackers. Bake at 375° for 18-22 minutes or until golden brown. Tie ends with chives. **Yield:** 2 dozen.

Editor's Note: Look for pepperoncinis (pickled peppers) in the pickle and olive section of your grocery store. This recipe was tested with I Can't Believe It's Not Butter Spray.

Berries 'n' Cream Torte

(Pictured at right)

It's easy to see why this fruity dessert always impresses dinner guests. I sometimes substitute the berries with sliced bananas.
— Tina Sawchuk, Ardmore, Alberta

1 cup butter (no substitutes), softened
1 cup sugar
2 eggs
2 cups all-purpose flour
2 teaspoons baking powder
1/2 teaspoon salt

FILLING:

1/2 cup sugar
4-1/2 teaspoons confectioners' sugar
4-1/2 teaspoons cornstarch
3 cups heavy whipping cream
4 cups sliced fresh strawberries
2 cups fresh blueberries
2 cups fresh raspberries

In a large mixing bowl, cream butter and sugar. Add eggs, one at a time, beating well after each addition. Combine the flour, baking powder and salt; gradually add to creamed mixture.

Line two baking sheets with parchment paper or greased aluminum foil; draw a 9-3/4-in. circle on each. Spoon a fourth of the batter onto each circle; spread evenly with a spoon to within 1/4 in. of edge. Bake at 350° for 8-10 minutes or until edges are golden brown. Remove to wire racks to cool completely.

Combine the sugar, confectioners' sugar and cornstarch. In a large mixing bowl, beat cream and sugar mixture until stiff peaks form. To assemble, place one cookie layer on a large serving plate. Top with 1-1/2 cups whipped cream mixture and 2 cups of mixed berries. Repeat layers twice. Top with remaining cookie layer and whipped cream mixture. Arrange remaining berries on top. Cover and refrigerate for 4 hours. **Yield:** 12 servings.

Nacho Popcorn

When I allow myself to indulge in a snack, I make this spicy popcorn. One batch doesn't last long at our house. You can add more or less red pepper flakes to suit your family's taste.
—Kay Young, Flushing, Michigan

　10　cups popped popcorn
1/4　cup butter *or* margarine,
　　　melted
　1　teaspoon paprika
1/2　teaspoon ground cumin
1/4 to 1/2　teaspoon crushed red
　　　pepper flakes
1/3　cup grated Parmesan cheese

Place popcorn in large bowl. In a small bowl, combine butter, paprika, cumin and red pepper flakes. Pour over popcorn and toss to coat. Sprinkle with Parmesan cheese and toss again. **Yield:** 10 servings.

Chewy Chocolate Cookies

These on-the-go goodies are great to take along to the beach, a picnic or on vacation. They have the great flavor and texture of brownies in a cookie shape.
—Mary Fravel, Langhorne, Pennsylvania

1-1/4　cups butter *or* margarine,
　　　softened
　2　cups sugar
　2　eggs
　2　teaspoons vanilla extract
　2　cups all-purpose flour
3/4　cup baking cocoa
　1　teaspoon baking soda
1/2　teaspoon salt

In a large mixing bowl, cream butter and sugar. Add eggs and vanilla; mix well. Combine the flour, cocoa, baking soda and salt; gradually add to creamed mixture. Drop by rounded tablespoonfuls 2 in. apart onto ungreased baking sheets.

Bake at 350° for 8-10 minutes or until edges are set and centers are puffed and cracked. Cool for 2 minutes before removing from pans to wire racks (cookies will flatten as they cool). **Yield:** about 5 dozen.

Soda Bottle Flower Vases

(Pictured above and on page 205)

DURING the dog days of summer, it's fun to take a break from formal entertaining. Casual summer get-togethers call for easy-to-prepare foods and effortless decorating ideas.

After you and your family enjoy some ice-cold soda pop, wash and save the bottles to use as homespun vases for the single-stem flower arrangements shown above. For best results, use flowers with long stems, such as daisies, gerberas, cosmos and carnations.

These charming table toppers can be grouped in an old-fashioned soda crate and displayed together on the buffet table. Or you can use them as individual centerpieces on picnic or patio tables.

They're so simple to put together that you can enlist older kids to help cut the flowers and fill the bottles while you're preparing the food.

Celebrate the Summer Olympics

IN 2004, the Summer Olympic Games return to Greece, the birthplace of these famed athletic events. Be a sport and kick off this historic occasion by planning a mouth-watering menu with a Mediterranean feel.

A successful Greek-style meal is off to a great start when you pass a platter piled high with Spinach Phyllo Bundles.

You'll be swimming in compliments (and recipe requests) when you serve succulent Garlic-Roasted Chicken and Vegetables.

Feta cheese and olives are flavorful additions that give Greek Tossed Salad an award-winning taste. (All recipes shown at right.)

MEDITERRANEAN MENU

(Clockwise from top left)

Spinach Phyllo
Bundles (p. 219)

Greek Tossed Salad (p. 220)

Garlic-Roasted
Chicken and
Vegetables (p. 218)

Garlic-Roasted Chicken And Vegetables

(Pictured on page 216)

The first time my Greek father-in-law made this chicken, he proudly shared the recipe with me. It's my favorite way to roast chicken.
—Jessica Pardalos, Shelton, Washington

 1 roasting chicken (5 to 6 pounds)
 4 tablespoons butter *or* margarine, softened, *divided*
15 garlic cloves, halved
 1 can (14-1/2 ounces) chicken broth, *divided*
1/4 cup olive *or* vegetable oil
1/4 cup lemon juice
 1 to 2 tablespoons dried oregano
 1 teaspoon salt
1/2 teaspoon pepper
1/4 teaspoon garlic powder
10 red potatoes (about 1-1/2 pounds), cut into large chunks
 2 cups baby carrots
 1 medium red onion, thinly sliced

Rub inside of chicken with 2 tablespoons butter. With a sharp knife, cut 16 small slits in chicken breast, drumsticks and thighs. Place a halved garlic clove in each slit. Place chicken on a rack in a roasting pan; tie drumsticks together. Place remaining garlic in pan. Pour half of the broth over chicken. Combine oil and lemon juice; pour half over chicken. Rub remaining butter over chicken. Combine the oregano, salt, pepper and garlic powder; sprinkle half over chicken. Cover and bake at 350° for 45 minutes.

Place the potatoes, carrots and onion in pan. Drizzle remaining oil mixture and broth over chicken and vegetables. Sprinkle remaining oregano mixture over chicken. Cover and bake 30 minutes longer; baste. Bake, uncovered, for 45-60 minutes or until a meat thermometer reads 180°, basting several times. Thicken pan juices if desired. Cover and let stand for 10 minutes before serving. **Yield:** 6 servings.

Phyllo Facts

PHYLLO (pronounced FEE-lo) is a tissue-thin pastry that's made by gently stretching the dough into thin fragile sheets. It can be layered, shaped and baked in a variety of sweet and savory ways. Handling it quickly is the key!

• Follow the manufacturer's instructions for thawing phyllo in the unopened package.

• Count out the number of phyllo sheets required for your recipe, place them on a smooth dry surface and immediately cover with plastic wrap and a damp towel. Gently pull sheets from the stack as you need them, keeping the remaining ones covered until needed.

Spinach Phyllo Bundles

(Pictured at right and on page 216)

Spanakopita is a Greek spinach pie made with phyllo dough. This appetizer version is always a hit at parties.
—*Eloise Olive, Greensboro, North Carolina*

1 medium onion, chopped
2 tablespoons plus 1/2 cup butter (no substitutes), *divided*
1 package (10 ounces) frozen chopped spinach, thawed and squeezed dry
1 cup (4 ounces) crumbled feta cheese
3/4 cup small-curd cottage cheese
3 eggs, lightly beaten
1/4 cup dry bread crumbs
3/4 teaspoon salt
1/2 teaspoon dill weed
Pepper to taste
1 package (16 ounces) frozen phyllo dough,* thawed

In a large skillet, saute onion in 2 tablespoons butter until tender. Remove from the heat. Stir in the spinach, feta cheese, cottage cheese, eggs, bread crumbs, salt, dill and pepper.

Use one package of phyllo sheets. (Save the remaining phyllo for another use.) Melt remaining butter. Layer and brush five phyllo sheets with melted butter. Keep remaining phyllo covered to avoid drying out.

Cut buttered sheets lengthwise into 2-in. strips; cut in half widthwise. Place 1 heaping tablespoon of filling at one end of each strip; fold into a triangle, as you would fold a flag. Place on an ungreased baking sheet. Brush with butter. Bake at 400° for 15-20 minutes or until golden brown. Serve warm. **Yield:** 28 appetizers.

***Editor's Note:** This recipe was tested with Athenos phyllo dough. The phyllo sheets measure 18 in. x 14 in.

Greek Tossed Salad

(Pictured on page 216)

A light dressing makes this salad a nice complement to any meal.
Feta cheese and olives are a fun addition.
—Valerie Belley, St. Louis, Missouri

6 cups torn romaine
1 cup chopped tomato
3/4 cup thinly sliced red onion
3/4 cup cubed cucumber
3/4 cup cubed feta cheese
18 pitted kalamata *or* ripe olives
3 tablespoons olive *or*
vegetable oil

1 tablespoon lemon juice
1-1/2 teaspoons dried oregano
1-1/2 teaspoons prepared mustard
1/4 teaspoon salt

In a bowl, combine the first six ingredients. In a small bowl, whisk the remaining ingredients. Pour over salad and toss to coat. Serve immediately. **Yield:** 6-8 servings.

Marinated Tomatoes

A dash of cinnamon gives these tasty tomatoes from our home economists
traditional Greek flavor. It's a super summer salad.

6 plum tomatoes, sliced
Red leaf lettuce
8 pitted kalamata *or* ripe olives,
chopped
1 tablespoon balsamic *or* red
wine vinegar
1 tablespoon olive *or*
vegetable oil
1 tablespoon grated onion
1 tablespoon honey
1 garlic clove, minced
1/2 teaspoon salt
1/4 teaspoon pepper
1/8 to 1/4 teaspoon ground
cinnamon
Minced fresh parsley

Arrange tomatoes on a lettuce-lined serving plate. Sprinkle with olives. In a small bowl, combine the vinegar, oil, onion, honey, garlic, salt, pepper and cinnamon. Drizzle over tomatoes and olives. Sprinkle with parsley. Cover and refrigerate for at least 1 hour before serving. **Yield:** 4-6 servings.

WHAT DO THE OLYMPIC RINGS MEAN?

DESIGNED in 1913 by Pierre de Coubertin, the five Olympic rings symbolize the five continents of Africa, Americas, Asia, Europe and Oceania.

The colors (black, blue, green, red and yellow) are significant because every country participating in the games has one of these colors, including the white background, in their national flag.

Olympic Rings Fruit Pizza

(Pictured at right)

Ring in the Olympics with this festive fruit pizza from our Test Kitchen. A chocolate cookie crust is topped with cream cheese frosting and colorful fruit.

1/2 cup butter *or* margarine, softened
1/2 cup shortening
1/2 cup sugar
1/2 cup packed brown sugar
 1 egg
 3 squares (1 ounce *each*) semisweet chocolate, melted and cooled
 1 teaspoon vanilla extract
 2 cups all-purpose flour
1/2 cup baking cocoa
1/4 teaspoon salt
 1 package (8 ounces) cream cheese, softened
1/2 cup confectioners' sugar
 2 cups whipped topping
1/2 cup fresh blueberries
1/2 cup fresh blackberries
1/2 cup diced fresh strawberries
1/2 cup pineapple tidbits, drained
 1 large kiwifruit, peeled and chopped

In a mixing bowl, cream butter, shortening and sugars. Beat in the egg, melted chocolate and vanilla; mix well. Combine the flour, cocoa and salt; gradually add to creamed mixture. Cover and refrigerate for 30 minutes.

Place waxed paper over a 15-in. x 10-in. baking sheet without sides. Shape dough into a flattened rectangle and place on prepared baking sheet. Cover dough with waxed paper; roll dough to within 1/4 in. of edges of baking sheet. Remove top sheet of waxed paper; invert dough onto another greased baking sheet. Remove remaining waxed paper.

Using a 4-1/2-in.-diameter plate or bowl and a knife, trace three touching circles along a long side of the dough. Trace two more circles centered below and overlapping upper circles by 1 in. Cut around outer edges of the rings; remove dough around rings and use to make cookies if desired. Bake rings at 350° for 14-16 minutes. Cool on a wire rack.

In a small mixing bowl, beat cream cheese and confectioners' sugar until smooth. Add whipped topping; mix well. Transfer cooled crust to a serving platter. Spread with frosting. On top rings, from left to right, place blueberries, blackberries and strawberries. Place pineapple and kiwi on lower rings. Store in the refrigerator. **Yield:** 12-16 servings.

Cranberry Baklava

*Living in the heart of cranberry country, I plan many meals around
that crimson-colored fruit. This is my spin on a great Greek favorite.*
— Darlene Alexander, Nekoosa, Wisconsin

1 package (16 ounces) frozen
    phyllo dough,* thawed
1 cup butter (no substitutes),
    melted
1-1/2 cups fresh *or* frozen
    cranberries, finely chopped
3 cups finely chopped walnuts
1 cup sugar
1 teaspoon ground cinnamon
1-1/2 cups honey

Grease a 13-in. x 9-in. x 2-in. baking
dish. Trim phyllo dough to fit pan.
Layer six sheets of phyllo dough in
dish, brushing each with butter. In a bowl, combine the
cranberries, walnuts, sugar and cinnamon. Sprinkle 1-1/4
cups over top layer of phyllo. Layer and brush six sheets of
dough with butter. Top with 1-1/4 cups cranberry mixture.
Layer and brush six more sheets of dough with butter; top
with remaining cranberry mixture. Top with the remaining
dough, brushing each sheet with butter. Using a sharp knife,
cut halfway through layers to make 24 pieces. Bake at
325° for 60-70 minutes or until golden brown.

In a small saucepan, heat the honey over low heat just until warm and thin. Pour over warm baklava. Cool on a wire
rack for 1 hour. **Yield:** 24 servings.

*Editor's Note: This recipe was tested with Athenos
phyllo dough. The phyllo sheets measure 18 in. x 14 in.

Garlic Lemon Dip

*When my father came from Greece to the United States about 50 years ago,
he brought this recipe with him. It's called Scordolia…"Scordo" means garlic in Greek.*
— Maria Coclin, Cranston, Rhode Island

1/4 pound day-old Italian bread,
    crusts removed and cut into
    large pieces
2 cups water
3 to 4 tablespoons lemon juice
2 medium red potatoes, peeled,
    cubed, cooked and cooled
5 to 6 garlic cloves, halved
1/2 teaspoon salt
1/2 cup olive *or* vegetable oil
Chopped walnuts *or* almonds,
    optional
Pita chips *or* crackers

In a bowl, soak bread in water for 15 minutes. Squeeze
bread and place in a small bowl (there should be about 1 cup
of bread); set aside.

In a blender or food processor, combine the lemon juice,
potatoes, garlic and salt; cover and process until smooth. Add
bread; cover and process until blended. While processing,
gradually add oil until blended. Transfer to a serving bowl;
sprinkle with nuts if desired. Serve with pita chips or crackers. Store in the refrigerator. **Yield:** about 1-1/2 cups.

Gyro Burgers

(Pictured at right)

The mild seasonings in these burgers give them mass appeal. Pita bread is a nice change of pace from the usual hamburger buns.
—Katie Koziolek, Hartland, Minnesota

2 tablespoons plain yogurt
2 garlic cloves, minced
1 teaspoon dried rosemary, crushed
1/2 teaspoon lemon-pepper seasoning
1/4 teaspoon salt
1 pound ground lamb *or* pork
4 pita breads, halved
Sliced cucumber
Cucumber Sauce (recipe below)

In a bowl, combine the yogurt, garlic, rosemary, lemon-pepper and salt. Crumble meat over mixture; mix well. Shape into four oval patties. Grill, covered, over medium heat for 6-7 minutes on each side or until meat is no longer pink. Serve in pita bread with sliced cucumber and Cucumber Sauce. **Yield:** 4 servings.

Cucumber Sauce

(Pictured above)

I'm Greek and my husband's Sicilian, so we use plenty of garlic in our cooking. We typically serve this traditiomal Tsatziki with lamb and chicken.
—Efy Leonardi, Massapequa, New York

4 cups (32 ounces) plain yogurt
1 medium cucumber, peeled, seeded and grated
1/2 teaspoon salt
1/4 cup olive *or* vegetable oil
1/4 cup white vinegar
2 garlic cloves, minced

Line a fine mesh strainer with two layers of cheesecloth. Place yogurt in strainer over a bowl. Cover and refrigerate for at least 4 hours or overnight.

Drain and discard liquid in bowl; set yogurt aside. Place cucumber in a colander over a plate; sprinkle with salt. Let stand for 15 minutes; discard liquid. In a small bowl, whisk oil and vinegar until blended. Stir in the garlic, yogurt and cucumber. **Yield:** about 2-1/2 cups.

25th Wedding Anniversary

IF YOU'RE planning a party to celebrate the 25th wedding anniversary of either you and your spouse or a close relative, you can spare the cost of a caterer and forgo the fees of renting a hall.

Just open up your home and celebrate in style! It's easy to entertain a large group when you turn to this chapter's crowd-pleasing recipes.

Turkey Breast Roulade is an elegant entree that features a hearty ham and artichoke filling.

Partner slices of the main course with Garlic Potato Bake and Mandarin Orange Spinach Salad.

Then leave a lasting impression by presenting an eye-catching Anniversary Cake. (All recipes shown at right.)

Garlic Potato Bake

(Pictured on page 225)

I created this recipe for an end-of-summer harvest picnic. Everyone loved it.
—*Shelly Lehman, Powell, Wyoming*

18 medium potatoes, peeled and
    diced
3 whole garlic bulbs, separated
    into cloves and peeled
3 cups (12 ounces) shredded
    cheddar cheese
1 package (8 ounces) cream
    cheese, cubed
6 eggs, beaten
1 tablespoon minced chives
1-1/2 to 2 teaspoons salt
1/4 teaspoon white pepper
Diced sweet red, yellow and
    orange peppers, rosemary sprigs
    and additional minced chives,
    optional

Place potatoes and garlic in a large kettle; cover with water. Bring to a boil. Reduce heat; cover and simmer for 15-20 minutes or until potatoes and garlic are tender. Drain.

In a large mixing bowl, combine potatoes and garlic, cheddar cheese, cream cheese, eggs, chives, salt and pepper; beat until smooth. Spoon into two greased shallow 3-qt. baking dishes. Bake, uncovered, at 350° for 30-35 minutes or until a thermometer reads 160°. Garnish with peppers, rosemary and chives if desired. **Yield:** 25 servings.

STEMWARE SERVERS

TO ADD a little elegance to a special-occasion dinner, present servings of Garlic Potato Bake in casual stemmed glasses (shown on page 225).

After baking the potatoes as directed, scoop servings into goblets or glasses. If you don't have enough of the same pattern, you can mix and match stemware.

Editor's Note: Do not use crystal stemware to serve hot food because the heat may cause breakage.

Lemon Burst Broccoli

This lemon dressing is great on any vegetable, especially broccoli.
—*Kim Morren, Carrollton, Texas*

3/4 cup lemon juice
3/4 cup vegetable oil
3 tablespoons sugar
3 tablespoons finely chopped
    onion
3 garlic cloves, minced
1-1/2 teaspoons salt
3/4 teaspoon paprika
6 pounds fresh broccoli, cut
    into florets

In a jar with a tight-fitting lid, combine the lemon juice, oil, sugar, onion, garlic, salt and paprika; shake well. Refrigerate for at least 1 hour.

Place broccoli in a steamer basket over 1 in. of boiling water in a large kettle or Dutch oven. Cover and steam for 8-10 minutes or until crisp-tender. Transfer broccoli to a serving dish. Shake lemon dressing and pour over broccoli; toss to coat. **Yield:** 24 servings.

Turkey Breast Roulade

(Pictured at right and on page 225)

The original recipe for this roulade called for tomatoes, which our son is allergic to. I substituted artichokes and mushrooms with wonderful results.
—Carol Earl, Brewster, New York

3 jars (7-1/2 ounces *each*) marinated artichoke hearts, drained and chopped
3 cans (4 ounces *each*) mushroom stems and pieces, drained and chopped
3 tablespoons chopped sweet onion
3 boneless turkey breast halves (3 to 3-1/2 pounds *each*)
2-1/4 pounds thinly sliced deli ham
1 cup butter *or* margarine, melted
1-1/2 teaspoons dried thyme

In a bowl, combine the artichokes, mushrooms and onion; set aside. With skin side down, cut a lengthwise slit through the thickest portion of each turkey breast to within 1/2 in. of bottom. Open the turkey breasts so they lie flat; cover with plastic wrap. Flatten to 3/4- to 1-in. thickness; remove plastic.

Place ham slices over turkey to within 1 in. of edges. Spoon vegetable mixture lengthwise down the center of the ham. Roll each turkey breast, starting from a side where the fold is in the center. Secure with kitchen string at 3-in. intervals. Place the turkey rolls seam side down in one greased 15-in. x 10-in. x 1-in. baking pan and one 13-in. x 9-in. x 2-in. baking pan.

In a small bowl, combine the butter and thyme; spoon over the turkey rolls. Bake, uncovered, at 350° for 1-1/4 to 1-3/4 hours or until a meat thermometer reads 170°, basting frequently. Cover and let stand for 10 minutes before slicing. **Yield:** 24-30 servings.

Mandarin Orange Spinach Salad

(Pictured on page 224)

With mandarin oranges and a slightly sweet dressing, this spinach salad is a refreshing change of pace. I frequently take it along to summer picnics.
—Georgiann Franklin, Canfield, Ohio

1/2 cup vegetable oil
1/3 cup sugar
1/3 cup white vinegar
 2 tablespoons minced fresh parsley
3/4 teaspoon salt
SALAD:
3/4 cup slivered almonds
4-1/2 teaspoons sugar
 7 cups torn romaine
 7 cups torn spinach
1-1/2 cups sliced celery
1-1/2 cups sliced green onions
 3 cans (11 ounces *each*) mandarin oranges, drained

In a jar with a tight-fitting lid, combine the first five ingredients; shake well. Set aside. In a skillet, cook and stir the almonds and sugar over medium heat until sugar is melted and almonds are coated. Spread on foil to cool completely.

In a large salad bowl, combine the romaine, spinach, celery and onions. Add oranges and sugared almonds; toss gently. Shake dressing; drizzle over salad and toss to coat. **Yield:** 24 servings.

Creamy Onion Soup

I enjoy inviting people into my home to sample flavorful foods like this creamy soup. You'll find it's a nice twist on the traditional version.
—Minnie Paulson, Stanley, North Dakota

 8 medium onions, thinly sliced
1/3 cup butter *or* margarine
 2 tablespoons all-purpose flour
 1 teaspoon salt
1/2 teaspoon pepper
 8 cups chicken broth
 1 cup (8 ounces) sour cream
1/2 cup milk
 12 slices French bread (1 inch thick), toasted
 1 cup (4 ounces) shredded mozzarella cheese

In a large kettle or Dutch oven, saute onions in butter until tender. Sprinkle with flour, salt and pepper; cook and stir for 1 minute. Gradually add broth. Bring to a boil; cook and stir for 2 minutes. Reduce heat; simmer, uncovered, for 30 minutes. Combine sour cream and milk. Stir into soup; heat through (do not boil). Place a slice of toasted bread in each soup bowl; ladle soup over bread. Sprinkle with cheese. **Yield:** 12 servings.

Ham Cream Cheese Balls

(Pictured at right)

It seems like I'm always hosting a shower, birthday party or other celebration. This spread is fast to fix.
—Jill Kirby, Calhoun, Georgia

2 packages (8 ounces *each*) cream cheese, softened
1 package (2-1/2 ounces) thinly sliced deli ham, finely chopped
3 green onions, finely chopped
2 tablespoons Worcestershire sauce
1 cup finely chopped peanuts
Crackers and raw vegetables

In a bowl, combine the cream cheese, ham, onions and Worcestershire sauce; mix well. Shape into 3/4-in. balls. Roll in peanuts. Cover and refrigerate until serving. Serve with crackers and vegetables. **Yield:** about 5 dozen.

Refrigerator Rolls

I taught my teenage son how to make these soft rolls for a 4-H project. Everyone was surprised when this big brawny fellow, who shows Brahman cattle, was named Grand Champion!
—Deanna Naivar, Temple, Texas

2 packages (1/4 ounce *each*) active dry yeast
2 cups warm water (110° to 115°)
1/2 cup sugar
1 teaspoon salt
6 cups all-purpose flour
1 egg
1/4 cup shortening

In a mixing bowl, dissolve yeast in warm water. Add the sugar, salt and 2 cups flour. Beat on medium speed for 2 minutes. Add egg and shortening; mix well. Stir in enough remaining flour to form a soft dough (do not knead). Place in a greased bowl, turning once to grease top. Cover and refrigerate overnight.

Punch dough down. Turn onto a lightly floured surface; divide into 24 pieces. Shape each into a ball. Place 2 in. apart on greased baking sheets. Cover and let rise in a warm place until doubled, about 2 hours. Bake at 400° for 12-15 minutes or until golden brown. Remove from pans to wire racks to cool. **Yield:** 2 dozen.

Three-Cheese Manicotti

Family and friends love the rich cheese filling tucked inside tender pasta shells.
— Vikki Rebholz, West Chester, Ohio

2 cartons (15 ounces *each*) ricotta cheese
5 cups (20 ounces) shredded mozzarella cheese, *divided*
1 cup grated Parmesan cheese
2 eggs, beaten
2 teaspoons dried basil
2 teaspoons dried oregano
1 teaspoon onion powder
1 teaspoon garlic powder
1 teaspoon seasoned salt
2 jars (26 ounces *each*) spaghetti sauce
20 manicotti shells, cooked and drained

In a bowl, combine the ricotta cheese, 3 cups mozzarella cheese, Parmesan cheese, eggs and seasonings. Spread 1 cup spaghetti sauce each in two ungreased 13-in. x 9-in. x 2-in. baking dishes. Stuff manicotti shells with cheese mixture; arrange over sauce. Top with remaining sauce.

Cover and bake at 375° for 35-40 minutes. Uncover; sprinkle with remaining mozzarella cheese. Bake 10 minutes longer or until cheese is melted and manicotti is heated through. **Yield:** 10 servings.

STUFFING MANICOTTI SHELLS

TO EASILY STUFF manicotti shells, place the filling in a large resealable plastic bag; seal the bag. Cut off a small part of one bottom corner. Squeeze the filling into each shell.

Stuffed Bread Appetizers

You may want to double the recipe for this hearty cold appetizer because
I've found that folks just can't seem to stop eating it!
— Tracey Wesstrom, Lansdale, Pennsylvania

2 packages (one 8 ounces, one 3 ounces) cream cheese, softened
1 cup chopped celery
1 cup (4 ounces) shredded cheddar cheese
1/2 cup chopped sweet red pepper
1/2 cup chopped water chestnuts
1 teaspoon garlic salt
1 loaf (26 inches) French bread, halved lengthwise
Mayonnaise
Dried parsley flakes
4 dill pickle spears
4 slices deli ham

In a bowl, combine the first six ingredients. Hollow out top and bottom of bread, leaving a 1/2-in. shell (discard removed bread or save for another use). Spread a thin layer of mayonnaise over bread; sprinkle with parsley. Fill each half with cheese mixture. Wrap pickle spears in ham; place lengthwise over cheese mixture on bottom half of loaf. Replace top; press together to seal. Wrap in foil; refrigerate overnight. Just before serving, cut into 1-in. slices. **Yield:** about 2 dozen.

Cheesecake Dessert Squares

(Pictured at right)

These creamy squares are a nice alternative for folks who are intimidated to make a cheesecake or other fancy dessert. Fresh fruit on top gives them a little more elegance.
—Sharon Skildum
Maple Grove, Minnesota

 2 cups graham cracker crumbs
   (about 32 squares)
1/3 cup sugar
1/2 teaspoon ground cinnamon
1/2 cup butter *or* margarine,
   melted
FILLING:
 3 packages (8 ounces *each*)
   cream cheese, softened
1-1/2 cups sugar
 1 teaspoon vanilla extract
 4 eggs, *separated*
Fresh fruit

In a small bowl, combine the cracker crumbs, sugar and cinnamon; stir in butter. Press into a greased 15-in. x 10-in. x 1-in. baking pan. Bake at 350° for 5 minutes.

In a large mixing bowl, beat cream cheese, sugar and vanilla until smooth. Add egg yolks; beat on low speed just until combined. In a small mixing bowl, beat egg whites until soft peaks form; fold into cream cheese mixture. Pour over crust. Bake for 28-30 minutes or until center is almost set. Cool on a wire rack for 30 minutes. Refrigerate overnight. Garnish with fruit. **Yield:** 24 servings.

Anniversary Cake

(Pictured on opposite page and page 225)

You can make this lovely single layer cake from our Test Kitchen with or without the cake topper. Flavor the cake as you wish, and if possible, tint the frosting to match the wedding colors.

ROYAL ICING:
- 4 cups confectioners' sugar
- 1/3 cup plus 2 to 3 teaspoons water, *divided*
- 3 tablespoons meringue powder*
- 1/2 teaspoon cream of tartar

CAKE:
- 2 cups shortening
- 3-1/2 cups sugar
- 6 eggs
- 5-1/2 cups all-purpose flour
- 6 teaspoons baking powder
- 3 teaspoons salt
- 3 cups milk

ADDITIONAL INGREDIENTS FOR YELLOW CAKE:
- 3 teaspoons vanilla extract

ADDITIONAL INGREDIENTS FOR LEMON CAKE:
- 4-1/2 teaspoons grated lemon peel
- 3 teaspoons lemon extract

ADDITIONAL INGREDIENTS FOR SPICE CAKE:
- 3 teaspoons ground cinnamon
- 1-1/2 teaspoons ground allspice
- 1-1/2 teaspoons ground cloves

BUTTERCREAM FROSTING:
- 1 cup butter (no substitutes), softened
- 1 cup shortening
- 12 cups confectioners' sugar
- 3/4 cup plus 3 tablespoons milk
- 3 teaspoons vanilla extract
- 1/4 teaspoon salt
- 2-1/4 cups lemon curd, raspberry filling, apricot filling, poppy seed filling *or* purchased filling of your choice

Gel *or* paste food coloring

In a mixing bowl, combine the confectioners' sugar, 1/3 cup water, meringue powder and cream of tartar; beat on low speed just until combined. Beat on high for 7-10 minutes or until stiff peaks form. (Keep icing covered at all times with a damp cloth to keep from drying out. If necessary to restore texture later, beat again on high speed. Prepare only half of the icing recipe if using store-bought candy roses or edible flowers to decorate.)

ROSES: Divide icing in half; set half aside. If using store-bought roses, refer to photo for position and attach roses to top of cake using a dab of icing. If making icing roses, cut a hole in the corner of pastry or plastic bag; insert round tip #12 and fill with remaining icing. Holding the bag straight up, pipe a dome-shaped mound of icing on the flower nail.

With petal tip #103 and icing, hold pastry bag at a 45-degree angle, wide end of tip down. Turn nail and squeeze bag to form bud. Holding pastry bag with narrow end farther away from the rose tip and turning the nail, pipe a row of three standing petals. Pipe a second row of petals, holding the narrow tip end at a greater angle. Repeat for a third row.

Gently slide scissor ends underneath rose and remove it from nail to waxed paper; let dry completely. Repeat with remaining icing to make 20-22 roses. (Flowers can be made several weeks in advance and stored in an airtight container.)

NUMERALS AND CAKE TOPPER: Set aside 1/2 cup of reserved icing. With round tip #4 and remaining reserved icing, pipe at least ten 3/4-in.-square "25"s, making sure to connect the two and five at the base of each.

For cake topper, place pattern of your choice under waxed paper; tape both to work surface. Completely outline edges; let dry for 10 minutes. To reserved 1/2 cup icing, stir in remaining 2-3 teaspoons water to thin. Fill in outline of cake topper with thinned icing, using the same tip. Let dry completely, then place in an airtight container to store before use.

CAKE: Line two greased 12-in. round baking pans with parchment or waxed paper; grease and flour paper and set aside. In a mixing bowl, cream shortening and sugar. Add eggs, one at a time, beating well after each. Combine the flour,

baking powder and salt; add to the creamed mixture alternately with the milk. Stir in additional cake ingredients based on the desired cake flavor. Pour into prepared pans. Bake at 350° for 50-55 minutes or until a toothpick inserted near the center comes out clean. Cool for 10 minutes before removing from pans to wire racks to cool completely.

FROSTING: In a large mixing bowl, cream the butter, shortening and confectioners' sugar until well combined. Beat in milk, vanilla and salt until mixture becomes light and fluffy.

ASSEMBLING: Split each cooled cake into two horizontal layers. Place bottom layer on serving plate; spread with a thin layer of frosting. Top with 3/4 cup filling of your choice. Spread a thin layer of frosting over the bottom of next layer; place cake, frosted side down, over filling. Repeat layers twice. Top with remaining cake layer.

Set aside 3 cups frosting. Tint remaining frosting with color of your choice; set aside 1/2 cup. Spread remaining tinted frosting over top and sides of cake. Place reserved tinted frosting in a pastry or plastic bag with round tip #4. Pipe lettering and outlines over cake topper. Let dry.

FINISHING: Place reserved white frosting in a pastry or plastic bag with star tip #21. Pipe eight vertical columns around sides of cake. With the same tip, pipe a shell border around top and bottom of cake.

Just before serving, use small dabs of frosting to attach numerals between columns and roses at top of columns. Stand cake topper up in center of cake; continue to hold while piping two large dollops of frosting on either side of cake topper. Position remaining roses with frosting around base of cake topper. Using leaf tip #69, pipe leaves around cluster of roses. (Dried decorations will collapse upon refrigeration. Remove to save.) **Yield:** 25-30 servings.

*Editor's Note: Meringue powder can be ordered by mail from Wilton Industries, Inc. Call 1-800/794-5866 or visit their Web site, *www.wilton.com.*

ASSEMBLING THE ANNIVERSARY CAKE TOPPER

1. Place cake topper pattern under a sheet of waxed paper; tape both to work surface. Pipe icing along outside and inside edges of the design; let dry.

2. Thin remaining icing with water. Pipe icing inside the edges of the design to fill in; let dry.

3. Using tinted frosting, pipe lettering and outlines over cake topper; let dry.

Peppered Rib Eye Roast

Roast recipes are a fuss-free entree to serve when entertaining. After marinating the meat overnight, simply pop in the oven and bake for a couple of hours. It turns out terrific every time.
—Ruth Andrewson, Leavenworth, Washington

1/3 to 1/2 cup coarsely ground
    pepper
  1 teaspoon ground cardamom
  2 boneless rib eye roasts (5 to 6
    pounds *each*)
  2 cups soy sauce
1-1/2 cups cider vinegar
  2 tablespoons tomato paste
  2 teaspoons garlic powder
  2 teaspoons paprika

Combine the pepper and cardamom; rub over roasts. Place each in a shallow baking dish. In a bowl, combine the soy sauce, vinegar, tomato paste, garlic powder and paprika. Pour over the roasts; turn several times. Cover and refrigerate overnight.

Place each roast in a roasting pan. Bake, uncovered, at 350° for 2 hours or until meat reaches desired doneness (for rare, a meat thermometer should read 140°; medium, 160°; well-done, 170°). **Yield:** 24-30 servings.

Vegetable Rice Casserole

As an avid gardener and occasional cook, I use fresh vegetables and herbs when trying out new recipes on my wife and children. This zesty rice dish always pleases.
—Blaine Baker, Kelseyville, California

  6 cups water
  2 tablespoons butter *or*
    margarine
  3 cups uncooked long grain rice
  2 tablespoons dried parsley
    flakes
  3 teaspoons dill weed, *divided*
  2 teaspoons celery salt, *divided*
  1 cup diced carrots
  1 cup diced fresh tomato
  1 cup diced green pepper
  1 cup diced onion
  1 cup diced celery
1/4 to 1/2 cup diced hot banana
    peppers *or* hot peppers of
    your choice
  2 tablespoons olive *or*
    vegetable oil

  2 cans (10-3/4 ounces *each*) condensed cream of
    chicken soup, undiluted
1/2 cup milk
  2 teaspoons dried basil
  1 teaspoon dried thyme
1/2 teaspoon pepper

In a large saucepan, bring water and butter to a boil; add rice. Cover and simmer for 20 minutes or until liquid is absorbed. Stir in the parsley, 2 teaspoons dill and 1 teaspoon celery salt; set aside.

In a skillet, saute carrots, tomato, green pepper, onion, celery and hot peppers in oil until vegetables are crisp-tender. Stir in soup, milk, basil, thyme, pepper and remaining dill and celery salt. Divide half of the rice mixture between two greased 11-in. x 7-in. x 2-in. baking dishes. Top with vegetable mixture and remaining rice mixture. Cover and bake at 350° for 45 minutes or until heated through. **Yield:** 24 servings.

Circle of Love Centerpiece

(Pictured above)

WHEN you celebrate the anniversary of two people who are the light of each other's lives, add a romantic touch to the dinner table with this easy-to-assemble luminary.

First, apply a strip of double-sided transparent tape down the length of a clear glass cylinder vase. Wrap parchment paper around the outside of the vase, securing the short ends over the tape. (We used off-white parchment paper, but you could use paper with a little more color or with a pattern corresponding to the colors of the day.) Wrap a colored narrow ribbon around the vase and tie in a bow. Place a small pillar candle inside the vase.

Set a small bowl upside down in the center of the table. Drape a cloth dinner napkin (in the same color as the table napkins you're using) over the bowl. Position a 12-inch round mirror on top of the covered bowl.

Place the vase in the center of the mirror. Add greens and fresh flowers in a circle around the vase. (We used leather and Italian ferns, purple wax flowers, tinted baby's breath and white tea roses.) Light the candles just before guests sit down to dinner.

There's very little last-minute preparation for this centerpiece. You can wrap the vase with paper, tie on the ribbon and set the candle inside the vase weeks in advance. The day before the party, set up the display on the table, but don't add the fresh flowers and greens. Those should be added just before guests arrive so they stay fresh longer.

You can put together this elegant display whenever you're entertaining. For Christmas, use a red or green napkin, pine boughs and holly berries. A wreath of silk fall leaves is great for Thanksgiving. And for a springtime celebration, a pretty pastel napkin and daffodils or tulips are a nice touch.

A Haunting Halloween

WHO SAYS Halloween is just for kids? The young at heart will have a ghoulishly good time when presented with this spooky yet scrumptious spread of grown-up goodies.

As guests arrive at your haunt, offer steaming mugs of Hot Apple Cider to chase away autumn chills.

Loaded with beef and vegetables, Pumpkin Stew will thrill every hungry ghoul and goblin attending your bewitching bash.

Put a spin on the traditional and pass a basket of breadsticks shaped like Witches' Broomsticks. Then toss some salad greens with Favorite French Dressing.

Getting into the Halloween spirit will be a snap when you serve Spiderweb Pumpkin Cheesecake. (All recipes are shown at right.)

Pumpkin Stew

(Pictured on page 237)

After our kids carve their Halloween pumpkins, I use the discarded pieces in this savory stew. My family eagerly looks forward to it every year.
—Christine Bauer, Durand, Wisconsin

1/2 cup all-purpose flour
1/2 teaspoon salt
1/2 teaspoon pepper, *divided*
 2 pounds beef stew meat, cut into 1-inch cubes
 2 tablespoons vegetable oil
 2 tablespoons butter *or* margarine
 1 large onion, chopped
 2 to 3 garlic cloves, minced
 3 medium carrots, thinly sliced
 2 celery ribs, thinly sliced
 4 cups water
 1 to 2 bay leaves
 1 to 2 teaspoons beef bouillon granules
 1 to 1-1/2 teaspoons dried thyme
 3 cups cubed peeled pumpkin

In a large resealable plastic bag, combine the flour, salt and 1/4 teaspoon pepper. Add meat, a few pieces at a time, and shake to coat. In a Dutch oven, brown meat in oil and butter. Add onion and garlic; cook and stir for 2-3 minutes. Stir in the carrots, celery, water, bay leaves, bouillon, thyme and remaining pepper. Bring to a boil. Reduce heat; cover and simmer for 1-1/4 hours.

Stir in pumpkin. Return to a boil. Reduce heat; cover and simmer for 20-25 minutes or until meat and pumpkin are tender. Discard bay leaves. **Yield:** 9 servings.

SPINNING A SPIDERWEB GARNISH

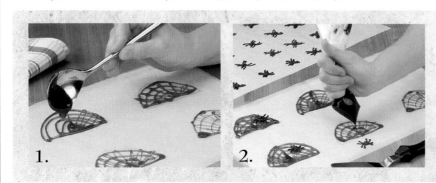

1. Carefully drizzle syrup over outlines in the pattern of a web. Cool completely.

2. Pipe 1-inch spiders onto parchment paper or foil; cool. Attach spiders to webs with remaining melted chocolate.

Spiderweb Pumpkin Cheesecake

(Pictured at right and on page 236)

This spiced cheesecake makes an appearance on my Halloween table every year. Folks get a kick out of the candy web and chocolate spiders.
—Bev Kotowich, Winnipeg, Manitoba

1-3/4 cups chocolate wafer crumbs (about 28 wafers)
1/4 cup butter *or* margarine, melted
FILLING:
   3 packages (8 ounces *each*) cream cheese, softened
3/4 cup sugar
1/2 cup packed brown sugar
   3 eggs
   1 can (15 ounces) solid-pack pumpkin
   2 tablespoons cornstarch
   3 teaspoons vanilla extract
1-1/2 teaspoons pumpkin pie spice
TOPPING:
   2 cups (16 ounces) sour cream
   3 tablespoons sugar
   2 teaspoons vanilla extract
SPIDERWEB GARNISH:
   1 cup sugar
1/8 teaspoon cream of tartar
1/3 cup water
   4 squares (1 ounce *each*) semisweet chocolate, melted

Combine wafer crumbs and butter; press onto the bottom and 1 in. up the sides of a greased 10-in. springform pan. Set aside. In a mixing bowl, beat cream cheese and sugars until smooth.

Add eggs; beat on low speed just until combined. Whisk in pumpkin, cornstarch, vanilla and pumpkin pie spice just until blended. Pour into crust. Place pan on a baking sheet. Bake at 350° for 60-65 minutes or until center is almost set. Cool on a wire rack for 10 minutes.

Combine topping ingredients; spread over filling. Bake at 350° for 6 minutes. Cool on a wire rack for 10 minutes. Carefully run a knife around edge of pan to loosen; cool 1 hour longer. Refrigerate overnight. Remove sides of pan; set aside.

For spiderwebs, draw six 3-in. x 2-in. half circles on two sheets of parchment paper. Place another sheet of parchment paper on top; tape both securely to work surface. In a saucepan, bring the sugar, cream of tartar and water to a boil over medium heat. Boil, without stirring, until mixture turns a light amber color and a candy thermometer reads 350°. Immediately remove from the heat and stir. Cool, stirring occasionally, for 10-15 minutes or until hot sugar mixture falls off a metal spoon in a fine thread.

Using a spoon or meat fork, carefully drizzle syrup over half-circle outlines and inside the outlines to form spiderwebs; reheat syrup if needed. Cool completely. Place melted chocolate in a resealable plastic bag; cut a small hole in a corner of bag. Pipe 1-in. spiders onto parchment or foil; cool completely. With remaining melted chocolate, pipe two or three dots on each web; attach spiders.

Remove sides of springform pan. Cut cheesecake; place a web on top of each slice and remaining spiders on the side. Refrigerate leftovers. **Yield:** 12 servings.

Editor's Note: We recommend that you test your candy thermometer before each use by bringing water to a boil; the thermometer should read 212°. Adjust your recipe temperature up or down based on your test. Webs and spiders can be made in advance and stored at room temperature in an airtight container.

Witches' Broomsticks

(Pictured on page 236)

My family loves bread, so I try to serve some with every meal.
Halloween isn't the same without these oh-so-good breadsticks.
—Nicole Clayton, Las Vegas, Nevada

2-1/3 cups biscuit/baking mix
2/3 cup milk
1 teaspoon Italian seasoning
3 tablespoons butter *or*
    margarine, melted
1/4 cup grated Parmesan cheese

In a bowl, combine biscuit mix, milk and Italian seasoning. Turn onto a lightly floured surface; knead 10 times. Divide into 30 portions; set half aside. Roll the remaining 15 pieces into 7-in. ropes for broom handles; fold in half and twist. Place on ungreased baking sheets.

Shape reserved pieces into 2-1/2-in. circles; cut with scissors to form a bundle of broom twigs. Place below each broom handle; pinch edges to seal. Brush with butter; sprinkle with Parmesan cheese. Bake at 450° for 10-12 minutes or until lightly browned. Serve warm or cool on a wire rack. **Yield:** 15 servings.

Sweet 'n' Spicy Halloween Munch

(Pictured on opposite page)

Kids of all ages love the sweet and salty blend in this fast-to-fix snack mix.
—Shana Reiley, Theresa, New York

1 pound spiced gumdrops
1 pound candy corn
1 can (16 ounces) salted peanuts

In a bowl, combine the gumdrops, candy corn and peanuts. Store in an airtight container. **Yield:** 2 quarts.

SNACK MIX SERVING SUGGESTION

INSTEAD of simply setting out bowls of Sweet 'n' Spicy Halloween Munch, place individual servings in edible containers like waffle cones and set them in a bowl filled with candy corn (as shown at right). This way guests will be able to munch as they mingle.

Or, instead of waffle cones, make paper cones (as in the photo on the opposite page). Take heavy-duty paper (we used origami paper) and roll it to make a cone shape. Secure with tape and fill with snack mix.

Jumbo Jack-o'-Lantern Cookies

(Pictured at right)

Every Halloween, I'd have a batch of these cookies waiting for my kids when they came home from school so they could decorate their own. Eventually, they started bringing friends home to join in the fun.
—Marlene Kuiper, Oostburg, Wisconsin

1 cup butter *or* margarine, softened
1 cup sugar
1 cup packed brown sugar
1 egg
1 teaspoon vanilla extract
2 cups all-purpose flour
1 cup quick-cooking oats
1 teaspoon baking soda
1 teaspoon ground cinnamon
1/2 teaspoon salt
1 cup canned pumpkin
1 cup (6 ounces) semisweet chocolate chips
Orange and green decorating icing *or* vanilla frosting and orange and green gel food coloring

In a large mixing bowl, cream the butter and sugars; add the egg and vanilla. Combine the flour, oats, baking soda, cinnamon and salt; add to the creamed mixture alternately with pumpkin. Stir in the chocolate chips.

Drop by 1/4 cupfuls onto ungreased baking sheets. Spread into 3-1/2-in. pumpkin shapes. Drop 1/2 teaspoon of dough at the top of each for stem. Bake at 350° for 15-18 minutes or until edges are golden brown. Cool for 1 minute before removing to wire racks to cool completely. Create jack-o'-lantern faces on cookies with decorating icing or tinted frosting. **Yield:** 1-1/2 dozen.

Hot Apple Cider

(Pictured on page 237)

A hot beverage like this is savored here when chilly weather returns after summer.
The clove-studded orange slices are so attractive.
—Sue Gronholz, Beaver Dam, Wisconsin

1 medium navel orange, cut into
    1/2-inch slices
50 to 60 whole cloves
6 cups apple cider *or* juice
1 cinnamon stick (4 inches)
2-1/4 cups unsweetened pineapple
    juice
1/4 cup honey
3 tablespoons lemon juice
1 teaspoon grated lemon peel
1/4 teaspoon ground nutmeg
Additional cinnamon sticks,
  optional

Cut orange slices in half. Using a wooden toothpick, poke holes in the peel of each orange slice at 1/2-in. intervals. Insert a clove into each hole; set aside.

In a large saucepan, bring apple juice and cinnamon stick to a boil. Reduce heat; cover and simmer for 5 minutes. Stir in the pineapple juice, honey, lemon juice and peel and nutmeg; return to a boil. Reduce heat; cover and simmer for 5 minutes. Discard cinnamon stick. Garnish with orange slices. Serve warm with additional cinnamon sticks for stirrers if desired. **Yield:** 8-10 servings.

Pumpkin-Face Ice Cream Sandwiches

These friendly faces will elicit smiles from friends and family.
You can use homemade or purchased sugar cookies in this recipe.
—Pattie Ann Forssberg, Logan, Kansas

3 tablespoons butter *or*
  margarine, softened
1-1/2 cups confectioners' sugar
1/2 teaspoon vanilla extract
1 to 2 tablespoons milk
Red and yellow liquid food coloring
48 round sugar cookies
72 raisins
Red and green decorating icing
1 quart vanilla ice cream,
  softened

In a small mixing bowl, combine the butter, confectioners' sugar, vanilla and enough milk to achieve spreading consistency. Tint orange with red and yellow food coloring. Frost the tops of 24 sugar cookies. Make pumpkin faces, using raisins for eyes and nose. Add a smile with red icing and stem with green icing. Let dry completely.

Spoon ice cream onto bottom of plain cookies; top with frosted cookies. Place in individual plastic bags; seal. Freeze until serving. **Yield:** 2 dozen.

Eyeball Soup

(Pictured at right)

My family has fun serving this creamy soup to unsuspecting guests and watching their reaction when they stir up an onion "eyeball". You can make the soup a day ahead and reheat it in the slow cooker.
—*Aleta Clegg, Pleasant Grove, Utah*

1/4 cup butter *or* margarine
1/4 cup all-purpose flour
  1 teaspoon salt
1/2 to 1 teaspoon coarsely ground
     pepper
  5 cups milk
  1 can (46 ounces) V8 juice *or* 4
     cans (11-1/2 ounces *each*)
     picante V8 juice
  1 cup frozen pearl *or* small
     whole onions, thawed

In a large saucepan, melt butter. Stir in the flour, salt and pepper until blended. Gradually whisk in milk. Bring to a boil; cook and stir for 1-2 minutes or until thickened. In another saucepan, bring V8 to a boil. Reduce heat; gradually whisk in white sauce. Add onions; heat through. **Yield:** 10 servings (about 2-3/4 quarts).

Editor's Note: If a smoother soup is desired, cool and puree in batches in a blender before adding the onions.

Favorite French Dressing

(Pictured on page 236)

This was the house dressing at a small restaurant near our home. When it closed, the owner graciously shared the recipe with me. It's fast to whip up on short notice.
—*Connie Knolles, Huntersville, North Carolina*

  1 can (10-3/4 ounces) condensed
     tomato soup, undiluted
  1 cup sugar
3/4 cup cider vinegar
3/4 cup vegetable oil
  1 teaspoon salt
  1 teaspoon pepper
  1 teaspoon paprika

  1 teaspoon ground mustard
  1 teaspoon Worcestershire sauce
  1 garlic clove
Salad greens and vegetables of your choice

Place the first 10 ingredients in a blender; cover and process until smooth and creamy. Serve with salad. Store in the refrigerator. **Yield:** 3-1/4 cups.

Black Widow Bites

Our home economists add even more fun to Halloween with these candy spiders resting on a chocolate cookie web. Little goblins will be delighted with these sweet treats.

Black shoestring licorice
  12 grape Jujubes
   1 cup vanilla *or* white chips
  24 red nonpareils
  12 chocolate wafers

Cut licorice into 96 pieces, about 1/2 in. long. Using a toothpick, poke one licorice piece about 1/8 in. into a candy. Repeat seven times to make eight spider legs. Repeat with remaining licorice pieces and candy.

Melt chips in a microwave or heavy saucepan; stir until smooth. Transfer to a heavy-duty resealable plastic bag; cut a small hole in a corner of bag. Pipe two small dots on one candy and immediately place one nonpareil on each dot to create eyes. Repeat with remaining candies.

Pipe a web on each chocolate wafer. Pipe a dot of melted vanilla chips onto the bottom of the spider and attach to wafer. **Yield:** 1 dozen.

COOKIE-CUTTER PUMPKIN CARVING

BEFORE YOU BEGIN, carefully cut a circle around the pumpkin stem, lift off the lid and remove the seeds from the lid and inside the pumpkin.

1. Place a cookie cutter on the pumpkin and tap firmly with a rubber mallet until at least half of the cutter has pierced the pumpkin's shell. (If the pumpkin shell is thin, the cutter may be pounded all the way through the shell.)

2. Remove the cookie cutter, using a needle-nose pliers if needed.

3. With a small serrated knife (or the serrated saw from a pumpkin carving kit), follow the pattern made from the cookie cutter to cut out the image, making sure to cut all the way through the shell.

4. With one hand inside the pumpkin, push out cookie cutter image from the pumpkin and discard.

Spine-Tingling Table Topper

(Pictured above and on page 236)

JACK-O'-LANTERNS glowing in a darkened room are a natural choice when decorating for Halloween. But instead of carving pumpkins in the same old way, use cookie cutters!

For an eerie evening effect, we used an assortment of star and moon cookie cutters. You could also use cutters with a fall theme, like leaves and pumpkins.

You may want to purchase an inexpensive pumpkin carving kit, which can be found at craft, hardware and variety stores during the Halloween season. Instead of a kitchen knife, we used the small serrated saw from the kit to cut out the cookie cutter image. The kit's plastic drill came in handy to create small circles on some of the pumpkins.

To make your pumpkins look their best for your party, cut them the day before. Rub a little petroleum jelly on the edges of the cutouts and refrigerate. The day of the party, place a tea light candle in each pumpkin.

Set the jack-o'-lanterns on the table along with your other decorations. We used a felt witch's hat, dried leaves, Indian corn and tree branches. Just before guests arrive, dim the lights, light the candles in the pumpkins and have a "spooktacular" Halloween!

REFERENCE INDEX

Use this index as a guide to the many helpful hints, decorating ideas and step-by-step instructions throughout the book.

GENERAL RECIPE INDEX

This handy index lists every recipe by food category, major ingredient and/or cooking method.

ALPHABETICAL INDEX

Refer to this index for a complete alphabetical listing of all recipes in this book.

Here's *Your* Chance To Be Published!

Send us your special-occasion recipes and you could have them featured in a future edition of this classic cookbook.

YEAR AFTER YEAR, the recipe for success at every holiday party or special-occasion celebration is an attractive assortment of flavorful food.

So we're always on the lookout for mouth-watering appetizers, entrees, side dishes, breads, desserts and more…all geared toward the special gatherings you attend or host throughout the year.

Here's how you can enter your family-favorite holiday fare for possible publication in a future *Holiday & Celebrations Cookbook*:

Print or type each recipe on one sheet of 8-1/2" x 11" paper. Please include your name, address and daytime phone number on each page. Be specific with directions, measurements and the sizes of cans, packages and pans.

Please include a few words about yourself, when you serve your dish, reactions it's received from family and friends and the origin of the recipe.

Send to "Celebrations Cookbook", 5925 Country Lane, Greendale WI 53129 or E-mail to *recipes@reimanpub.com*. Write "Celebrations Cookbook" on the subject line of all E-mail entries and *include your full name, postal address and phone number on each entry.*

Contributors whose recipes are printed will receive a complimentary copy of the book…so the more recipes you send, the better your chances of "being published"!